FAMILY GAMES

FAMILY GAMES

**General Models of Psychotic
Processes in the Family**

MARA SELVINI PALAZZOLI
STEFANO CIRILLO
MATTEO SELVINI
ANNA MARIA SORRENTINO

VERONICA KLEIBER, Translator

W.W. NORTON & COMPANY   NEW YORK   LONDON

Published simultaneously in Canada by Penguin Books Canada Ltd.,
2801 John Street, Markham, Ontario L3R 1B4

Printed in the United States of America.

First Edition

Library of Congress Cataloging-in-Publication Data

Family games : general models of psychotic processes in the family /
    Mara Selvini Palazzoli . . . [et al.] ; Veronica Kleiber, translator.
    — 1st ed.
      p.   cm.
    "A Norton professional book"— P.
    Bibliography: p.
    1. Family psychotherapy.   I. Selvini Palazzoli, Mara.   II. Title:
Psychotic processes in the family.
RC488.5.F3245 1989
616.89′156—dc19   88-22556

ISBN 0-393-70070-4

W. W. Norton & Company, Inc., 500 Fifth Avenue, New York, N.Y. 10110
W. W. Norton & Company Ltd., 37 Great Russell Street, London WC1B 3NU

1 2 3 4 5 6 7 8 9 0

Acknowledgments

WE OFFER OUR first dutiful thanks to Giuliana Prata, who shared with Mara Selvini Palazzoli the first exciting years of the experimentation with the invariant series of prescriptions. We express our gratitude to Maurizio Viaro, whose cooperation proved itself to be precious both in the continuous exchange of ideas and in the critical revision of the manuscript of this book.

We acknowledge our indebtedness to Veronica Kleiber for her invaluable help in working on the English text.

Stefano Cirillo, Matteo Selvini, and Anna Maria Sorrentino want to thank the colleagues of the Centro di Terapia dell'Adolescenza of Milan.

Giuliana Mauro Paramithiotti was, as always, our righthand woman in her secretarial work.

Contents

Contents

Preface

FOR 20 YEARS NOW, in my work with a succession of therapeutic teams, I have been pursuing one and the same foremost objective: to shed some light on the mystery of psychosis, that most grievous of the so-called mental disorders. I have concentrated on studying these disorders as they appear during infancy and adolescence, not only because my professional caseload afforded many such instances but also because it is at this age that the dramatic developments we are so eager to be able to forestall and avert are at their most tragic. This goal was prompted by my enthusiasm for the new systemic ideas I began to delve into during the sixties. My "discovery" of Gregory Bateson led me to envisage a radically new approach to my work, though I soon became painfully aware of the tremendous difficulty of recasting this innovative way of thinking in terms of clinical practice for dealing with the difficult problems I was facing every day in my office.

The feeling that I was on a promising new track was enhanced by a new way of working: I joined up with other colleagues to form a team. Teamwork brought with it a number of advantages, such as direct supervision, co-therapy, the possibility of alternating the role of therapist with that of supervisor, and a collaborative rapport that had everyone on an equal footing. A team develops a collective mind and renders possible self-correcting, self-reflecting, and self-appraising processes otherwise not easily come by. The intellectual vitality and creativity of a team was a great improvement on my previous way of working as an individual therapist, in which all I had to guide me was indirect supervision and occasional seminars.

In the early seventies, when the team had devised the so-called paradoxical interventions, we were rewarded by our first instances of spectacular therapeutic success. They were episodes, of course, but quite astounding when seen from the perspective of my long years of clinical experience. As time went by, however, our excitement over these initial achievements tended to wane and give way to a growing realization of the inordinate difficulty of answering the crucial questions: what exactly had made us successful, what could increase our chances of succeeding and where to look for the error when we failed.

After we had gradually abandoned paradoxical methods and invented an entirely new therapeutic technique (the first chapters in this book chronicle how my subsequent teams went about this), a new project began to take shape in our imagination. We had to contrive to elaborate a system of road signs, an Ariadne's thread to guide the therapist through the maze-like intricacies peculiar to the family with a psychotic child.

Great teachers such as Lyman Wynne and Jay Haley had shown us that significant aspects of schizophrenia could be conceptualized in relational terms; suffice it here to recall the time-honored adage: "Whenever there are disturbed children there is a disturbed marriage, although all disturbed marriages do not create disturbed children."[1] Yet, despite all this pioneering spade-work, here we were, still a long way from understanding what special kind of marital disturbance was capable of bringing on such a devastating effect and what the reasons and the circumstances leading to the child's involvement in his parents' distress might be.

Now, precisely this concern has been with me throughout all these years and continues to preside over my research on psychosis today: *How are we to link a parental couple's malfunctioning with that of their child?* Here in a nutshell is the substance of all the investigating I have done since the days of *Paradox and Counterparadox*. There have been several changes of direction and we have explored along a variety of charted courses, but our efforts have at all times pursued our prime objective with strict theoretical and clinical coherence. As methods changed, new strategies and therapeutic instruments came into being, yet the final purpose was and is the same: to seek out the roots of what is commonly spoken of as mental illness.

This new course of therapeutic action strengthened my resolve to abide by another fundamental choice I had made: I was determined to work in isolation, with a small group of collaborators. Getting institutionally involved in a complex establishment such as a university, hospital, foundation, training school, or some other such structure would, I felt, be disruptive of our peace of mind and curtail our freedom to speculate, theorize, and experiment as we thought best. Limiting the scope of our endeavors to what we could personally oversee meant that our scenario would have to be a perfectly straightforward family therapy consulting room. It entailed keeping our research within self-appointed and self-supporting dimensions: We needed to work as "artisans," in a workshop setting. I was convinced from the outset that this apparent drawback would prove a blessing in disguise. In fact, it freed us from bureaucratic trammels and gave us

[1]Framo, J. (1968). Rationale and techniques of intensive family therapy. In J. Boszormenyi-Nagy, J. Framo (Eds.), *Intensive family therapy*, New York: Harper & Row, p. 154.

plenty of leeway to develop *the imaginative and creatively artistic side of our work, which is just as much an essential part of science as is rigor* — especially where research on human beings is concerned. Most important of all, we had all the time we required to thrash things out and think things over about every case we dealt with. Given the present state of knowledge about psychosis, research conducted on a large number of patients seems less illuminating than painstaking in-depth study of the individual case.

Can what we have done be termed scientific? Morin (1982), speaking of the science of complexity, stresses how clear, "closed-end" concepts once considered universally binding have of late come under much critical fire and warns of the implausibility of drawing a sharp boundary between science and non-science. This has a bearing on our work, insofar as *the object we are researching is a unique one, namely, the human being.* The failure of all attempts to colonize the human sciences with models borrowed from natural science is by now an undisputed fact. Biomedical analogies, which in those early days seemed to me to hold out so much promise, have in the meantime revealed their inadequacy. A human being cannot be contrasted with a cell, nor can a family be equated with an organism. The intrinsic complexity of the self-reflecting, self-aware strategic systems that are the province of behavioral science — i.e., individuals, groups-with-history, societies — resists all attempts to constrain it into physical or biological models. This silences the myth of a preeminence of the rigorous methodology peculiar to hard science: The criterion simply does not apply to the object we are examining, which is qualitatively different. Has an electron ever wanted to be told whether it is a particle or a wave? Our patients definitely do want to be told about themselves; they want us to counsel, to explain, and to bring about change.

Our position is unique also with regard to other branches of human science such as anthropology and sociology, given the special clinical context in which we operate: We do so only "on demand." Only if there is an explicit request can we take action. This is why the "artisan's workshop" dimension, rather than a setting with full institutional trappings, is mandatory if we are to succeed not only in studying those with whom we become personally involved but also in experimenting. The latter is something we can safely set out to do only as long as our absolute priority remains the sacrosanct one of therapeutic gain. This is by no means limiting; in fact, it yields an equivalent gain in knowledge.

So, how far have we come on this long road of ours? We are at the point where we can propose general diachronic and synchronic models which, when we fit them accurately into the web of variables proper to the individual family, help us reconstrue in detail the particular interactive process which at a given time erupts into a son's or daughter's undesirable behavior. These are general models — definitely *not* generic ones. We are constantly at pains to submit ever more detailed and concrete descriptions and definitions to scientific scrutiny. Our findings are specific, open and above-board, which exposes them to permanent critique and possible disproval — or, as Popper says, to "being falsified." Only sweeping generalities, in fact, are allowed to eschew clinical control and remain on the level of unassailable doctrine. By willingly rendering our results vulnerable to clinical control we hope to encourage a debate among our colleagues and possibly swell the ranks of those engaged in relational research into psychosis.

DSM-III-R SPECIFICATIONS

In this book, we have made the broad and ill-defined term "psychosis" synonymous with "severe mental disorder" and have also used it to cover several cases of anorexia and bulimia included in our research. At least 90% of the cases on which we report may safely be said to fall within the loose category of severe mental disorders. For the sake of clarity, we indicate a diagnosis according to the *DSM-III-R* (American Psychiatric Association, 1987) specifications for each case. From June 1979 to June 1987, our center dealt with 290 cases of young patient(s) living within the parental home. The table lists only one diagnosis in each case, the main one on which we based our treatment. To simplify matters we have neglected the type of course foreseen for the disorder as well as other specifications pertaining to the 4th or 5th digit, and the III, IV and V axes.

The families in our study were actually 283, 7 of them having presented two children as patients. The invariant series of prescriptions was issued entirely or in part to 149 of these families. Of the total 157 cases were treated by the team of Mara Selvini Palazzoli and Giuliana Prata and 133 by the team that authored this book.

Table 1
DSM-III-R DIAGNOSIS OF PATIENTS
SEEN FROM JUNE 1979 TO JUNE 1987

Agoraphobia	2
Anorexia nervosa	93
Attention deficit hyperactivity disorder	2
Autistic disorder	45
Bipolar disorder	6
Bulmia nervosa	11
Chronic motor or vocal tic disorder	1
Conduct disorder	5
Dysthymia	3
Elective mutism	1
Functional encopresis	3
Functional enuresis	2
Gender identity disorder of childhood	1
Identity disorder	1
Major depression	18
Obsessive-compulsive disorder	5
Opioid abuse	5
Oppositional defiant disorder	6
Overanxious disorder	2
Pervasive developmental disorder	4
Psychological factors affecting physical condition	5
Schizoid personality disorder	5
Schizophrenia catatonic	3
Schizophrenia disorganized	7
Schizophrenia paranoid	16
Schizophrenia residual	14
Schizophrenia undifferentiated	9
Separation anxiety disorder	1
Somatization disorder	1
Stuttering	1
Tourette's disorder	3
Trichotillomania	1
V codes for conditions not attributable to a mental disorder that are a focus of attention or treatment	8
	290

PART ONE
The Invariant Prescription

CHAPTER I

The Paradox Proves Unsatisfactory

B Y THE LATE SEVENTIES, we had started having misgivings about so-called paradoxical methodology. Although we had run up impressive, almost instant successes, some of our results were doubtful at best and there had been quite a number of downright failures. Moreover, we were perplexed by the frequency of relapse in the wake of brilliant initial response.

This chapter, written 10 years later, reports on how we gradually came to spell out the reasons for our mounting dissatisfaction with paradoxical technique. We will start by illustrating our current views on the subject.

THE STRATEGIC PARADOX

Paradox, as we use the term, conforms to the operative meaning given by Rohrbaugh et al. (1977, p. 1): " . . . the specific tactics and maneuvers which are in apparent opposition to the goals of therapy, but are actually designed to achieve them." In other words, an intervention is paradoxical if it entails: explicitly prescribing the symptom, appraising it favorably, attaching a positive connotation to it, encouraging it, expressing the fear that it will disappear too rapidly, etc. We do not, on the other hand, think of paradox as being " . . . a contradiction that follows correct deduction from consistent premises" (Watzlawick et al., 1967, p. 188), nor do we subscribe to such notions as "consistent deductions from Aristotelian premises yield paradoxical results because the premises are invalid"[1] (Dell, 1981, p. 40), since elegant abstractions of this kind have not proved expedient and have only muddled the clinical picture.

---

[1] An important subject, unfortunately beyond the scope of this work, is the unproven and operatively tenuous connection between theory and practice that has characterized a good deal of the evolution of family therapy: Ranging from certain theoretical dicta of Watzlawick to Maturana's epistemology to Prigogine to nth order cybernetics, astrophysics and whatever, there has been much theoretical glitter but precious little clinical gold.

The problem will be better understood by referring to the nine examples taken from clinical practice given in *Pragmatics of Human Communication* (Watzlawick et al., 1967, p. 242). If we examine these instances of "therapeutic double bind" we notice two main characteristics, aside from one common to them all, i.e., the symptom having been prescribed. These are:

(1) *The therapist retains control of the therapeutic relationship.* One of the nine examples has the therapist taking his paranoid patient's suspicions at face value and joining him in searching the room for hidden microphones; this has the effect of inducing the patient to talk about his real problem, which centers on his marital relationship.

(2) *The therapist modifies the previously attempted solution.* There has been an attempt to solve the problem which has worsened matters. The therapist then effects change by using a variety of techniques:

(a) interventions designed to neutralize the anxiety which triggers specific symptoms such as insomnia, migraine, tics, bed-wetting, stuttering, obsessions, etc. This amounts to applying a logic of "reductio ad absurdum." An obsessive patient, for example, may be instructed to intensify his disturbing thoughts during some specific hour of the day,[2] or the insomniac may be enjoined not to sleep till a certain hour of the night.

(b) interventions that redefine the problem. In Watzlawick's example, the spouses are encouraged to fight, on the grounds that the more a couple fights the more they love each other.

(c) interventions aimed at influencing the special family behavior that sparks off the patient's symptom. Watzlawick tells of ordering the wife of an alcoholic to systematically drink just one little glass more than her husband.

As these examples point out, the strategic paradox represents a strong tool for maneuvering to control the therapist-patient relationship.

In such strategy the connection between controlling the relationship and effecting therapeutic change is never explicitly stated: Control appears to be an end in itself, as though the therapist's proficiency hinged on his

[2]This manner of prescribing the symptom strikes us as better suited to an individual therapy context and adequate only for a number of very specific symptoms. It diverges substantially from the more usual paradoxical provocation. Rohrbaugh et al. (1977) distinguished between prescribing the symptom on the assumption that it will be obeyed (as in point (a) above) and (as in all the other examples) acting on the presumption that the patient will fail to comply.

ability to place the patient in a paradoxical situation and thereby bring about change.[3]

The strategic therapist (Haley, 1963, 1976; Rabkin, 1977; Weakland et al., 1974; Watzlawick et al., 1974), we feel, remains in the ranks of those who "act without understanding" in that he fails to address an issue we consider paramount, namely: Why has the patient we are now observing in the context of his web of relationships developed these particular symptoms at this particular time? The strategic therapist contends that the answer is not to be sought in terms of a time-related process: " . . . [strategic therapists] flatly deny that for the purposes of therapy there is essential value in discovering the relation between causative events in the past [pathogenesis] and the present condition [pathology], let alone in the need for the patient himself to grasp this connection, that is, to attain insight" (Fisch, Watzlawick, Weakland, & Bodin, 1972, p. 605). Diversely, the strategic therapist may limit his answer to overall generalities, referring to dysfunctions in evolution (citing biological analogies) or linking the symptom as it appears here and now to communication deficiencies inherent to the system (double bind).[4]

What fails to emerge is an adequate relational explanation for the concrete evidence encountered in each single case. The strategic therapist has no interest in individual diagnosis. This is a natural outcome of embracing a strictly systemic-holistic approach. Nor is he overly concerned with diagnostically classifying the families he sees: His outlook is purely pragmatic and directive and all his efforts are aimed at inventing tactics for each session and elaborating final prescriptions. The Palo Alto school sanctions only such prescriptive interventions as are designed to alter the sequence of behaviors centering around the symptom and especially interventions aimed at counteracting precisely those previous attempts to solve the problem that have worsened it.

A NOVEL CONCEPT OF PARADOX

The team that co-authored *Paradox and Counterparadox* (Selvini Palazzoli, Boscolo, Cecchin, & Prata, 1978) restated the concept of therapeutic paradox, placing it within the traditional framework of strategic thinking consistent with Palo Alto theory. However, they went on to elaborate an

[3]It is interesting to note, in this context, how Jackson and Haley (1963, p. 363) consider psychoanalysis a paradigmatic example of psychotherapy technique that, without being aware of doing so, places the patient in precisely such a paradoxical situation.

[4]As in this definition, for example: "It is possible to describe symptoms as communicative acts that have a function within an interpersonal network" (Haley, 1977, p. 99).

entirely original point of view. In fact, they never tested the strategic
approach in clinical experience, possibly due to an almost instinctive reluctance to adopt a too simplistic method.[5] However, strategic thinking influenced the authors of *Paradox and Counterparadox* to a remarkable extent,
as is obvious from the emphasis placed on *the need to keep the therapeutic
relationship firmly in the hands of the therapist.* The perspective is clearly
directive-prescriptive throughout the book. Indeed, the idea of attaching a
positive connotation onto the behavior of *all* family members started out as
a device for steering the course of therapy and protecting the therapist.
During the team's first psychoanalytical ventures into family therapy (1967
to 1971) a number of interventions proved "offensive" to the parents, who
reacted with blunt hostility or by dropping out. Positive connotation, aside
from its subtly "tongue-in-cheek" coloring, was first and foremost born of
the need to avoid embarrassing, counterproductive clashes with the family
and to shield the therapist.

Still another and more significant influence on the authors of *Paradox
and Counterparadox* was the neo-cognitivistic content of strategic thought.
Watzlawick, in *The Language of Change* (1978, p. 42) quotes Epictetus: "It
is not the things themselves that worry us but the opinions that we have
about these things." The ultimate purpose of therapy, then, was to alter the
family's self-image, its perception of its own plight and of the special problem that had made it seek therapy. Circular epistemology, to be instilled
into the family's dysfunctional pattern in place of its long-standing pathogenic *linear* epistemology (by means of relational hypothesizing, circular
questioning, etc.) was nicely consistent with neo-cognitivist thinking, and
the same held true of the concept of startling, unexpected interventions
(Selvini, 1988, p. 45). With regard to this neo-cognitivistic line of thought,
see Maurizio Viaro's remarks (Viaro & Leonardi, 1986, p. 14) on how standard session conduct assigns great importance to each family member's
point of view on the problem.

What set the *Paradox and Counterparadox* team's approach apart from
purely strategic thinking was the absolute priority given to the question:
"Why is this particular member of this particular family exhibiting this
particular symptom at this particular time?" A strategic therapist, on the
other hand, will attach prime importance to the question: "What can I do
to get this client to change?" or 'What is it in the family system that keeps
the problem alive?"

The original team set out to do clinical research in a very clear-cut area,
namely that of the more severe mental disorders of infants and adolescents.[6] To this end, then, the team adopted paradoxical intervention as
auxiliary to their principal concern, namely the study of the family. Taking

---

[5]Minuchin's definition of the Palo Alto school as "minimalist" (1984, p. 28) strikes
us as particularly felicitous.

Kurt Lewin's advice, i.e., if you want to know how something functions, try to change its manner of functioning, the team concentrated on attempting to change the symptom-ridden families in order to detect the organization's modality of their relationships. The therapists' main interest, in fact, was family, not therapy; whereas strategic therapists tend to place therapy itself at the center of their scrutiny—one only needs to glance through the titles of some major works in the field to confirm this (Haley, 1963, 1976; Rabkin, 1977; Weakland et al., 1974; Watzlawick et al., 1974). This different focus may at first blush seem a fine shade of meaning; however, we consider it of the utmost importance. To have staked out our claim as researchers intent on studying psychosis rather than as academic coaches for training family therapists implied following an entirely different line of reasoning, even though both operators will be using family therapy.

HOW PARADOX EMBRACES
INTERPRETATION AND PROVOCATION

The paradoxical interventions presented in *Paradox and Counterparadox* were designed to provide the family with an explanation (interpretation) of the reasons for the patient's having developed the symptom. As is well known, this implies relationally redefining the symptom in terms of a protective-sacrificial conduct the patient is said to be enacting for the benefit of someone else in the family. It was not clear for a long time to what extent paradoxical interventions reflected the therapist's true ideas about the cause of the family's distress instead of consisting mainly of provocative statements aimed at stimulating change-inducing reactions. At the time, the team was wholeheartedly committed to the notion that acquiring proper systemic thinking required a shift in focus from an alleged purpose (intrapsychic reasoning) to the discernible pragmatic effect (observable in the system's functioning). Such a shift apparently settled the dilemma posed by the obscure unutterable nature of *intent*, as opposed to directly observable *effects*.

This neo-behaviorist criterion (observing black-box input and output) was adopted by the team as remedial for their previous causal conditioning: It proved the mainspring of subsequent in-session research on the symptom's pragmatic effects. Questions such as, "Which one of you is most worried and upset by Maria's symptom?" or "What does Mom (Dad) do when Maria does this or that?" could reveal that the offspring's plight had succeeded in reuniting a couple of squabbling parents or had very intense-

[6]See the Preface to this book. Mara Selvini Palazzoli never deemed it useful to write off classical nosological definitions such as anorexia, schizophrenia, etc. She firmly believes the prime concern should be to discover what relational process lead to the appearance of those severe symptoms (Selvini Palazzoli, 1983, p. 48).

ly involved the mother, and so on. At this point the team would perform a complete turnaround and fall back on those presumably unutterable intentions, given that the symptom's pragmatic effects were nothing other than the patient's secret—and possibly "unconscious"—purpose. By impeding his own autonomization, the patient was, in fact, offering himself up as a sacrifice on the altar of his parents' marital harmony, his mother's psychoemotional sanity, or whatever else.

The team members failed to realize that they had fallen into a tautological trap: A disturbed child is *always* a child who is not achieving autonomy and is therefore compelling his parents to cling to their parental roles and even exacerbate them. It is quite unrealistic, however, to attribute the inevitable effect this has on the family's life cycle to any real intention on the child-patient's part (mistaking the effects for the intention).

Take a situation of this kind: In a family in which one child enjoys particular prestige, one of the other children starts exhibiting intolerable psychotic behavior. This behavior, if its intentional aspect is considered, will be seen as a series of strategic moves aimed (a) at chastising the parents for having bestowed their preference (even though they strongly deny this) on the prestigious sibling and (b) getting the prestigious one to decamp. The pragmatic effects are: The strategy backfires dramatically, the favored one stays firmly put and is more than ever convinced that he is irreplaceable, especially now that "the problem" has arisen. This may suit one of the parents very nicely; however, one cannot realistically assume that the patient actually intended to benefit this parent. Intent and pragmatic effects, therefore, proceed along separate tracks. The intention or goal behind a move may well be at cross purposes with the ensuing pragmatic effects.

In the early days, learning to think in terms of pragmatic effects was a necessary form of mental training[7] for unlearning psychodynamic thought patterns, even those that take relational aspects into account (Guntrip's ego psychology (1961), Sullivan's (1966, 1968) and Horney's (1937) social psychology, and Berne's (1964) transactionalism), all of which assign logical and causal priority to individual personality structures and view relational and intrapsychic variables as subordinate. Such undue emphasis on pragmatic effects, however, led to systemic-holistic reductionism. Focusing exclusively on intrapsychic causes (structures, i.e., intentions or needs) had given way to an equally one-sided interest in pragmatic effects, which were taken as indicators of the system's ostensible needs, first among which was the overworked concept of homeostasis.

A further perturbative element compounded the age-old confusion between the pragmatic effects and the intentions of symptomatic behavior: a tendency to consider paradoxical reframing as *interpretation* rather than

---

[7]On page 108 we show how asking, "Who does the patient especially want to nail to the cross?" yields a precious clue for unravelling the tangled family game.

provocation. Systemic-biological analogies (such as the adage, "all subsystems of an organism are finalized to the survival of the organism as a whole") and others borrowed from first-order cybernetics (preponderance of negative "conservative" feedback), all widely prevalent during the seventies, endorse the notion that the patient, however unconsciously, *really* does sacrifice himself for the system. This is not so. The original team perceived from the outset that paradoxical reframing worked for the patient by provoking him into changing on the wave of his/her indignant reaction. Still, for many years, due to an almost religious reverence for the black-box taboo that barred all intrapsychic hypotheses, no one dared to come out and say so. It was only in 1985, after she had parted with her former colleagues, that Mara Selvini Palazzoli wrote an article in which she explicitly offered this explanation for the patient's change.

PARADOXES IN THE FIRST SESSION

Work with paradoxes aroused a great deal of enthusiasm in those early years. However, the sensational therapeutic results achieved at first became fewer and less substantial as time went by, and in some cases the initial success proved short-lived. Verifying our results entailed intense, time-consuming autocritical examination and laborious tracking-down. A first flaw was found to reside in the arbitrary and stereotyped way the paradox was presented to the family, namely by routinely stating to all concerned that the patient was sacrificing himself for the good of the whole family. Moreover, paradox apparently possessed therapeutic value only where the therapists succeeded in coming up with very specific, often made-to-measure logical underpinnings for their (positive) explanation of how and why the symptom had surfaced. This implied finding a link between the particular symptom at hand and the parents' discomfort or that of some other family member. For example, if there was a past history of marital strife and the couple planning to divorce had reunited as a result of the child's distress, the symptom could be presented as the patient's attempt to bring his parents together again. In the case of an apparently congenial couple, on the other hand, featuring a mother wholeheartedly involved in her child's predicament and a father affecting a distant, apathetic stance, it was more expedient to make a distinction and describe the patient as being engaged in two separate sacrifices, one for his mother's benefit (say, catering to her need to play the self-denying martyr) and the other for his father (perhaps setting him free, by keeping his wife tied down at home, to pursue some undertaking of his own). Quite a repertoire of variations on this basic theme was available, including the need to stand in for some recently deceased significant relative (Selvini Palazzoli et al., 1978, p. 77) or to enable another sibling to leave the family (Selvini Palazzoli, 1975, p. 99).

The paradox, then, was therapeutically valuable by virtue of being specific. It was of prime importance to avoid the temptation to repeat successful interventions again and again on the grounds that they had worked so well the first time (Selvini, 1988). Likewise, family therapy trainees needed to resist the urge to carry over into their practice secondhand paradoxes molded on those they found in *Paradox and Counterparadox*. For some highly original paradoxical therapies, see the work of Savagnone (1978, 1985, p. 13), who, having grasped the essential concept, put his own creative talent to brilliant use.

The need to concentrate on specificity raised anew the issue of data-gathering, especially that of sorting out key information. Later Mara Selvini Palazzoli, in a letter to B. Speed (1984, p. 511) stressed the fundamental importance of not generalizing: "Too often people wanting to do family therapy are hastily seeking after a ready handbook (recipes) of interventions, and what they do is totally ineffectual because it is generic. The modelization of the game that is going on in the family must consider all members of the family in their actual specific position, exactly as we have to do in recomposing a jig-saw puzzle. If a piece is lacking or put in a wrong place, it is from that lacuna that the family slinks away."

Another source of error was found lurking in a different area, that of the nature of the request for therapy. A paradoxical intervention, no matter how ingenious, will miscarry unless there is a strongly motivated request for help. The same holds true in a context where the therapist's prestige is weak. Some of us worked for a time in a public psychiatric care center on the outskirts of Milan, in conditions apparently not very dissimilar to those prevailing at the Morrisiana Mental Health Center (Bronx, New York) and described in a series of interviews in *Family Therapy Networker* (January–February 1986, p. 23). In a context of this type, paradoxical interventions are likely to be met with contempt and frequently induce the family to break off their relations with the center. The status of the referring person also had decisive bearing on the effectiveness of paradoxical therapy. Several of our failures could be traced to just this issue.

A further notion gradually came to the forefront of our reasoning: a number of failures could be ascribed to interventions that were nonsystemic in that they failed to involve *all* members of the family. This aspect was thought to be as relevant to success or failure as that of specificity. The assumption was that the more all-encompassing a paradox was in linking together the behaviors of all family members (including a prestigious grandfather, perhaps, or an aunt), the greater its therapeutic value would be (Selvini Palazzoli et al., 1975, p. 137), hence the tendency to avoid basing interventions on the patient's sacrificial behavior functionally trained on only *one* family member. This raised a new batch of problems. For example, the advantage one parent stood to gain by the patient's symptomatic behavior might show up very clearly, whereas that accruing to the other parent or to the patient's siblings was far less conspicuous. In attempting to define ways in which the symptom favored each and every family member, the original team ran the risk of elaborating overly sophisticated interventions and issuing arbitrary messages that undermined credibility.

A further hazard lay in fostering the patient's view of himself as a martyr, since he would usually be very eager to fasten onto any such encouragement (Selvini, 1988).

The search for the reasons for failures also touched on linguistic-communicative matters. On this issue (i.e., speaking the family's own language, adopting their choice of words in order to make oneself immediately understood, etc.) the same criterion holds as for the need for specificity— here, too, when "evidence" is conjured up to bolster the paradox's credibility, the use of stereotyped linguistic clichés must be avoided.

A basic tenet of the time held that the therapeutic message conveyed in winding up the session should be synthetic and essential. Fundamental intentions pursued by the intervention needed to be stated beforehand, in order to use shock to render it virtually impossible for the family to make retort or have the last word. It was deemed theoretically sound for the therapist to leave the stage as speedily as possible after having dropped the intervention on the family like a bombshell, thus wriggling out of any interaction with the family. The basic idea was not to afford the family the chance of prevaricating about the message or watering it down.[8]

BRINGING PARADOX INTO PLAY AFTER THE THIRD SESSION

Our second thoughts about how the first few sessions should be conducted and the likelihood of making mistakes during that particular phase of therapy carried less weight with us than the crucial problem connected with the subsequent course of therapy. The truth was that if first- or second-session interventions failed to produce any significant results, the problem was how to proceed from there. Further recourse to paradoxical intervention was of no avail and sometimes even grotesque. We therefore resorted to reparatory alternatives, focusing on first one and then another member of the family, with the uncomfortable sensation of playing blind man's buff. The process would gradually get out of hand altogether and every session would be a first session. We came to dread the endless chore of thinking up opening gambits like the chapters in Italo Calvino's *If on a winter's night a traveller*, each of which was the beginning chapter of a separate novel. Therapeutic case histories, however, are not innocuous plots to be juggled around at will.

[8]At present we consider such frantic recoiling from interaction with the family as mainly a sign of our own unease.

Looking for a solution, the therapists settled on very brief therapies: During the second or third session, especially if the family was particularly evasive or inaccessible, the therapists would either come forth with some shocking piece of reframing or induce a crisis in the family while bidding them farewell, for instance, by announcing, "The so-called healthy members of your family are in great danger and we, as social psychiatrists, cannot run the risk of curing one of you only to plunge the rest into even deeper misery." The idea here was to forestall the piling up of incoherent interventions eventually leading to the family's dropping out of therapy. Such do-or-die tactics were discarded, however, once they were in danger of becoming the rule instead of the exception.

In this sense, paradoxical reframing proved suitable only for therapies requiring very few sessions: The fact is that it either works or it doesn't, and if it doesn't there is absolutely no point in insisting. Moreover, our experience taught us that if a paradoxical intervention is brought into play following a series of lame, wishy-washy sessions, it will usually fall flat.

It is not surprising, then, that many family therapists hailed the premises of *Paradox and Counterparadox* with great enthusiasm but employed its basic ideas in their work mainly as "therapy for the therapy," i.e., in order to overcome an impasse. Weeks and L'Abate (1982) and Stanton (1981) advise starting therapy with a conventional (prescriptive or structural) approach, relying on direct, collaborative technique and bringing in paradox only as a last resort if everything else has failed or the client is hopelessly refractory.

The *Paradox and Counterparadox* team used still another line of attack in aiming for significant results, one common to a number of strategic authors: This consisted of basing therapy on *prescriptions* usually handed out after the first few meetings with the family. These generally involved assigning specific tasks to the family members which, if properly executed, would bring about change. The most effective of these therapeutic processes were those in which a balance was struck between paradox and prescription and therapy was allowed to develop logically and consistently over a reasonable length of time. While we were redimensioning the interventionism of the paradoxical phase in favor of prescriptions, another idea came to us: Could a certain manner of conducting the session be effective not only in yielding key information but also in inducing change per se?[9] As will be seen later, Mara Selvini Palazzoli and Giuliana Prata, after the split in the original team, came to consider such hypotheses as unrealistic, especially from the point of view of their usefulness as therapeutic instru-

---

[9]See the concluding paragraph of Hypothesizing, Circularity, Neutrality (Selvini Palazzoli et al., 1980b), where the authors deal exhaustively with the pragmatic neo-cognitivist approach previously referred to, which is one that Boscolo and Cecchin, as well as numerous other authors, including Lynn Hoffman, still endorse.

ments with families of seriously disturbed children. Mara Selvini Palazzoli and Giuliana Prata therefore decided to recast the whole subject and shift their sights onto experimenting with a novel prescriptive strategy. They gradually abandoned paradoxical reframing altogether. By 1983 a few paradoxical-type interventions were still being used in first sessions, where they occasionally served as an opening gambit. Paradox had now become a tool for getting and keeping the family intrigued; but there were no expectations as to its direct power to effect change.

The following example is taken from the first session with the family of an anorectic who had turned symptomatic following her parents' divorce.

THERAPIST   What about you, Palmira (the patient)? How did you understand that you had to invent anorexia to give your father . . . definitely your father, but I don't know about your mother, maybe both of them . . . the chance to see each other even if they are separated? In fact, here we are now, in a cosy little group, etc. Because usually when people separate they say friendly good-byes and that's that. Instead, with this problem of your vomiting, these two are always hearing from each other . . . probably at a cost to you because you're not having much fun. So, how did you manage to realize that you had to create the reason for them to see each other, to meet up, to talk to each other? . . . When did you work it out?

PATIENT   Me? (almost laughing) I've got nothing to do with it. I haven't . . . I don't . . . What do you mean, "understand"? Anyway, I can't understand what you're saying now. (Viaro and Leonardi 1983, p. 22)

As to paradoxical reframing itself and its use as a therapeutic instrument, Mara Selvini Palazzoli (1985b) gives a description and a theoretical discussion of a recent successful and repeatedly implemented example of this, showing how its therapeutic value is limited to a very specific situation.

USING PARADOX TO DISCLOSE THE ONGOING FAMILY GAME

Summing up paradoxical reframing as undertaken by the first team and later by Mara Selvini Palazzoli and Giuliana Prata was original and significant because, unlike the interventions of the strategic school, each paradoxical reframing was based on painstakingly detailed analysis of intrafamiliar relationships. This discloses the ongoing family game as well as the patient's covert intentions. As Lynn Hoffman so aptly puts it in her discussion of the Milan approach:

> What is beginning to be clear, however, is the importance of 'reading' the internal (and external) politics of the family. One must study the coalitions

and apparent power balances or imbalances in relation to the symptomatic behavior. This is why the most important contribution of the Milan group may not be their most visible signature, the systemic paradox, but their detective work in devising a hypothesis that will explain the symptom in the family and how all the pieces fit. (1981, p. 293)

Quite so. Paradoxical interventions will in all instances point to the connection between the child's symptom and the parents' marital difficulties. Even in the sympathetic ambience created by positive connotation (i.e., neither parent has ever really demanded sacrifice from the child), the intervention is always a potent, implicit unmasking device that can show up both the severely warped relations between so-called healthy members of the family and their detrimental effect on the patient. The various bits of evidence then laid before the family in order to add credibility to paradoxical redefinitions were considered at the time to be merely instrumental devices, rhetorical fireworks at best. Today we are reassessing them in terms of their value as intuition of "pieces" of family games.

HOW PARADOX IMPEDES ACCESS
TO THE COMPLEXITY OF
PSYCHOTIC GAMES

We have until very recently refrained from making public our reasons for gradually drifting away from paradoxical technique. For too long a time our dissatisfaction with these methods and the search for an alternative tool were confusedly interwoven in our thinking. What clinched the matter was, as usual, a pragmatic consideration. Paradox had shown itself of little therapeutic relevance in numerical terms and the results it elicited had, in the long run, proved short-lived. Beset by failures, we had taken a fine-tooth comb to our records and searched for "ad hoc" explanations. We attempted to lay the blame for the fiascos on our ineffective use of an effective instrument. This accounts for the laborious effort we put into refining our "paradox technique," as we have described here. Now, of course, we perceive quite clearly that our progressive disgruntlement with paradox was nothing but a healthy becoming aware that the subject into which we were researching—psychotic games in the family—was of inordinate complexity. The haphazard, absolutely unpredictable nature of the results due to ever-changing paradoxical interventions certainly did not add anything to our knowledge, as comparing one course of therapy to another was virtually out of the question.

Thus, it was not so much the frequency of our failures that disheartened us as the realization that, despite our diligent efforts to refine our technique, we were obtaining no sizeable cognitive gain. This line of research was no major improvement on our basic hypothesis concerning psychosis,

a concept on which the team had founded its entire work. On balance, we had elaborated a huge array of stratagems and techniques and obtained a few interesting results, yet very little truly original insight into the relational groundwork of psychosis had materialized. This principal reason for our dissatisfaction is analyzed in greater detail in Part Four. In other parts of this book we refer to the various considerations that eventually led us to discard paradoxical methods.[10]

Despite all we have said here, our experience with paradoxical therapies was clinically very fruitful indeed. It was probably a stage we could not avoid going through, and we have no intention of reneging on our past enthusiasm.

Our new experimental approach—and the game metaphor—seem currently to be providing us with greater insight into how paradoxical therapies really function, and this in turn makes us understand more clearly our present therapeutic strategy and techniques.

In Chapter II we illustrate this new method, which engendered new concepts. Here, too, our findings will be presented in the chronological sequence that mirrors the course of our research during the past few years.

---

[10]As we shall see, we have gradually discarded our reticence, an excessively contentious spirit that takes over the therapeutic relationship and a doctrinaire adherence to technical precepts, all of which can impair the patient-therapist relationship.

CHAPTER II

Enter the Prescription

THE MARSI FAMILY

IN FEBRUARY 1979, the Marsi family crossed the team's path. This encounter triggered much speculation. The Marsis were a middle-class family. The parental couple had for years been locked in serious marital conflict. Maria, their firstborn daughter, was 20 when we first met her, and a chronic anorectic. Her problem severely affected the family's home environment, especially due to several dramatic attempts at suicide. The first three sessions with them, rather chaotic, mainly called attention to the highly aggressive manner in which the three daughters, all of them in their late teens, interfered in their parents' affairs. The team made a series of laborious attempts to grasp the nature of the family game.

At the end of the fifth session, seeing that they had got nowhere, the team members decided to summon only the parents to the following session and to do so in a cryptic manner, without supplying any reason for having split up the family group. The idea was to find a nonverbal way to prevent the girls from meddling into their parents' problems. We came up with the following prescription, which we handed to the parents during the session that followed:

> Keep everything that has been said during this session absolutely secret from everyone. Should your daughters ask questions about it, say that the therapist has ordered everything to be kept only between her and the two of you. On at least two occasions between now and your next scheduled appointment, you are to "disappear" from home before dinner without any forewarning. Leave a note worded as follows: "We shall not be in tonight." Each time you go out, pick some place to meet where you are reasonably sure no one will recognize you. If, when you get back home, your daughters ask you where on earth you've been, simply smile and say: "That concerns only the two of us." Each of you is also to keep a sheet of paper, well out of everyone's sight, on which to jot down personal observations on how each of your daughters has reacted to her parents' unusual behavior. At our next meeting, which will again be with only the two of you, each of you will read your notes out loud.

A month later, the results were amazing: the parents had scrupulously carried out our orders, Maria had shed her symptomatic behavior, and the whole family had already changed. At this point the team decided that summoning the girls again would contradict the logic underlying the intervention. Therapy proceeded for another three sessions with only the parents attending. During this time the couple did a number of lengthier "disappearance acts" and the daughters started becoming independent. The girls' rapport with each other, too, took a decided turn for the better. A year later, our follow-up showed that the results achieved were stable: Maria had resumed her studies after many years and was also highly successful in sports. Three years later her parents informed us that she was happily married.

THE PRESCRIPTION BECOMES "INVARIANT"

Up to this point, there had been no special upheaval in our research. All we had done was devise a prescription that broke up a hitherto obscure family game. The carrying-out of our prescription had headed the family game off in an entirely new direction. As far as our experimental technique was concerned, the turning point came later, when we realized that this same prescription, by acting on multiple levels, was able to cut through the knots of a game even when we had not yet deciphered and reframed it.[1] From this moment on the prescribed sequence was routinely issued to all families of anorectic or psychotic children, and we came to call it the *invariant prescription*.

As will be seen, the new tool we had thought up meant significant therapeutic gain but it also, perhaps more significantly, represented an important stride forward in our ongoing research. Less than a year later, in May 1980, Mara Selvini Palazzoli and Giuliana Prata reported on the daring change of course they had imparted to their research project and invited others to check these findings in their own clinical work.

TOWARDS META-THERAPY:
PRESCRIBING AT MULTIPLE LEVELS[2]

Introduction

I am happy to have the opportunity of presenting something really new to this conference. What follows is a pre-print report on the research

[1]Mara Selvini Palazzoli was hinting at this in the title and subtitle of a paper she presented at the Lyons meeting (see below).
[2]The following section is a transcript of Mara Selvini Palazzoli's presentation to the International Conference on Family Therapy, Lyons, France, May 1980. The paper was written with Giuliana Prata.

Giuliana Prata and I started a year ago in order to tackle a problem we had been pondering for years without finding a solution. The problem is: What are we to do with the parents of a patient once we have separated them from the rest of the family? In a number of cases simply labeling the parents as "patients" and leaving the younger generation at home had very quick therapeutic effects on the patient's condition. This approach, however, left a number of problems unsolved and even ushered in a few new ones. The parents would invariably adopt the semblance of a desperate case and display their hopelessly negative marital rapport, so that we were forced to face an inexorable logical impasse: The parents refused to accept what amounted to an explicit accusation. If the child were to shed his symptoms and the parents' conflict remain unchanged, the causal link between marital conflict and symptom would stand disproved.

The prescription we have chosen thus represents our effort to implement as cryptic an intervention as possible, without attaching any blame to the parents or offering pedagogical truisms on how to act as — or to "be" — a "good" couple. Therapeutic emphasis thus shifts to the younger generation, on the assumption that the children are meddling into their parents' lives and tending to pit them against one another. The blurring of generational dividing lines, in fact — or, worse, their effacement — is a constant in families with severe patients. This prescription has shown itself particularly potent for re-establishing them.[3]

Preparing for the Prescription

In our current practice the prescriptive stage is reached after a preparation that ends with the second session. Let us follow the itinerary from its beginning: Every Monday morning, from 9 to 11, one of the therapists is on hand to take all telephone calls related to requests for an appointment. If such calls are made at other hours of the day or on other days, the secretary will simply ask the caller to contact us at the appointed time. During the first contact the therapist tries to gather as much information as she can about all those who live in the family home, including grandparents and other relatives. All these members of the household are then summoned to a first session.

This is not all the therapist tries to do over the phone. She also inquires whether other influential people are involved in family matters, even though they may not live in the home. This is frequently the case with grandparents, who either live in or have raised and looked after the chil-

---

[3]This remark, included in the paper presented in Lyons, led some colleagues to believe Mara Selvini Palazzoli had joined the structuralists!

dren, or play an important role in family affairs. The therapist, in setting the appointment, will summon any such "suspects" along with the members of the household. If necessary, she will firmly insist that the presence of these "suspects" is important, and will even go to the extent of changing the appointment to make sure these significant others will be able to attend, thereby assigning the greatest importance to their presence.

If, when the group shows up for their first meeting, one of the "live-in" members is missing, the session will immediately be adjourned. Should one of the influential "outsiders" fail to appear, the session will take place nonetheless, but an absence of this sort, regardless of the alibi that is offered, is always important information that the therapist will skillfully probe into. Our experience tells us that grandparents who do not live with the family usually show up. These the therapist treats with the greatest consideration and respect.

The first session ends in the following manner: After discussing the case with the team, the therapist joins the group and addresses those who are not members of the nuclear family, whether they live in or not: "Normally, at the end of a first session, we are able to say whether we believe family therapy is or is not advisable. In this case, however, despite everyone's excellent cooperation [this is said even when there has been nothing but obstinate reticence], we have not come to a definite conclusion and require a further meeting with the family. The next appointment will be on such and such a day, at such and such an hour. You will stay home; we will see only the family. We wish to thank you so very much for having come today and for being so helpful." During leave-taking the therapist again makes a point of stressing how grateful she is for the help of those who from now on will be excluded.

We consider that this important intervention produces a twofold effect. One has a bearing on therapy itself and the other is connected with the amount of information it calls forth. From the point of view of therapeutic action, it provides what is quite likely this group's first experience of an irrevocably fixed demarcation line drawn around the nuclear family. In the case of severely disturbed families — in growing order of morbidity, this means those with psychotic offspring, young schizophrenic members, anorectic-bulimic cases, and rapidly degenerating anorectics — setting up well-defined permanent boundaries around the nuclear family occasionally produces extraordinary effects of its own. By the time the group returns for the next session, the patient may show astonishing improvement. By drawing this dividing line, the therapist establishes beyond doubt who is and who is *not* a member of the nuclear family, thereby reinstating the patient as a member in good standing of his family group.

As for the yield in information, it will be manifest in the immediate countereffects coming from all those present, and especially from those who are being dismissed. A further response will be observed during the second session, which will essentially be devoted to the following agenda:

(a) a circular inquiry (friendly, relaxed, and totally non-inquisitorial) about the reactions of those dismissed, including what any of them may have had to say on the subject;

(b) noticing how the behavior of those present may have changed from that exhibited during the first session, and specifically whether they seem more at ease or more uptight — more communicative or more reticent — now that the others are missing. One member may take this opportunity to "spill the beans" about someone who has been dismissed. Someone — or everybody — may assume an adamant defensive stance;

(c) additional inquiries about matters not yet touched upon or not entirely clarified during the first session.

Throughout this session, the therapist will maintain a strictly neutral manner and carefully avoid blaming anyone for anything.

If there are no "suspects" — whether or not they live in the family home — only the nuclear family will be summoned to the first session. At the end of this meeting, too, the therapist will announce that the team has not been able to reach a definite decision and that a further session must be held. This second session, as in the first case, is aimed at gathering information and also at "hooking" the family by the unexpected and intriguing way the therapist goes about this data-gathering. This is very important for everyone in the family but especially for the younger generation, who are now to be dismissed after they have entered into a meaningful rapport with the therapist. We will not go into further detail here about how we conduct such a session, as we have described this fully elsewhere (Selvini Palazzoli et al., 1980b). Instead, let us now look closely at the prescription itself.

The Prescription

1. In winding up the second session, with only the nuclear family present, the therapist reunites with the family, following the team discussion, and announces: "This time we are in a position to tell you that the team considers family therapy appropriate in your case. Our next session will be on such and such a date, at such and such a time. You [addressing the children by their first names, in order of their ages] will stay home. Only you two [to the parents] will come." After this, the family is dismissed. Team members will pay great attention to the various verbal and nonverbal reactions unleashed by this last announcement.

2. The following session, with only the parental couple attending, is

structured[4] mainly around the following questions that the parents are asked to answer in turn:

(a) Right after our last meeting, during the days that followed and up till today, how did A, B, C [each of the children] react to the fact that only the two of you would be coming here today?
(b) What was *your* reaction to this? How did you account for it?
(c) Have you talked about it together?

3. In winding up the session, the therapist joins the couple after discussing the case with the team and announces in solemn, emphatic tones: "We have come to the conclusion that we shall really have to issue you a prescription today. We have discussed the matter at long length, as we are well aware that it will be very difficult for you to carry it out. However, it is imperative that you do your best to comply with it, since this is of the utmost importance for the work we are doing. It is a complex prescription that has four parts to it."

4. "Once you get home, you must commit yourselves to keep everything about today's session absolutely secret from everyone. If either of you is questioned separately by one or more of your children as to what took place here, you must answer using these precise words: 'Doctor X has ordered that everything said in the session be kept a secret between her and ourselves.' Your tone of voice should be calm and unperturbed. If the child (or children) questions the two of you when you are together, whichever one of you feels more inclined to do so can give this standard answer. It will also be given in exactly the same manner to anyone else who inquires—your parents, relatives, the family doctor, friends, etc. The secret is to be kept equally from everyone."

5. "Roughly one week after this session, you will begin going out now and then during the evenings. I will tell you later how often you are to do this. Your outings are to follow this pattern very strictly: Once the two of you have decided on a suitable evening, you will make an appointment to meet somewhere outside the home during the late afternoon, and in any case before your usual dinnertime. On the kitchen table at home you will leave a note saying: 'We shall not be in tonight.' You will take turns in actually writing out this note, but it is not to be signed. You will not come home before 11 p.m., nor will you prepare any dinner. You yourselves will have had dinner when you get home. You can organize these outings as best you please. The main thing is for you not to go to places or with people that will allow for later identification of where you went and what

---

[4]We no longer insist on such structuring today, as dismissing the children has lost its cryptic implications (see Chapter XV).

you did. Not even I need to know how you spend your time." Having said this, the therapist prescribes the exact number of required outings. They will be proportionate to the time interval before the next appointment. We favor a rather long period, at least five weeks.

6. "Should your child/children ask where on earth you've been and what you've been up to, answer very calmly: 'These are matters that concern only the two of us.'"

7. "Lastly, you will each keep a personal notebook well out of sight somewhere, in which you will enter the data and every piece of verbal or nonverbal behavior, on the part of your children or of anyone else, that you feel is caused by—or in some way related to—your carrying-out of this prescription. We urge you to be very precise and careful about your note-taking, as it is of the greatest importance for you not to omit anything. At our next meeting we will again see only the two of you, and you will report on what has happened."

If the parents, when they show up, have complied with the terms of the prescription, this first stage in the sequence will be followed by another involving "weekends," i.e., "disappearances" that last over one or two nights. The couple will be asked to leave a note saying, "We will be back after 11 p.m. on such and such a date." The third and last stage requires a far lengthier absence from home—at least a week, or even a month. Having left the usual note, they are to refrain from calling home or in any way contacting the rest of the family while they are away.

Remarks on the Prescription

We shall now examine the several parts of the prescription in detail, in order to point out its theoretical rationale as well as its purpose in terms of pragmatic and therapeutic effects. It will be clear how this prescription, based on a series of set behavior pieces and verbal expressions arranged in a precise time sequence, unleashes a tidal wave of two-way information that flows into the family-therapist system in a steady crescendo. The team members who thought it up (as usual, in a flash of intuition and with amazing immediate results) felt they had found a springboard to hoist them straight to the heart of the problem, bypassing a mass of detail that tended to sidetrack them into the blind alley of linear punctuation.

The unusual thing about this new prescriptive method was that we decided almost at once, even before we had framed a theoretical founda-tion for it, to make it a set formula, much like the formula of a drug to be used in clinical medicine, that is not varied or adapted to the individual case but administered to a large number of cases, after which its effects can be registered. This was exactly the opposite of what we had done, case by case, with paradoxical methods or family rituals, which had been extremely specific. Rather, it bore some resemblance to a ritualized prescription we had called "even days and odd days," also applied unvaryingly to a number of cases. The two devices have a common purpose: "Even and odd days" aims to deal with parents' mutual interfering in the matter of "what to do with the child," a situation often encountered in the case of particularly intractable children. The prescription we are introducing here is mainly designed to deal with the universally pathogenic phenomenon of blurred intergenerational boundaries.

Regarding effectiveness, however, there is no comparison between the two prescriptions: "Even and odd days" was likely to be disqualified and disobeyed, especially by families with a rigid dysfunction, whereas the new prescription, if correctly administered, is very rarely discredited or ignored, and its effects are astounding. We attribute its inordinate potency to the minute attention to timing, order of sequence, etc., which clearly marks the therapeutic context and the subcontexts, thus reducing to a minimum the risk of elusive or manipulatory maneuvers.[5]

We shall now comment on the separate parts of the prescription and on its precise wording.

Point 1. "This time we are in a position to tell you that the team considers family therapy appropriate in your case. Our next session will be on . . . at. . . . You [addressing each of the children in turn by their Christian names, in order of their ages] will stay home. Only the two of you [the parents] will attend." The bomb-like effect of summoning only the parents is often evident from the immediate nonverbal response it elicits and is due to the entirely unexpected exclusion of the children. Hadn't we all just been talking about the advisability of *family* therapy? The fact that the therapist offers no explanation for this bizarre move allows each member of the family to think up his/her interpretation. This may later be quite a rich source of information.

It is extremely important that the therapist follow the ritual we have described down to the last detail, in the same carefully calibrated, terse and resolute style, enunciating the various bits of information in order of their growing importance (i.e., first the date of the next appointment, then the names of those to be excluded, and lastly, the announcement of those who are to be present). This gives a dramatic slant to the procedure and also shows that the therapist is perfectly sure of what she is doing. It is important to follow the verbal expressions word for word, as even the slightest departure from the text may, for example, let the family believe that summoning the parents alone will apply only for the next session — as would be the case, for instance, if the therapist were to say: "In our next session we

---

[5]As our research proceeded, it became clear that many parents, especially of "schizophrenic" children, will fail to carry out the prescription no matter how skillful the therapist may be.

will be seeing only the two of you." The sequence of communications we have worked out leaves the matter open to any number of interpretations.

Point 2. The parents are asked to answer in turn:

(a) "Right after the session, and during the days that followed, up till today, how did A, B, C [the children] react to the fact that only the two of you would be summoned today?"
(b) "And what was *your* reaction to this? How do you account for it?"
(c) "Have you talked about it together?"

This session will be structured around the gathering of specific information. In answering the first question, most parents will report that their children reacted favorably and seemed relieved, sometimes even delighted. Answers to the second question will differ widely and will be strained and hesitating: This, for the couple, is the real climax of the session. As to our third question, only very rarely will spouses actually have discussed the matter between themselves.

An important fact should be mentioned here: The information thus elicited will on no account be used by the therapist when winding up the session. This is a departure from our usual manner of working, in which the therapeutic conclusion is based on whatever information has been obtained during the session. Why, then, do we hold such a structured session? The first reason, and the most obvious one, is that a prescription usually follows a circular interview. So, to stick to our routine, we might just as well take this time for a prearranged, standard interview. The information it yields will in any case contribute to a better all-round acquaintance—or, at least, so we thought at the time. As we acquired more experience, we became ever more convinced that the structured interview was needed in order to make it easier for the parents to accept the prescription that followed it. The prearranged questions, in fact, especially the second of these, caused the parents' answers to reveal, by their wording or by nonverbal behavior, a culturally conditioned expectation on their part that they were about to be taken to task for some sort of misbehavior and then given instructions on how to avoid such misconduct in the future. This is an unpleasant expectation, and even when it is belied by the therapist's amiable, neutral attitude, it somehow seems to hang in the air. It therefore comes as a huge and very welcome surprise when the forebodings conjured up by the questions are dispelled by the liberating prescription.

Point 3. "We have come to the conclusion that we shall have to issue you a prescription today. We have discussed the matter at length, in order to carefully elaborate it, and because we are well aware that it will be a very difficult one for you to carry out. However, it is imperative that you do your best to comply, since this is of the utmost importance for the work we are doing. It is a complex prescription and has four parts to it."

This "preamble" was chosen for its pragmatic effect. If the therapist were to appear to be handing down, from the height of her authority, a prescription she considered perfectly feasible, there would be infinite ways of sabotaging it. Instead, the therapist acts like an expert reluctantly compelled by the exigencies of therapy to issue a prescription she knows will be very difficult for the couple to obey. Likewise, on behalf of this therapeutic requirement, she will urge them to do their best to carry it out. By so doing, the therapist places herself in a complementary position with regard to a pressing therapeutic dictum, and it is not surprising that one of the spouses will often hasten to reassure her that the prescription isn't really all that unfeasible.

We should like to point out that the "preamble" is worded in order to make the prescription appear tailor-made for this particular family instead of a set routine.[6]

Point 4. "When you get home, you are not to say a word about the session. If either of you, separately, is asked by one or more of your children about what has gone on here, you will answer using these exact words: 'Doctor X has ordered us to keep everything said in the session strictly secret *between her and ourselves.*' Your tone of voice should be very calm. If you are questioned while the two of you are together, whichever one of you feels more inclined to do so will answer. The same answer exactly will be given to anyone else (parents, relatives, friends) who questions you on the matter."

At this point the therapist is apparently getting down to the actual contents of the prescription, by ordering that something be done. In fact, on a meta-level, she is marking a context. She is using this "something" to establish the terms of a compact between herself and the parents. The drawing-up of a contract marks the context as one defined and structured for collaboration. Its scope is very precise and specific and comprises the three partners to the radical exclusion of everybody else. The exclusive nature of the contract is further underlined by the explicitly voiced and accepted obligation to keep the secret and to convey to all "others" that such a compact has been entered into.

The pragmatic benefit of an encouragement to carry out the terms of the contract is added to a covert incentive to compete[7] by the remark: "Whichever one of you feels more inclined to do so may give the answer."

Point 5 and 6. "Roughly one week after this session, you will begin going out now and then during the evenings, for a number of outings that I will prescribe later. This is how you are to do this: Once the two of you have decided on a suitable evening, you will make an appointment to meet

---

[6]This we have since stopped doing.
[7]This notion of stimulating competition, however covertly, was later abandoned in order to foster a cooperative spirit between the spouses.

somewhere outside the home, in the late afternoon or in any case before your usual dinnertime. On the kitchen table at home you will leave just a note, reading as follows: 'We shall not be in tonight.' You will take turns in actually writing out this note. You will not come back home before 11 p.m. You can organize these outings as best you please. The main thing is for you not to go to places, or with people, who will later allow your child/children to identify where you went and what you did. Not even I need to know how you spend your time. Should your child/children inquire where on earth you've been and what you've been up to, you will answer quite calmly: *'These are matters that concern only the two of us.'"*

These last two parts of the prescription represent a major turning point: The two have now become a couple. They were summoned as parents and are being sent home primarily as spouses. This highlighting of the couple as a well-defined, separate entity is again the result of a shared secret, one not even the therapist needs to know about and that strongly tends to tag this same meaning onto the prescribed behavior sequences as well. Actually, it is of no importance what the spouses do on their escapades; what is crucial is that they manage their outings in such a way as to avoid any later leaks in information. The note they leave in announcing their departure, couched in typically adolescent style, signals that they resent any control over their lives by their offspring or by anyone else, and by alternately writing out the note they show they are both in this together.

With regard to the hierarchical level of context-marking, we can observe the following: Once the therapist-parents context has been defined as hierarchically superior (due to the therapist having ordered that everything about the session be kept secret), the secret meetings receive the marking of a subcontext, one that is the couple's own and will signal to their children that their parents are claiming their legitimate right to privacy. The subcontext ranks below the main context in hierarchy, since the outings are undertaken on the couple's initiative and not on orders from the therapist. This is amply borne out by the reactions of those excluded from the secret. The first part of the secret, i.e., the parents' statement that they have been told by the therapist to keep everything about the session to themselves, is usually met by an "ah" from the children that can mean any number of things but normally dissolves into respectful acquiescence. The secrecy surrounding the outings, on the contrary, will arouse great curiosity, much insistent questioning and sleuthing, a lot of loud indignant protesting, sarcasm and the non-too-veiled suggestion that such unspeakable conduct might have been "respectable" had it been called for by doctor's orders.

The lower position in hierarchy of this latter ploy, however, has a salutary side-effect: It can call forth "retaliatory" moves, such as, "If you can have your secrets I can have mine." Thus, a most expedient way to induce parents to grant their children autonomy would seem to be to have them claim some autonomy and privacy for themselves.

Point 7. "Lastly, each of you will separately keep a notebook well out of your children's reach, in which you will enter the date and all verbal and nonverbal behavior on the part of each or all of your children that you feel may be due to or connected with your carrying-out of the prescription. We entreat you to be very precise and careful about your note-taking, as it is of the utmost importance for you not to omit anything. At our next meeting we will again see just the two of you, with your notebooks, and you will report on what has happened."

This all-important point strongly accentuates the marking of the main (i.e., parents–therapist) context, by stressing its contractual nature. Not only have the parents had to keep a secret and go on a few outings, but now they are actually called upon to *work for* the therapist and to take over from her in carefully observing and registering what goes on. The purpose of all this work is to provide the therapist with information about the very people she has dismissed from the session! This information is highly specific, since it is limited to the response that appears to have been elicited by the couple's compliance.

The task assigned to the parents shifts their attention away from whatever interpretation they may have attributed to their secret outings: These will now be perceived as a provocative maneuver designed to stimulate revealing behavior on the part of those not in on the secret. The outings are designed to furnish the therapist with clues she can work on. This engenders an extraordinarily important pragmatic effect: It protects the therapist against disqualification by the couple—by any couple, even those who display themselves as "hopeless cases"—because of the fact that the therapist is considered to be prescribing the outings as a sacrificial act for someone else's benefit. Moreover, and most significantly, by assigning the parents their task in this particular fashion, the therapist manages to stay perfectly cryptic without in any way impairing the collaborative spirit of their compact.

It often happens that one of the parents (usually the one most disgruntled by the prescription) will ask to be told "what the therapist is aiming at." If the therapist has not assigned the "homework" with the notebooks, she will be in a fix. She will either have to declare what she is aiming at, thereby forfeiting the therapeutic dividend, or she will need to adopt a highhanded manner and say something like, "Not to worry—that's my business," which would adversely affect the collaborative marking of their contract. Instead, the "homework" allows her to reply in cool, unruffled tones, perfectly attuned to the context, "I am aiming at a chance to study the observations you will register for me in your notebooks."

An equally unruffled answer can also be given to the various "what ifs" liable to be forthcoming, such as: "What if my daughter reacts by getting worse?" "What if my son runs away from home?" The answer, given with a gentle, reassuring smile, can be: "Just write it all down in your notebooks; those notes are what really matters." By repeatedly urging the couple to be most diligent and thorough about their note-taking, the therapist reinforces the basic logic underlying the entire intervention. Lest this should not have been made quite clear, we repeat that once the prescription procedure has been adopted, therapy will carry on with only the parents attending; the children will not be summoned again, nor will there be any further contact with them, either by letter or over the telephone.

Reactions to the Prescription and a Word of Warning to the Therapist

We have now been applying this prescription for a year, and have treated 22 families by this method. There has not been a single dropout. Up to now, all parents turned up for their planned sessions. Obviously, the responses to the prescription have been very different. We can classify the couples into three general types, namely:

1. *Those who faithfully comply with the prescription and carefully register the reactions of their children or of any significant others.* The session, in this case, will be entirely devoted to discussing the contents of their notebooks and any discrepancies found between the two versions. In turn, the spouses are called upon to comment on the reactions they have observed, while the therapist tactfully keeps her interventions to a bare minimum. Quite a variety of things will be reported as regards the couple's outings. More than half our couples refrained from commenting at all on where they had been or what they had done. In a few cases, the spouses expressed satisfaction at the improvement in their rapport. There was one case that remained unique, that of the parents of an only child suffering from a severe case of chronic anorexia. This couple would meet at the flat of an acquaintance, who had left it in their custody while on a trip abroad, and engage in passionate sex. All information about the outings is acknowledged by the therapist without any comment, so as to let the couple know that she considers it to be of very little importance.

Vitally important information, on the other hand, is provided by the parents' notes on the reactions and spontaneous behavior of their offspring, and by their own counterreactions hereto. This will shed much light on the family game. The therapist will find that she holds a master key that can spare her much anxiety and effort during the first sessions. She no longer has to go all out to try and understand as much as she can about the family game, since she knows in advance that the really valuable information will come via the prescription or, rather, via the various reactions it elicits. With a couple of this type, the therapist will wind up the session by handing out "more of the same,"[8] i.e., she will add a few weekend "disappear-ances" to the evening outings. These, too, are to be arranged so as not to allow for any leaks of information. If at all possible, the parents are to vanish after leaving the usual terse note saying, "We will be back on Sunday night," or else announce their departure only a few minutes before they leave the house. They are to keep mum, of course, about where they go.

2. *The couples in this group have complied only in part with the prescrip-tion.* They have kept the secret about what went on during the session, as per the therapist's orders, but they have been on a fewer number of outings than were prescribed. They adduce a variety of alibis, such as sudden illness or some other practical hitch in their plans. Or they have made "mistakes," such as making up a story instead of simply disappearing with-out any explanation.

One mother "forgot" to hide her notebook, so that it was discovered and read by her daughter. However, all this is not related triumphantly, in order to provoke the therapist, but in an abashed, apologetic manner. We are dealing here with families whose intergenerational dividing lines are much more entangled than is the case with those in the first group. The strength of this intergenerational bond will be manifest in the couple's difficulty in complying with our orders, but also in the vehement, highly interesting reactions the children show to the couple's attempts, however incomplete, to carry out the prescription. These can be spectacular. The therapist, despite a partial lack of success, will show no impatience or displeasure, but collect as much information as possible and then, in winding up the ses-sion, prescribe exactly the same all over again.

3. *These couples have either totally disregarded the prescription or man-aged to disqualify it by, say, telling their children where they went and what they did.* All this is announced in snooty, irritating tones, deliberately de-signed to irk the therapist. The therapist must not appear in the least upset but proceed to gather information in a friendly, neutral way, as though she simply wanted to hear what happened, without passing judgment. This attitude, which serves to usher in the next move, signals to the couple: "This is your problem, folks, not mine. I have done everything I could to help, but I'm perfectly willing to accept defeat. It's not my job to be right every time."

We learned that these couples also lay another trap that must be avoided besides that of trying to get us to rise to their provocation: One is in danger of keeping one's cool throughout the session and then taking it out on them at the end by thrusting on them the same prescription, or even an aug-mented version of it. There is a theoretical explanation for why this is a wrong move: When the parents flaunt such provocative behavior, they are

[8]This no longer holds true today: if and how we prescribe each stage of the pre-scription will always depend on the outcome of the stage that preceded it.

marking the context and defining their relationship with the therapist in a manner exactly opposite to that which the therapist established in the first session. The context will then cease to be therapeutic, since not only has the request for collaboration been ignored but, more significantly, the relationship with the therapist, on an analogical level, has been marked as contentious (symmetrical). Should the therapist fail to realize this and go on insisting *as though* the context were still one of collaboration, failure will be bound to ensue. The only proper thing for the therapist to do is take the initiative of remarking the context and redefining the relationship, so as to leave the way open for future recontracting. Let us see how this can be achieved.

The therapist joins the family after the team discussion, and sits down, saying, "The team, at this point, would like to know what your wishes are." (The tone should be that of a friendly air hostess inquiring of first class passengers what they would prefer to have for dessert.) "More precisely, we need to know whether you are satisfied with matters the way they are now, and feel that you would prefer to interrupt our work at this point. If so, we will respect your decision and end our meetings with this session. If, on the other hand, you prefer to carry on, we must warn you that in order to work further on the problem that brought you here, we will have to issue prescriptions, as they are the basic tools with which we work."

Such a categorical statement will always call forth much information, both about the family system and about the system involving the couple plus the therapist, mainly on a relational level. The couple may decide to carry on or to call it quits. There are times when they will be cunning enough to confront the therapist with two opposite decisions, one for each spouse: This is especially true of "schizophrenic" systems. In that case, the therapist will keep matters in abeyance anyway, by suspending treatment until the two of them have reached a unanimous decision that satisfies them both. She will be very careful not to tag a "good" label onto the one who prefers to carry on or a "bad" one onto the one who wants to quit. We know all too well that roles of this type are assumed at random and are short-lived and interchangeable, whereas what is equally predominant in both parties is a strong fear of change.

Now for a word of warning about couples such as these, whose divergent behavior has both practical consequences and theoretical implications. During leave-taking, one of the spouses (the "good" one, of course) will be apt to say to the therapist: "But now I'll have to tell the children what has happened, since we won't be coming for any more appointments." This is an obvious attempt to heap ignominy on the head of the "bad" spouse. The therapist's quick rejoinder will be: "Oh no you don't, you're not to tell your children anything at all. The terms of our contract are still binding. In our last meeting you both agreed to keep everything that goes on here a secret between the two of you and me. The children have nothing whatsoever to do with this agreement of ours. Take your time, think things over, and when you have reached a joint decision, I shall be here to listen to what you have to say." This puts a very strong emphasis (and no time limit) on the parents–therapist compact. Such a message is very important; it may not prevent a dropout but it leaves the door open for a "physiological" resumption of therapy.

Closing Remarks

It is probably impossible to pinpoint and fully grasp the many facets of this prescription and the several levels on which it acts. Let us concentrate on the element of secrecy it entails and on the fact that the therapist enjoins the parents to inform everyone that what goes on in the session is a secret they must never reveal. It was quite some time before we realized that the prescription could rule out only the parents' verbal disclosures. The truth of the matter is, the session *has* taken place, and the therapist may have aroused an unexpected awareness, carrying with it a high content in information not only for the therapist but for the parents as well. If this is so, the parents, when they get home, will be very likely to convey, albeit only by subtle changes in their behavior, the nonverbal messages that are known to have such striking repercussions. These are transmitted right along with the explicit verbal messages the parents have been taught by the therapist and the implicit communication that the couple has entered into a compact with her. Once we had understood this, we were more positive than ever that the therapeutic efficacy of this prescription, and others of its kind, hinges fundamentally on a special hierarchical arrangement of communications on a nonverbal level.

THE THERAPEUTIC IMPACT
OF THE INVARIANT PRESCRIPTION

A few comments on the paper presented in Lyons and included as the preceding section may help point out the multiple ways in which the prescription acts as therapy. These are:

1. The preeminence awarded to the parental couple. The whole intervention is based on the dismissals, first of the elder generation (grandparents) and later of the younger one (children).
2. The setting-up of a hierarchy of subsystems. By avoiding explicit comment, the therapist strongly characterizes the therapeutic system as symmetrical, that is to say, governed by its own options. She hands out the prescription without any explanation. The parents, in turn, stress the asymmetry of the parents–children subsystem by

their secret outings, signaling to their children that they are claiming their right to some leeway and privacy for which no permission or agreement is required from anyone.

3. The collaborative compact that the therapist and the middle generation (parents) enter into via the secrecy. The therapeutic relationship thus established is totally different from that which characterized our "paradoxical" period. The parents are strongly tied to the therapist by a bond that is, on the one hand, an explicit alliance *against* the "interferers" (the extended families, the children) and, on the other, more importantly, an alliance *in favor of* the disturbed child's recovery and the entire family's well-being. Much of the reticence and two-way maneuvering that beset the therapist-family relationship during the days of "paradox" thus begins to subside.

4. The constantly fluctuating manner in which the couple is defined. They are alternately seen as parents and as spouses, implicitly labeled as co-responsible for their child's pathology yet explicitly acknowledged to be the victims of their child's pathological power. The cryptic summoning of only the parents already sets off all kinds of speculation: Have they been summoned alone because they are bad parents who have harmed their child? Or has the patient been left at home so that the therapist can discuss him more freely with his parents? The structured interview concerning their reactions to the children's dismissal then makes the parents feel they are going to be called to order. Instead, there comes a surprising secret prescription that takes all the onus off secrecy. Moreover, the two of them, who have been summoned as parents, are sent home, after receiving the prescription, with the feeling of having been ordained as a married couple, one that shares a secret not even the therapist needs to be let in on, since she does not especially want to know what they do on their outings. The couple will also lose their suspicion that the therapist is using the outings to make an idyll out of their marriage, since she is quite obviously interested mainly in their note-taking and the real purpose of all they are doing is to provide information on how others react to their behavior.

THE INFORMATION LODE
OF THE INVARIANT PRESCRIPTION

The report presented at Lyons was still brimming with our enthusiasm for the prescription's therapeutic powers. We had given little attention at the time to its value as a source of information, and we were still uncertain about how the information it elicited, which shed so much light on the family game, might be used in therapy. It seemed as though, in each case, only that quota of information was being used which allowed us to foresee and forestall the difficulties of getting that particular family to accept therapy.

A year and a half later, in October 1981, at the Heidelberg conference, Mara Selvini Palazzoli and Giuliana Prata reported on further progress in the team's understanding of the threefold effect accruing to the prescription, to wit: (1) it is therapeutic, (2) it provides information, and (3) it advances our research. In the following section we quote the salient parts of this paper from the published version listed in the bibliography (Selvini Palazzoli & Prata, 1983).

A NEW METHOD FOR THERAPY AND RESEARCH IN THE TREATMENT OF SCHIZOPHRENIC FAMILIES

The primary objective remains to devise a method to collect the largest amount of crucial information. Accordingly, since May 1979, we have devoted ourselves to a new research program with families presenting schizophrenic patients. This research is ongoing and is expected to continue for a long time. During this period we have treated, and are still treating, 19 families (six presenting patients with chronic infantile psychosis, ten presenting chronic schizophrenic patients, and three presenting acute delusional patients). All of these patients represented extremely serious, discouraging cases.

One must keep in mind that, even though we are speaking of research, our primary goal is therapeutic change. Our primary objective is the improvement of the family. Our current method is radically different from our previous one. Previously our therapeutic interventions varied in accordance with the multifarious situations in the different families. Now all families are treated in an identical manner: They are given the same prescription. . . .

The question is, On what hypothesis is this new method based? Giving the schizophrenic families a fixed, invariable prescription structures for the therapists a repeatable context. A repeatable context supplies the optimal condition for learning about "schizophrenia."

This time again, as it so often happened in the history of our work, we were inspired by Gregory Bateson (1972). Here I am particularly referring to his essay "The Logical Categories of Learning and Communication." In this original theorization on the different logical levels of learning, Bateson maintains that the passage from learning level zero to learning level one is constituted by the appearance of the process of trial and error. This happens when a choice which has been shown to be wrong is substituted with a different choice. Wrong choices can thus become profitable errors inasmuch as they "provide information to the organism which might contribute to his future skill." He refers to this as a stochastic process. But, Bateson notes, in order to have this learning take place it is necessary to assume a repeatable context. Quoting Bateson, "Without the assumption of repeatable context . . . it would follow that all learning would be of one type, namely would be zero learning." But that's not all.

Bateson also asserts that we think and know solely through differences and comparisons. So, the fact of giving one and the same prescription to different families allows us to compare their various reactions. It is evident that, in so doing, similarities and differences provide us with high quality information. . . .

After these cursory, but very significant, conceptual comments, we would like to clarify some of the most interesting repetitive phenomena that we have observed.

Let us begin from what we observe when the parents faithfully keep the secret and the three progressive stages of the prescription. The identified patient shows an immediate improvement, and progressively abandons his symptomatic behaviors. *The prescription seems to break the ongoing game without it being necessary for the therapist to first understand what game has been going on.* The family Marsi was first seen in May 1979 and we devised for the first time this prescription. We realized at once its powerful effect. The family presented a chronic anorectic daughter, aged 21, with repeated suicidal behaviors. Immediately after the parents had completed the first stage of the prescription (after the fourth session), the girl stopped her anorectic behavior. Later, while the parents completed the subsequent stages of the prescription, her behavior improved consistently until she moved away from home, started a relationship with a boy, and got involved in sports. At present she is doing well as a student at the university and has become a regional champion in one of her sports. All the relationships in the family have changed considerably.

There have been changes like these in 10 out of the 19 families we have treated or are now treating. One of the cases with which we were most pleased was that of the family with a 31-year-old, chronic schizophrenic, the only son of two elderly teachers. The son had suffered his first psychotic crisis shortly after having reached the age of 20, while he was in military service. He had been living for years at home under heavy medication. His most interesting activity seemed to be that of holding redhot political meetings behind the closed door of his room. He conversed at length with imaginary adversaries whom he attacked with a thundering voice, addressing himself to the wall. The parents, deeply motivated, faithfully fulfilled the prescription. There was immediately a noticeable improvement—the son got a job. However, the radical turning point was reached when the parents, summoning up all their courage, obeyed the last and most difficult stage of the prescription. They disappeared from home for longer than a month. When they came back they were met by a young man who not only had been able to organize himself, but had found a more important job and had even begun a romantic relationship. During the 10th and last session, which took place with the parents, we were told about a peculiar incident. Having quarreled with his girlfriend, the former identified patient, on returning home, had tried to revive his psychotic behavior by attempting to stage a rather melodramatic suicide. But his attempt was not successful. Better said, it was so clumsy that he lacked credibility, so much so that the parents could not help but laugh.

However, we do not want to speak of only successful cases. We think it is highly interesting to list a number of other phenomena repeatedly observed with different families. We shall report the bare facts succinctly to avoid the temptation of adding interpretive comments.

One observation that has recurred with all 19 families: *It has never been the identified patient who shows the most dramatic reaction to the disappearance of the parents and later to their refusing to give any information about it.* Confronted with the disappearance of the couple and the laconic and impersonal written note "tonight we'll not be in," an unexpected character suddenly emerged from the juggler's hat of the schizophrenic family. Sometimes it was a son or a daughter who had been considered perfectly sane. In some other cases an unexpected and apparently insignificant type jumped out, or somebody whose existence had not even been mentioned before. Such is the magic informative power of this prescription of ours! I shall supply an example.

The following episode took place during the family therapy of a psychotic girl aged seven. Besides the members of the nuclear family we had invited an aunt, the mother's sister, to take part in the first session. We suspected the aunt to be an important character because, as she lived across the street, she often visited the family. However, despite our focused efforts she did not supply any information. Consequently we felt that the aunt was less significant as a member of the extended family system. We proceeded to work with the parents, prescribing their disappearances in the evening. The couple courageously fulfilled the prescription, leaving the two girls — that is the seven-year-old identified patient and her sister of ten — alone. Well, it was that "insignificant" aunt who reacted dramatically to the disappearance of the parents, *not* the girls. When she came to her sister's home, at 9, her usual time, she found the two girls alone. Without any drama they had managed to prepare a simple dinner. Even though she had read the message left in the middle of the table, the aunt acted as though there had been tragedy. To do such a thing — without informing her beforehand! She decided that her sister must have planned a double suicide. She alarmed the village with dramatic phone calls and finally went downstairs into the basement looking for bodies. It had been necessary to give the prescription to learn that aunt was far from being an unimportant member of the extended family!

In some other cases, feedback providing high quality information is evident immediately following the prescription. In a session with parents of an obese and psychotic identified patient, the mother at once reacted to the prescription of disappearing in the evening, exclaiming: "But that's impossible! How can we avoid informing Emilia beforehand? She'd be terribly offended!" We thus discovered that the family, in compiling the telephone chart, had not even mentioned among its members this Emilia, an old but very important aunt who not only had always lived with the family, but who also held the keys to the pantry, ruled in the kitchen, cooked every meal. Since the identified patient was seriously obese, the presence in the home of a respected, nurturing aunt was important in the family system.

These two cases lead us to an important fact. We previously said that a key element in conducting a competent session using our approach is the gathering of significant information. During the first session we literally try to fascinate our families with our type of questions, with our competence. The families with schizophrenic members despise incompetent people; they get easily bored and drop out. But in spite of all the trouble we take, it is only the prescription which forces the schizophrenic families to give us information. This is a further proof, if proof should still be needed, of the effectiveness of making the family *act* instead of making the family *talk*.

Two further types of phenomena generated by the prescription are important and warrant comment. Four of the 19 couples have fulfilled only once the first stage of the prescription, that of disappearing in the evening. But all four stopped, either revealing the secret to one of the children, or keeping the secret but declaring in the following session their intention to stop the prescription. All four of these couples actually made the following unexpectedly sincere statement: "We don't want to risk losing the sane child (or children) in order to help the sick one." A statement like that throws at least some doubt on the so frequently alleged great love for the identified patient! The loss they feared evidently was that the healthy children, imitating the parents, would also disappear from home, profiting from the newly acquired liberty. But, compelled by the prescription to come out into the open, these families went so far as to offer the therapist to exchange the prescription against some other proposal made by themselves and meant to improve the conditions of the identified patient. We had a similar case with the parents of a chronic psychotic child, 18 years old, behaving as a mentally retarded boy. These parents got such a fright from the fulfillment of the first stage of the prescription that they jumped for safety by breaking the secret. Still they did come to the following session, with a proposal that would have been unthinkable at an earlier date, that of freeing the identified patient from a torturing and useless school attendance and finding him a job. The plan was carried out at once and produced very positive results. A fifth family, who had immediately broken the secret, was dismissed.

Last but not least, there are three cases about which we still have doubts. These parents followed the first stage of the prescription, reporting a definite improvement of the identified patient. But, on passing to the second stage, that is to the more prolonged disappearances, they stopped because of a sudden, sometimes dramatic relapse of the identified patient. We suspect, chiefly on account of the analogic behaviors, that the couple, or one of the parents, had broken the pact of secrecy, revealing every-thing—perhaps only by means of hints or tacit inferences—to some members of the nuclear or extended family. They do not confess to having done so. In our view, the sudden relapse of the identified patient is the pragmatic effect of the breach of secrecy. Once again, the patient becomes the one who does not know while the others know. Somehow feeling cheated, he reacts accordingly.

Our hypothesis—*the identified patient somehow feels cheated*—is the central point of our research. This hypothesis could explain the first explosion of the psychotic behavior as a dramatic protest and it could explain the relapse we had observed during the later stages of our prescription.

We use this hypothesis as Ariadne's thread with which we step forward in the labyrinth which is the organization of families presenting with a schizophrenic member.

ORIGINALITY AND SHORTCOMINGS
OF THE HEIDELBERG REPORT

The reader will note that the paper quoted in the preceding section represents a further step towards our recognition of the method's informa-tion-yielding value. It illustrates how issuing the prescription and carrying out its several stages sets off a whole string of surprises: Family members who have hitherto been ignored or considered insignificant suddenly burst onto the scene with telling bits of behavior that hint at the part they may be playing in the family game. As for the game itself, pieces of the intricate puzzle will begin to take shape, even though they are still disconnected. The implications for research were that this was the first time a method-ologically more correct experimental procedure was being used for learning about "schizophrenia" or, rather, about the patterns of relationship coexist-ent with the presence in a family of a "schizophrenic" member.

As to its value as therapy, the percentage of success it afforded is re-markable, considering the dishearteningly grim condition of these patients.

A weak point can be found in the explanatory hypotheses we put forward here in order to try to account for our four failures. This was clearly the afterglow of a former unwavering faith in the prescription's miraculous properties. Instead of seeking out the reasons for our failure in the team's own mistakes (today, of course, these would include not having tackled the spouses' stalemate), we tended to blame failure on the families, by assuming they had let out the secret, although this was never really proved.

CHAPTER III

Only the Parents are Summoned and Secrecy is Prescribed

THE PRESCRIPTION UNDERGOES
A MAJOR CHANGE

A FEW MONTHS AFTER the Heidelberg meeting in October 1981, Mara Selvini Palazzoli and Giuliana Prata substantially modified their method. The two parts of the prescription were now to be issued separately, i.e., "secrecy" would come first, with the "evening outings" following at a later stage, depending on the outcome. This new development was inspired by the case study of the parents of a young chronic schizophrenic: The couple let the secret leak out, thereby causing a deeply frustrating therapeutic setback. The team took a clue from this smarting defeat and resolved that secrecy needed to be emphasized by prescribing it alone and basing all subsequent interventions on the reactions it elicited.

Splitting the secrecy from the outings had a further consequence, one the team had failed to anticipate, namely a twofold increase in the prescription's information lode, which obtained whether the injunction was properly carried out or not. If it was fulfilled, the behavior of the various family members, as depicted in the parents' notes, could unequivocally be taken as the reactions of the "left-outs" to secrecy having been first stated and then faithfully kept. If it was not fulfilled, such noncompliance revealed that, for this particular family, declaring and keeping a secret were unacceptable. This information made it easier to probe into the reasons for this and thereby come closer to deciphering the underlying family game, whereas, when both parts of the prescription were issued simultaneously, a favorite high-sounding excuse of parents who disregarded it would be that they couldn't possibly leave their children at home alone. Separating the "secrecy" from the "disappearances" allowed the team to identify the cases in which secrecy itself was the real obstacle, as we shall see later.

OUR THERAPEUTIC METHODOLOGY
ACQUIRES RELIABILITY

This modification provided therapy with a very precise structure, at least as far as its first, decisive phase was concerned. Briefly, therapy starts with a first consultative session, usually with one or more members of the extended families present along with the nuclear group. A second consultation follows, to which only the nuclear family will be summoned, which ends with the therapist announcing that family therapy is warranted and that the children are now to be dismissed for good. The third session, with only the couple attending, ends with the prescription of secrecy. If secrecy is obeyed, the fourth session will see the parents appointed co-therapists, and the evening outings will be prescribed. The following sessions will entail prescribing ever lengthier outings each time the parents have fully executed the task previously assigned to them, and this goes on until the symptom has disappeared and the family game has been modified accordingly.

The new pattern was strictly followed by two teams working alongside each other, one of them comprised of Mara Selvini Palazzoli and Giuliana Prata and the other, a new one, made up of Mara Selvini Palazzoli, Stefano Cirillo, Matteo Selvini, and Anna Maria Sorrentino. On different days of the week, these two teams used the same setting to pursue an identical research project. In June 1985, the team of Mara Selvini Palazzoli and Giuliana Prata came to a parting of the ways, with Giuliana Prata embarking on a program of her own and Mara Selvini Palazzoli carrying on with the three collaborators mentioned above.

TECHNICAL ASPECTS OF
THE INITIAL INTERVIEW

As was outlined in the Lyons report (see Chapter II), therapy will normally begin with a first consultative session to which one or more prominent members of the extended families are invited along with the nuclear family. Whether or not to hold the first session in this manner was then, and is now, left to the discretion of the therapist who fills in the telephone chart (Di Blasio et al., 1986). He will be the one to sound out the relationship between nuclear and extended families and decide who, if anyone, looks like a valuable source of information. It is counterproductive as a rule to invite members of both family clans to the same session, as this will only make them feel ill at ease and induce them to be reticent. One therefore needs to decide beforehand whether to choose, say, a paternal grandmother who has very close ties to the family and lives in the flat opposite theirs but does not get along with her daughter-in-law, or a maternal grandmother who speaks to her daughter every day on the phone and has in the past looked after the children while their mother was at work.

No matter who is finally chosen, he/she will be viewed during the session as a privileged source of information. The therapist will address such persons with great consideration and respect and carefully avoid attaching any blame to them. However, he will refrain from exploring the parental couple's marital rapport in their presence, as this would encourage them to interfere (this is particularly likely in the case of families with a psychotic member). Instead, he will focus on topics concerning the transgenerational relationships. For example, he will ask the grandfather to describe the changes he has observed over the years in each of his grandchildren's behavior towards each parent.

At the end of the session, as we said earlier, those who are not members of the nuclear family will be taken leave of amidst effusive expressions of gratitude for their splendid cooperation. This, we hope, will send them off with very warm feelings towards us, so that we will have them on our side (instead of as highly dangerous, uncontrollable enemies who could do much harm), at least until we establish solid ties with the nuclear family. However, we must be very careful not to mention the advisability of family therapy while these members of the extended families are present; we will therefore wind up the session with the noncommittal formula cited verbatim in the Lyons report (see p. 17). It would be a great mistake, in fact, to make so momentous and decisive a statement in the presence of the very people we are excluding.

Dismissing the relatives without making our intentions clear and inviting only the nuclear family to the following session, on the other hand, is a move we still see as charged with great therapeutic potential. Implicitly, it is tantamount to declaring, "You are not a part of *this* family."

If no members of the extended families have been invited to the first session, obviously nothing will stand in the way of proclaiming the team's intention of undertaking therapy there and then, provided enough information has been obtained at this stage to allow for such a decision. As a rule, however, it will always take two sessions to be able to do this. Since the family has been told over the telephone that the total number of sessions will be ten, in summoning them to this second consultative session we will assure them that this "extra" consultation will not increase the total number of sessions. Since this is a private center and they are paying for therapy, this information is essential.

SESSION TWO: THE CHILDREN
ARE DISMISSED

The second session had—and still has—a set beginning, consisting of a structured inquiry into the relationships with the extended families. Someone will often take this opportunity to "spill the beans" about one relative or another, especially one present at the previous session. The therapist jumps at this chance to extract further significant information on how specific members of the extended family are involved in the family game, by noticing who speaks up and who keeps silent on the subject, and if and how, on either a verbal or an analogical level, two opposing factions seem to be shaping up.

An important remark is in order here: For a number of years—roughly from 1979 to 1985—we were in doubt as to how this session was to be conducted. There were obviously no misgivings about devoting it primarily to work with the children, since this was to be the last time we would meet with them. We would usually be out to impress them with our skill and send them home enthralled by our expertise. What perplexed us was the scope this session should have. For a long time we carefully limited our efforts to exploring relationships with members of the extended family and touched fleetingly and indirectly on the subject of the couple's marital rapport. We were anxious to avoid casting even the slightest blame on the parents, as this would have left the children with the triumphant illusion that only the *real* patients (i.e., the parents) would be summoned next time. These reservations would at times lead us to adopt a passive stance, encouraged by our blind faith in the magic powers of the prescription that was to follow. On more than one occasion, these fond expectations were dashed precisely because the crucial session with the children had no real edge to it.

In Chapter XVI we describe in detail how we now conduct this session.

SESSION THREE: ONLY THE PARENTS
ARE PRESENT

The third session starts off with the therapist coming in to face two thoroughly baffled parents. To a greater or lesser degree, they are defiant, wary and mistrustful: Hadn't there been all this talk about family therapy? So how come only the two of them have been asked to attend today? Why has the "sick" member been left home? These are some of the queries probably running through the parents' thoughts as they wait in uneasy silence for the therapist to make the next move. True, they may have come to the conclusion that the therapist has tactfully arranged to leave the children at home so that they will all feel freer to talk about the patient's problems. Such a notion will sometimes hark back to a similar experience in individual therapy, which routinely includes a session for only the parents if the patient's age or condition should warrant it.

Thoughts of this kind will no doubt be troubling the parents as they sit waiting for the therapist to appear, and the last of our set questions, i.e., "What did *you* think of the fact that only the two of you were summoned today?" will do nothing to help bring their misgivings to the surface. As for the children's reactions at having been left home, inquiring about this will normally elicit evasive answers calculated to take the sting out of the question—the couple will affect insouciance. One of them may occasionally report that a child has said, "Oh, it's *your* turn next time, eh?" or even, "See? *You're* the sick ones!" Remarks of this sort are plainly relayed to the therapist in hopes of receiving a denial, which, however, will not be forthcoming.

Another reason why this third session was a source of considerable embarrassment to us was that we dreaded to touch too deeply on the couple's marital problems, as we feared this would annul our efforts to first establish a collaborative relationship with them and then seal off the session with stage one of the prescription. On the other hand, we were aware that a forceful and enlightening session, by adding to our credibility, would be more likely to induce the couple to comply with our injunctions. As we acquired more experience, we learned to juggle these various risk factors with increasing ability and to take plenty of time in issuing the first part of the prescription. We realized that this was something to do without any hurry, so as to enable us to observe (and, if necessary, calmly and sympathetically encourage) each spouse's reaction to our move.

SECRECY IS PRESCRIBED

The prescription comes as a reward for everyone. The context immediately changes from what it was only a few seconds earlier. We will have shifted from an interrogation, albeit gentle, to an offer of active collaboration. The therapist comes back into the room wearing a pleased smile and announces that the first stage of therapy has now been completed and that we have finished with the "talking" part of our work, which was necessary in order to understand what is going on in the family. We are ready to move on to the "doing" part.

The parents will heave a sigh of relief and, having all this time been bracing themselves for a lot of pedagogic sermonizing about the symptom and related subjects, will sit back and relax. The therapist surprises them by instructing them to tell their family that "Dr. X has ordered us to keep the secret equally from everyone." He even hands them a memo on which the statement is typed out. He makes very clear that this same message is to be given in answer to anyone's questions or, should no one ask questions, to be volunteered by the spouses on the evening of their return, when everyone is seated at the dinner table. The same communication is to be made to all significant members of their extended families (the therapists will refer to these by name and define, in each case, whether they are to convey the news personally or over the telephone), but always with both spouses present. The therapist goes on to say that this very same sentence, and nothing else, must be repeated in answer to any and all attempts to elicit further information, such as: "Did you talk about me at all?", "Did he say the case was serious?" or "Has he given you any hope?" and the like. If people outside the family know about the therapy, they, too, are to be given the standard answer, but only if they ask questions. The sentence will be spoken as calmly but firmly as possible and should not come as a discourteous brush-off but rather as what it really is, i.e., a faithfully carried out precept.

Mara Selvini Palazzoli (1986) has examined and reported on a series of cases where the parents at this point voiced reluctance or even inability to keep the secret, generally from some particular member of the extended family. This reluctance is all the more significant since the therapist has stressed that this task is being given to test whether they are eligible for therapy. He also tells them that in a case such as theirs, this procedure, the first part of which involves their keeping a secret, is the only tool the team has at its disposal for helping them. If one or the other spouse still refuses, this is a revealing clue to be examined carefully. The spouse willing to go along with the prescription will of course be a help, not only on account of his/her attitude in itself but also because it, too, will yield information.

A refusal will lay bare important parts of the game that is keeping the patient's symptom alive. This is why any information thus obtained offers the therapist the chance to attempt a very powerful intervention, one that can bring on a crisis. As we already know, handing out the prescription ends with the therapists' entreating each of the spouses to accurately report in a notebook on everybody's reaction to the announcement of the secret. After this, the couple is handed an appointment slip for the next session, which will again be for only the two of them, and the therapist clearly states that the date of this new appointment is the only thing about the session not covered by the secret, as it is important for everyone to know that therapy is proceeding.

SESSION FOUR: THE PARENTS ARE RESUMMONED AND APPOINTED AS THEIR CHILD'S CO-THERAPISTS

The fourth session marks a turning point in therapy. The parents are told that we will work only with them in future. No one else, not even the patient, will be summoned again. When this is made explicit, it usually has repercussions on the couple's attitude towards therapy. Such a message will first of all be a token of esteem. The therapist, after having checked that the couple has complied properly with the requirements of secrecy, gravely and formally raises them to the rank of co-therapists. By so doing he implicitly absolves them of any guilt that may have accrued to them in the past and enables them to join forces in a venture that, by ignoring the past, engages them actively in the future. There is a technical detail to be observed here: The therapist should make a point of referring sarcastically to the inevitable know-it-alls who will no doubt have plenty to say and object to this strange notion of summoning only the parents, when it is obviously the child who is ailing. Communications such as this prediction reinforce the parents' resolve by granting them greater authority, especially since the therapist has now come out firmly and wholeheartedly on the side of the middle generation, i.e., the people sitting in front of him. This is something we had vaguely foreseen at the time of *Paradox and Counter-paradox* (1978, p. 110–111):

> In the first years of our research, we made the repeated and obstinate error of believing that an adolescent couldn't get "better" unless one was able to change the intrafamilial relationships, especially that between the parents. In order to accomplish this, our only course was to enter into the problem in a direct and verbal manner, interpreting everything that occurred during the session, in the intergenerational relationship as well as that between the couple with the intention of changing whatever was "wrong."
>
> Besides the fact that in doing so we only succeeded in receiving negations and disqualifications, and, at best, a superficial progress, our more serious error lay in the implicit message we were directing to the adolescent: the condition sine qua non for his growth was the parents' change. We had not yet understood that the symmetric pretense of "reforming" the parents makes up the core of adolescent disturbances, psychotic disturbances included. As a matter of fact, there does not exist a disturbed adolescent who is not convinced that he is doing poorly because his parents are in some way wrong. The parents have the same belief, with this variant: each is firmly convinced that the true fault is in the other partner.
>
> It is important to note that in rigidly dysfunctional systems, such as those in psychotic transaction, the children (not only the patient) seem to willingly assume the role of "reformers": by indicating an oppressed parent, by tying down a potentially fugitive parent, or by trying to take the place of an unsatisfactory one. We observed an extreme case of this last in an adolescent girl who went so far as to adopt the role of an "ancestral father," that is, by becoming violent, vulgar, and uncouth in order to take the place of a father who appeared weak and ineffectual. A role thus willingly assumed is also assigned by the system, although always in a hidden manner, through secret coalitions and factions which are immediately denied or dissolved according to the requirements of the game.

At the time, despite these far-seeing observations, we had not yet come to fully appreciate their consequences for methodology, which are: *With a family in this phase of their life cycle, it is a serious mistake to pursue treatment to its completion with the entire nuclear family attending.* We feel very strongly that the adolescent children must, at a certain point, get disentangled from their parents' problems. For a therapeutic imperative such as this to be effective, however, explanations or exhortations are of no use: What is needed is tangible, decisive action, namely dismissing the children after two or three sessions and continuing to work with the parental couple alone. The therapeutic alliance, in fact, is an essential element and one that can be established only with the parental couple: they are the ones, except for a few cases that must be carefully looked into, who have called to request treatment and, in the case of a private center such as ours, it is they who will foot the bill.[1]

The choice of working with the parents is a realistic one to make, since this middle generation, if genuinely motivated, is the one we can ontologically rely on. Choosing to work with the transgenerational subsystems could mean treading the beaten path of ingrained transhierarchical patterns actually responsible for the family's dysfunctioning, while choosing the offspring subsystem would give us the appearance of stepping forcibly into the parents' shoes, thus accusing them of incompetence at the very least. This reasoning holds true for the single-parent family as well, although the situation requires some special precautions, to which we shall refer later (Chapter IV).

The choice of working with the parents alone, since it is an analogical communication, may, as is well known, take on contradictory meanings. Third parties—but also the parents themselves—may equate their being summoned for therapy with being labeled sick, guilty or both. This brings to mind an amusing episode, which does not really fall into this particular category: It concerns the husband of a young mother of two, who for years had been exhibiting severely delirious psychotic behavior. After two sessions with the grandparents and children also attending, the wife openly declared her lack of motivation and staunchly refused to take any further part in the proceedings, thereby obliging us to carry on therapy with only the husband. We worked on the hypothesis that the latter was unwittingly fostering his wife's delirious behavior. Therapy worked like a charm: At its conclusion, our client told us that his bar cronies were teasing him by saying; "Well, your wife's real well, now that you have been getting yourself cured." In short, working exclusively with the parents tends to render them responsible, which in turn favors therapeutic cooperation by stressing the couple's power to redeem rather than their pathogenic influence.

[1]There is a difference in the case of a chronic patient over 20, if we see that the parents are by this time entirely demotivated. Should the patient be motivated, the therapeutic alliance will be offered to him (see in Chapter XV the section, "Contraindications for dismissing the patient"). The case in which the referring person (and the only motivated member of the family) is one of the siblings has been dealt with by Mara Selvini Palazzoli (1985b).

PARTIAL CARRYING-OUT
OF THE PRESCRIPTION

It has been pointed out earlier that once proper compliance with their assignment has been verified, the parents are appointed co-therapists. Let us see what happens in the opposite case. If the secret has been let out, the therapeutic relationship will have been broken. As our experience has increased, cases of total noncompliance have disappeared. On the other hand, incomplete compliance is a very frequent occurrence. One of the spouses, for example, may have "forgotten" to inform someone in the extended family about the secrecy pact. Such an alleged oversight may escape the therapist's notice, especially if this has not seemed to be a very significant relative. An omission such as this must always be seen as a sign and accurately investigated, as it will often point to valuable information. Or else, a spouse may say, in any number of ways — nonchalantly, ruefully or with the intent to provoke — that he/she has decided not to inform a certain relative about the secrecy pact, as this would reveal the fact that the family is undergoing therapy. This places us in a ticklish position: If it is our purpose to keep the extended families from interfering in the spouses' game, should we insist on a move that will arouse the curiosity of the very people we are trying to keep at a distance? As a general rule, the answer is yes. A relative such as this usually entertains a highly relevant rapport with the spouse in question.

Consider the case of a father in his mid-forties. His mother, an old lady by now, has from childhood on treated him with withering contempt and the wound still festers. He will be loath to let her know that his family is seeking therapy, for fear of the scathing comments she is bound to make. This dilemma of the father's, however, which will certainly be reflected in his own family's behavior patterns, would never, but for the incomplete carrying-out of the prescription, have been brought out into the open where it can be worked on.

Focusing on how our order to keep the secret has been executed will yield information that must always be studied immediately. It helps reveal hitherto undetected aspects of the family game and provides the team with an operative gain far exceeding that of the prescribed secrecy itself. It will also allow the team to plan the intervention for the end of the fourth session, i.e., to decide whether to interrupt treatment after providing a reasonable explanation for doing so, to reiterate the partially fulfilled secrecy pact, or to proceed to the next stage of the prescription: the "disappearances." If this third alternative is chosen, it will make a turnabout in how the couple is defined: They are now no longer parents, but spouses. We deal with the effects of this in the following chapter, where we show how this momentous change in the couple's identity is due to their having declared that they are keeping a secret.

"TO KEEP THE SECRET
IS TO GET MARRIED!"

Explicitly announcing that they have accepted the therapist's prescription of secrecy, and then obeying it, strongly denotes the spouses' status as a couple and binds them together more thoroughly than any rite or token of legal sanction could do. Here is a convincing example:

This couple was living together. They were both in their thirties and came to us, looking absolutely miserable, for help with Alex, a scrawny twelve-year-old who for some time had been behaving in an ever more obnoxious fashion, both at home and at school. His conduct was seen as verging on the psychotic. Alex was the woman's son, born when she was very young of her stormy passion for a ne'er-do-well her own age with a jail record of several sentences for larceny. Soon after the boy was born, his father left her.

This young schoolteacher, who came from a respectable white-collar family, apparently took great delight in belying her honorable background, first by this disreputable affair and later by going to live with another man. However, as the session unfolded and we took a closer look at things, a very different picture emerged. Throughout the years, Isabella had maintained close ties to her mother, who after her husband's death had been entrusted with caring for Alex for long periods at a time. There was a long history of daily telephone calls, ritual Sunday lunches, endless quarreling and, last but certainly not least, financial dependency. All this came to light during the first session, when the therapist discovered, and was quick to veto, the circumstance that Grandma was paying for therapy.

Giuseppe, who had been living with Isabella for seven years now, was a civil servant with a modest income, and any extra expenses the family had to face depended on Grandma's generosity. The old lady never failed to complain that all this largesse towards the young couple was sorely depleting her finances. The dowager was invited to the first session but failed to turn up, pleading ill health.

During the first three sessions the team worked with the threesome, mainly trying to understand why this couple had gone on for so many years without getting properly married. It seemed odd for a schoolteacher not yet with tenure and a low-ranking civil servant to be defying public opinion so stubbornly in a small town, where such unconventional conduct was sure to meet with much disapproval. Isabella was adamant about this: She cared nothing, she said, for being formally married. As for Giuseppe, he mumbled a confused explanation: Marriage was apparently being put off until such a time as Isabella would have tenure and earn a steady income.

All this reticence, possibly due to Alex's being on hand, prompted the therapist to drop the subject and instead take advantage of the little boy's presence to check an idea that had suddenly hit her: Might it not be that

Isabella's haughty defiance of her mother by her disreputable behavior had induced the old lady to get back at her daughter by setting Alex against Giuseppe? And might Alex have responded by rendering himself insufferable to everyone, but especially to Giuseppe, whom he is trying to evict? Giuseppe's exit would make an honest woman out of Isabella and entitle her to go back and live with Alex in her mother's home. When the therapist voiced this hypothesis, Giuseppe looked a great deal more persuaded than Isabella. Alex was totally expressionless. He neither agreed nor denied anything. His behavior in session was that of a rather dull and definitely mixed-up child.

We came to the third session empty-handed. It was to be the last before the summer holidays. The therapist, together with the team, had decided to use the session to make out what the real relationship between Giuseppe and Alex might be. To this end, she proposed the following exercise of the imagination to the trio: Should Alex, thanks to his provocative behavior, succeed in getting Giuseppe to decamp, how would he then behave towards his mother, once the two of them were on their own? At this, the grown-ups looked puzzled, but Alex immediately reacted with a long, desperate bout of weeping. The therapist waited in respectful silence for this to subside. The mother's face stayed cold and hard throughout this crisis, whereas Giuseppe looked thoroughly shaken. In this highly emotion-charged moment, the therapist told herself that Alex might in actual fact have a strong attachment to Giuseppe, which his mother was in some way forbidding him to have.

Instead of commenting on this insight, or even making it explicit, the therapist decided to hand the trio a prescription: During the coming summer holidays, the two male members were to share some kind of sports activity which Alex's mother was to organize for them. An implicit message was tagged onto the prescription by warning the mother that she would have to try and bear the feeling of being left out, which would be bound to affect her while the "men" were off doing their thing. Only Isabella and Giuseppe were invited to the next session. The team's forecast was optimistic, since we supposed that Alex's desperate weeping, plus the sagacious prescription we had thought up, would certainly bring about change.

What ensued was total disaster.

When the couple turned up in September, they were absolutely distraught. In the few weeks of his first term in lower high school, Alex had managed to get himself expelled by the principal. He had constantly upset classroom procedure, played idiotic pranks on his classmates or pinched their genitals, taken to heaving deep sighs for no reason whatsoever, and engaged in nauseous feats such as smearing his nose-pickings over his books and notebooks. As for his conduct at home, it was as much as Giuseppe could manage not to beat him to a bloody pulp. In fact, Giuseppe was so worried about not being able to control his anger that he was thinking of leaving the household, in order to avoid rash behavior that might land him in jail. What about the prescription given in the previous session? Oh, yes, well, they hadn't been able to carry it out . . . not even one single time. . . . Alex hadn't been too well and they had decided sports wouldn't have been good for him.

This fourth session was a dramatic one. The therapist recontracted the couple's willingness to stand by the terms of treatment: She told them they would now have to choose whether to go on steadily propelling Alex into an inevitable career as a juvenile delinquent, maybe by shutting him away in reformatory, or whether to give a new slant to therapy and start looking into their rapport as a couple. It was Giuseppe who took the initiative. He bitterly expounded on Isabella's morbid attachment to her mother. He asked himself how he could possibly marry a woman whose every mood depended on her mother's. Isabella was quick to retort that he, too, had always kowtowed to his mother, who looked down on Isabella and her "bastard" and had always disapproved of the couple's liaison. Giuseppe cut Isabella's remonstrances short very decidedly by telling the therapist that he was perfectly willing to leave the household if this was necessary—to which the therapist countered that he would have done this long ago if he had really been up to it.

The team held a long, heated discussion. Among the several suggestions, there was one that advocated taking a legalistic stance and advising the couple to get married. Finally, however, one member of the team, who up until then had kept silent, came out with the following: "Why aren't we using the tool we always use with couples who are raising a psychotic child? What's going on here, anyway—have we suddenly all become sticklers for propriety? Whether or not they hold a marriage license is no concern of ours. They have come here for us to save Alex—so, let's prescribe secrecy. To keep the secret is to get married. If they both commit themselves to this and leave their sacred mothers out of it, we shall have accomplished something for Alex—otherwise, we've all had it." Everyone agreed at once. The therapist rejoined the couple and with due solemnity prescribed secrecy. The couple was amenable.

After a month or so, Isabella and Giuseppe appeared for their fifth session. They were quite transfigured and wide-eyed with wonder. A miracle had occurred. Alex had changed completely and turned into an intelligent boy who listened to reason, was able to discern right from wrong, and readily admitted to his mistakes. He had torn into his school work, to make up for lost time. One day, when his mother was insisting that he wear a blue sweater rather than a red one, the child unexpectedly exclaimed: "You never used to make any decisions at all, but for about a month now, you've been making a whole lot of important ones, it seems. Well, now you'll have to decide whether you want me to go on being a baby or to grow up." This was the only time Alex hinted at what was going on.

How this change came about was clearly described in Isabella's careful notes on everything that happened. We learned how Alex, for the first time in his life, had seen his mother treat Giuseppe like a husband and a parent and challenge her mother in doing so. No amount of tears or recrimination could sway her. Isabella had written:

> The moment we got home, I told Alex about the secrecy. Giuseppe was present. I told my mother the following day, when we went to her place for lunch. She and I were alone in the kitchen, Giuseppe and Alex were in the parlor and I left the door ajar so they could hear every word. My mother reacted indignantly: "*What* secret?" she yelled, "and what's all this only the two of you know about? What about *me*? Who am I, a stranger? After all I've done for you. . . ." She burst out sobbing and begged me to tell her, but I stuck to my guns. It was a hell of a day. You could have cut the air in that house with a knife. It was as though a bomb were ticking away somewhere, ready to go off any minute. At table, my mother wouldn't speak to Giuseppe, not even to ask him to pass the salt. Instead, she got up to fetch it, reaching across him ungraciously. She was raving mad at Giuseppe as well.

As the couple were leaving, they announced to the therapist that they had filed for a marriage license.

CHAPTER IV

Prescribing the "Disappearances"

ILLUSTRATING THE PRESCRIPTION

AT THE END OF THE FOURTH SESSION, once the parents have proved their commitment to secrecy, they are appointed co-therapists, and the "disappearances" are brought into play, in the manner we described previously (pp. 21–22).

This is a complicated, manifold prescription and we will devote much time to explaining it to the couple in full detail. A memo summarizing the steps to be taken is also handed them when we bid them good-bye. First of all, we make perfectly clear that "disappearing" does not involve simply leaving the house. It means leaving without getting caught in the act and without any advance notice. We illustrate this by relating a number of stratagems other couples have used, such as walking about the house in slippers and leaving one's shoes on the landing, where they can be put on at the last minute, or calling up the lift a few minutes beforehand, so as not to be found waiting for it by the children. Such precautions will obviously come in handy especially after the first disappearance has taken place and the children are likely to be on the alert and keeping close watch on their parents' every move. The family's particular routine must be studied as regards work schedules, as, for instance, the long hours of a family shop. These are concrete items to be considered when planning how best to "disappear."

We strongly advocate that the same spouse not always be the one to actually go out and meet the other, as the children may otherwise hold only this parent responsible for the escapades. We also advise the spouses to plan their outings (four of them are usually indicated for roughly a month's interval between sessions) on different days of the week, in order to rule out the idea of some prearranged, regular engagement. For this same reason we turn down the parents' plea to shift the outings to the early after-noon: We prefer them to take place when shops, offices, and the like are closed, so that any notion of the couple's going on an errand will be invalidated.

Great care is given to the notice the couple is instructed to leave. Each spouse in turn must write out the message, to show that both are conniving in this behavior. The notice is to be posted with tape where it cannot be overlooked. This is done to make the children realize at once that their parents have gone somewhere of their own free will, and there is no need to call the police. We repeat the exact wording to be used and stress that nothing is to be changed or added.

As for the evening meal, we instruct the parents to leave a normal food supply in the refrigerator but no prepared dishes, such as roasts or fancy salads. When they get home, the parents will check whether the children have eaten and what they have chosen (this, to be sure, will be of special interest to the mother of an anorectic!), but will refrain from asking ques-tions either about this or about anything else, in order to forestall a very likely retort, such as, "If you *really* want to know what goes on, all you have to do is stay home."

The parents will obviously not use their outings to visit with friends or relatives, who are sure to let the children know about it sooner or later. Instead, they are to go where they will not easily be recognized and no one is likely to tell the children that they have been spotted. We urge the spouses to come home wearing sunny, satisfied smiles on their faces, even though they may have spent the whole time sitting somewhere in their car, wringing their hands in anguish at the thought of the poor children alone at home.

Any question, whether from the children or from anyone else, concern-ing where they have been, why they didn't say anything before leaving, etc., must in all cases be met with one and the same answer, namely, "That's our business," stated calmly and with no intention of being rude. When we touch on this issue, in order to avoid any misunderstanding, we are quick to point out how this set answer differs from what we have instructed them to give in reply to questions concerning the session, which was: "The therapist has ordered us to keep everything about the session secret from everybody." The "disappearances" are something the spouses should seem to have thought up for themselves, without the therapist having anything to do with it. If someone asks outright whether the thera-pist ordered the couple to go on the outings, or if this explanation is stated as a given fact, the answer is always to be, "That's our business." Obviously, the "secrecy" formula will still apply whenever there are questions about what went on during the session.

The spouses will keep records in their separate notebooks on the verbal and nonverbal behavior they notice when they return from their escapades (such as, the children were wide awake, very much alarmed, they'd notified their grandparents, etc., or else the children were fast asleep, the kitchen was tidy, the kitchen was in a fearful mess, and so on) as well as any unusual behavior they observe on the days immediately following the outing that might be attributed to it (such as long faces, sullen silence, unusually affectionate attitudes, changes in the symptomatic behavior, etc.). We stress that everyone's reactions to the outings, not only those of the children, are to be carefully recorded.

When all the children in a family are very small, instead of a notice being left, a babysitter is asked to arrive at the home immediately before the parents leave. She should be a perfect stranger both to the children and to the family's relatives. We recommend hiring someone from a specialized agency. The babysitter will not be informed as to where the couple is going, so that she will be unable to supply this information to others.

THERAPEUTIC EFFECTS OF THE "DISAPPEARANCES"

Prescribing the disappearances, like prescribing secrecy, has a twofold effect: It is substantially therapeutic and it supplies the therapists with a great deal of information. The therapeutic efficacy of "disappearing" is due to a number of factors, to wit:

1. The parents steal away from home like two adolescents, without asking anyone's permission and without accounting to anyone for what they do while they are away. Thus, they act out behavior that for many of them is quite unprecedented. This is the reason why our announcement of the prescription frequently calls forth excited, conspiratorial reactions and exclamations such as, "Wait till my mother gets wind of this!" Also, amidst much mischievous laughter, one or the other spouse will often say, "This is something we ought to have started doing long ago!"
2. If "secrecy" has not been effective in doing so, this part of the prescription definitely *will* sever any remaining ties with people who are interfering with the couple's rapport. A spouse will often have picked a member of his/her family of origin, or one of the children, as a special confidant to be pitted against the rival spouse. Occasionally, this role will be played by a friend or a business acquaintance. The fifth session, in any case, will demonstrate clearly that it is rarely the patient who shows the strongest reaction to the outings, but usually the confidant, that is, the relative or sibling who has been holding a privileged position.
3. This, then, tends to place the patient on an equal footing with the

other members of the family group and gets him/her extricated from the web of deceit and tangled alliances that has been built up about him/her. It is important to say that if one of the spouses has been entertaining a privileged rapport with some third party—a sibling, perhaps—this relationship will have constantly been fostered by assigning the care and assistance of the "sick" one to this privileged person's ministrations: The fact that the parents now disappear from home without entrusting the "sick one" to, say, the prestigious sibling, in one and the same move frees the former from his role as "patient" and the latter from that of protector.

4. In families with more than one child, the parents' absence will engender a kind of fraternal complicity, hitherto lacking or long forgotten. The siblings have been placed on an equal footing and have a certain number of hours to share, all on their own. This often leads to forms of organized activity that will become more manifest and well-defined later, during the prolonged absence required by weekend disappearances.

5. In the extremely controlling situation usually found in families with an anorectic daughter, the circumstance of the parents' leaving the field (and relinquishing control) calls forth astonishing effects. If the patient is considered capable of looking after herself one night a week, there does not seem to be any very plausible reason for her being watched over the other six nights. This will then allow the child to follow her parents' example and shift her attention from their affairs to her own.

RELUCTANCE TO "DISAPPEAR"

The "disappearance" stage of the invariant prescription will prove an especially rich source of information even when the family refuses to comply or encounters great difficulty in carrying out the prescription.

Some parents may put up strong resistance when faced with the prospect of having to "disappear"; this may be evident from the moment the idea is put to them. This will give rise to a delicate situation in the session: The therapist will need to sound out very tactfully exactly what strategy it is, in the parents' game, that is being placed in jeopardy if the prescription is carried out. Obviously, one (or both) of the spouses has sensed immediately that disappearing from home would be a mortal insult to the privileged confidant and offend him/her on two counts: Not only would he/she be treated in the same manner as the patient, but "disappearing" with the other spouse would also be tantamount to a betrayal, all the more serious since the confidant has probably for years now been the repository of endless complaints against the other spouse. To top it all, this privileged ally has also been cajoled into believing that he/she shares the responsibility of caring for the "sick" one.

Such an elaborate affective structure, so painstakingly built up day after day, is not easily thrown over, especially as it is the only bulwark against a frustrating married life. The idea of giving all this up is frightening, particularly in view of what one stands to get in return: the dismal prospect of four hours with a spouse whose very presence one has come to loathe and to whom one no longer has anything to say. And why should one need to put up with all that heavy sarcasm, sullen silence, the humiliation of heavy sighs of boredom? Why betray a trusted ally on the off chance that the "sick" one might get better? Anyway, who says he will get better? The therapist? Who knows if the therapist is reliable?

We can imagine all these thoughts running pell-mell through the mind of each of the parents as both sit glued to their chairs, listening to this ominous prescription. Each of them now faces one of life's more difficult decisions. Accepting the proposal will entail abandoning the known for the unknown. There is the risk of antagonizing one's mother, or of speeding a privileged child (perhaps fondly imagined as the staff of one's old age) towards emancipation. This on the unlikely probability that the "sick" one will recover—this creature who has by now become a "case," and a very exasperating and burdensome one indeed. What's more, this hypothetical recovery is to come about via a specious reconfirmation of marital harmony—how anachronistic and far-fetched, only the spouse really knows.

The therapist will now very tactfully and sympathetically explore what is really behind the reluctance to accept the prescription. Without fail, the excuse will be that the parents are afraid to leave their children at home alone. The therapist will turn to the parent who seems less adamant about refusing to disappear and ask this spouse to help her understand what the other is really afraid of. She will sometimes receive valuable assistance; however, on other occasions the one who seemed more inclined to accept will turn out to have acted so only because he was positive the other would refuse.

If all this slow, patient probing eventually leads the couple to a genuine acceptance of the risk, we, too, will take the risk of issuing our therapeutic instrument. If no consensus has been reached, however, we will certainly not do this: It is far better, at this point, to dismiss the couple and express our hope that they may some day feel more strongly motivated.[1]

Nothing feels more akin to a numbing loss of therapeutic power than having to face spouses, in the fifth session, who have sabotaged our pre-

---

[1]The families who come to us have often read our books; this is why some parents blithely reject the prescription, convinced as they are that this will oblige us to pull some less formidable trick out of our hat. The dismissal, in such cases, works by therapeutically inducing a crisis.

scription in every possible way. There will be the excruciating pantomime of two spouses reading out a lot of trivial notes, which point all too clearly to the fact that, say, the privileged son has been unmistakably notified of what was going on, if only by deep sighs and significant looks ("Your poor Mom here has had to spend another of those atrocious evenings with that beastly father of yours . . . the usual torture, but for your sister's sake I am forced to grin and bear it, I suppose . . . "). Moreover, such parents are likely to put the blame for the prescription's failure on the therapist's shoulders, since they, too, feel ever more frustrated and impotent. It is therefore imperative to concentrate on the preliminary spadework, in order, whenever possible, to achieve genuine therapeutic collaboration and, if such is not forthcoming, at least to get scent of this in time.

BARGAINING OVER THE RISKS

There are cases when the therapist senses that the parents' misgivings about leaving their children at home alone are not altogether unfounded. The difficulty concerns mainly the lengthier outings, especially the weekends. However, it may arise also with regard to an evening outing, in the case of patients in an acute or chronic condition whose conduct is apt to be violent or suicidal. The parents will then be likely to conjure up dire fantasies of a child jumping out of the window or setting the house on fire, smashing the furniture or even harming a little brother. This is where the therapist must make a very clear statement: Yes, there definitely are risks to be taken, there is no denying that, and it is not our task to make light of them. All we can do is assure the parents that in our experience with hundreds of families, in which we applied this same method, not once has there been anything like a disaster, or even a serious accident. However, we say, the parents are the only ones qualified to make a decision; it depends on how they personally feel about running the risk. We urge them to weigh the pros and cons by considering the opposite danger as well, namely that of the patient lapsing into chronicity. Should the patient already be a chronic case, we explain that they are quite free to choose among the alternatives open to them and decide whether it is worth giving our treatment a try in the hopes of offering their child a more tolerable life (albeit risking that the child may instead choose to die) or whether it is preferable for the patient to eke out his/her miserable existence, in and out of hospital, just as long as he/she is alive.

Therapy reaches a dramatic climax here. Parents of severely afflicted children face the several hazards of death, chronicity, or a life of endless misery for their child, for themselves, and for any other children in the family. After careful consideration the parents will often choose to run the risk and fall in with our plan. If they decide not to, this is often — though not always—due to considerations of the type we have described in the foregoing paragraphs, to wit: There is, of course, their anxiety about a more or less realistic danger threatening their child, but parallel to this, and running beneath it, there will be the parents' deep fear that by accepting our prescription they will be placing their entire relational strategy in jeopardy. Bringing this fear to the surface, where the therapist can work on it, will be extremely beneficial.

"DISAPPEARANCES" USED
TO COUNTERACT
PATHOLOGICAL POWER

If they have accepted the double jeopardy attending the prescription— the threat to their own strategy and their anxiety about the child—the spouses will come back for their fifth session with a victory to their credit. If the patient's symptoms have even partly receded, this victory will be tangible, although the parents, as is well known, will be inclined to belittle such results or even neglect to report them, engrossed as they now are in their newfound preoccupations, i.e., a tendency on the part of the extend- ed family to disengage, the "healthy" offspring's growing drift towards emancipation, and a change in their marital rapport. Some of these cir- cumstances—or, indeed, all of them—will have been sparked by their car- rying out of our prescription.

Even if the symptom has not subsided at all (which will obviously oblige the therapists to revise their starting hypothesis concerning the ongoing game), the parents will in any case have learned by experience that they can, for a while at least, elude their child's control, which will produce the parallel effect of loosening their control over him/her. The session will therefore be given over in part to the crucial issue of the pathological power the patient has acquired and to deciding what strategies to imple- ment in order to counteract it.

It is only in this phase of therapy that the therapists can hope to enlist the parents' collaboration and have them stop giving in to, say, their suicid- al daughter's blackmail, to wit: "Unless you do things my way, I'll kill my- self." The parents will now have experienced, in the almost symbolic lapse of time of a single evening, the stirring possibility of achieving both their own *and* their daughter's autonomy. They have even acquiesced, at least in principle, to the idea that their daughter just might be using this newfound autonomy to push her resolve to kill herself to the fatal limit. And so, for the first time, they feel sufficiently sure of what they are doing to be able to tell her, through their behavior, that her life is in her own hands and that she is the only one with any say about whether she will live or die.

It is in this session, therefore, that the time-honored, ingrained patterns based on the parents' enslavement to their offspring's pathology must be broken up. We are thinking here of the tremendously taxing feeding rituals an anorectic will impose, or of the obsessive rituals and stereotypes of a psychotic, who will bully his parents incessantly and make incredible demands on them. The eye-opening discovery that they can elude their child's watchful tyranny, albeit for a few hours once or twice a week, does much to strengthen the parents' self-confidence, and they will feel encouraged to attempt even bolder and more diversified acts of insubordination — indeed, some couples, when they come for their fifth session, have already carried out such unprecedented behavior quite spontaneously.

We should remark here on our special working context: A private family therapy center is quite obviously a self-selecting enterprise. We see a special type of family and consequently a special repertoire of family games. Except for the very rare case, our team will not see families in which the parents reject or mistreat the child-patient, or whose attitude to the latter is hostile and violent. The great majority of the families about whom this book was written features parents who place their offspring at the center of their lives.[2] These are parents whose very identity is essentially reflected in their children's successful development, which is the key to their personal fulfillment. They are closely tied to their children by such behavior patterns as overprotection, morbidly anxious attachment, overindulgence, etc.

In the public health service, on the other hand, which tends to cater to a demand for control, medical care, hospitalization and the like, we often encounter family games involving thoroughly hostile and rebuffing parents and occasionally some who resort to physical violence. In this family therapy center, due to the high proportion of families in which the child-patient wields pathological power over the parents, it is of the utmost importance to get the spouses to join together in reinstating the patient in a position of responsibility.

A very important point must be made here: *Countering pathological power must never be the only track along which therapy proceeds.* A strategy that openly contrasts the symptom and defies family rituals while neglecting to implement any truly radical changes in the games that the family and the couple are playing is doomed to failure. There is a major risk of setting off a dramatic escalation that may lead the patient to perceive the tragic possibility of winning the tug-of-war with his parents by aggravating his symptom and resorting to self-destruction, as in his impotent rage he fails to find any other way out.[3] Hence, therapy will need to proceed along

[2]See Chapter X, "The Anorectic Process in the Family."
[3]For an illustration of this, see p. 231 in Chapter XVI, "Constructing Synchronic Models."

two parallel tracks and also pursue its main objective, that of deciphering and modifying the pathogenic game.

The reactions written up in the parents' notebooks, i.e., the way each parent has described them and any difference in the spouses' attitudes towards therapy, will be valuable material for proceeding with the main task — the battle against a pathogenic game that shows up time after time in every session, in the same or in differing modalities. If we abide by and respect the conditions the parents have indicated, the battle against pathological power will be seen in a positive light, by both the patient and the parents. The patient will sense that the game is changing and spontaneously find new territory and new moves beyond the constrictions of the miserable pathological power he has been clinging to so desperately. For their part, the parents will avoid the trap of taking our advice (to be firm) to mean engaging in a tug-of-war with their child, with all the attending dangerous, aggressive, and provocatory attitudes; instead, they will be induced to dodge the patient's insistent demands, firmly but without any show of defiance. They will plead exhaustion, appear depressed, and tell the child that they have become aware that their failure, in the past, was due to their constant catering to his every whim. Their attitude will give back to the child the responsibility for himself.

"DISAPPEARING" OVER THE WEEKEND

The fifth session ends with the therapist prescribing "more of the same." The evening outings will now be replaced by a longer absence from home, i.e., a weekend. The parents will be instructed to leave home on a Friday evening and return Sunday night, thus spending two nights outside the home.

The new prescription will be issued at the end of the session, in the usual fashion: The session with the couple will be interrupted while the therapist joins the team for a discussion; the spouses will meanwhile sit waiting for the therapist to rejoin them. The closing intervention will then wind up the session. This sequence of events allows us to avoid the mistake we had occasionally made of viewing the weekend prescription as an automatic extension of what we had prescribed before.

By strictly following the sequence given above, we are pursuing two different aims: In the first place, we are reminding ourselves of the need to carefully test the parents' motivation to continue with therapy (by using the detectors previously referred to) so that we will not be tempted to proceed mechanically from one stage of the prescriptive series to the following. Our second purpose is to define very clearly for the family a fundamental difference: During the session, we have offered advice and encouraged certain rules of conduct related to the struggle against pathological power. These must be taken by the family as our suggestions on how to counter the child's power play, the carrying-out of which we leave to them, jointly and individually. The prescription, on the contrary, has a mandatory character.

Increasing the dose of our "medicine" will reinforce any results hitherto achieved. Should there not have been any, the prescription will signal to the family a message that is absolutely unambiguous in defining the issues listed above, namely: establishing the spouses' undisputed claim to privacy and time of their own; severing any ties that tend to interfere with this claim; placing the patient on an equal footing with his siblings and providing an opportunity for the children to share a feeling of mutual belonging; getting the parents to relinquish control over the symptom and simultaneously delivering the parents from control by the patient. A lengthier absence will greatly emphasize the several meanings implicit in the message being conveyed.

We need only briefly mention the connotation of intimacy that will characterize a married couple's staying away on their own for two nights, or the relatively long period of time that the children, especially if they are adolescents, will be left to organize as they please while their parents are gone. The written notice serves a twofold purpose: On the one hand, it reassures the children that their parents have not disappeared forever, and on the other it tells them that they will *not* be back before the appointed time, i.e., "late on Sunday night." So, while in the case of families with small children we will often observe striking positive effects following the evening outings (usually related to the message such conduct conveys to members of the extended families), in families with adolescent children or young adults the most conspicuous results will be forthcoming once the "weekend" stage has been reached.

The invariant series of prescriptions also foresees an even more prolonged absence, perhaps covering a whole month. This is mostly implemented in the case of young adults who have become chronic cases and to whom the parents must make a very clear move of granting them autonomy and freedom of choice in all that concerns them, including the choice of living or dying. We should state that for the past four years now we have never once had to resort to this last phase of the prescription.

FAMILIES WITH SPECIAL STRUCTURAL CHARACTERISTICS

In the extensive use we have made of our invariant series of prescriptions, we have also treated a few situations that posed special problems, such as those of the single-parent family, the reconstituted family, and the adoptive family.

The single-parent family does not normally present unsurmountable difficulties. The parent is entrusted with the secret (and keeps it to himself) and is then appointed co-therapist to the child. He/she can carry out the "disappearances" alone. In this case, too, the prescription is able to strike at key aspects of the ongoing game (while revealing them). We had a particularly gratifying success with the family of a 22-year-old anorectic girl who was also an alcoholic and a bed-soiler. The girl's mother had died after the onset of her daughter's anorexia but before the other complications had appeared. The girl had an older brother and a younger one, both of them still unmarried and living with the family, although they were often away on business. The therapist told the father to think of the prescribed "outings" as the sign of a secret love-life. This, he was told, would destroy an erroneous image his daughter had of him, namely that this father of hers, still strong and attractive, was trying to get his daughter to take the place of his dead wife, even sexually. The fact that the girl recovered so completely was probably due quite specifically to the cessation of subtle paternal seduction maneuvers, which the girl could not have failed to sense and which she had warded off by making herself utterly repellent by getting drunk and soiling her bed.

We treated five single-parent families by this method and were successful in four cases. The fifth was a painful failure, due to our having overlooked a problem connected with the referral.

In the case of separated parents, we start with a joint consulting session and then proceed to work with whichever parent lives with the patient, but only if there is strong motivation for therapy.

In reconstituted families, where the parent with custody of the child has a new spouse or companion, we find ourselves faced with the problem of imposing the "disappearances" also on the one who is *not* a parent. Before we make our decision, therefore, we need to gather a lot of information and carefully examine the situation, in order not to take counterproductive action.

The adoptive family is a crucial problem for us. Very rarely will adoptive parents truly accept the responsibility our method imposes on them. They always have a convenient loophole for shirking responsibility, namely; the child's symptoms are the product of his natural parents' chromosomes or can be chalked up to those first traumatic years (months) of his life. Therapy is thus very likely to fail, and should never be undertaken without a painstaking probe into the prevailing family myths.

THE PARENTS' NOTEBOOKS
ARE DULY HONORED

From the time we first started developing our new method we realized that a place of honor in the proceedings, also on a formal level, needed to be given to the notes written by the parents at our request. Starting with the session following the one in which we prescribe secrecy, the therapist would open the conversation by saying; "Let's begin with your notebooks. Who wants to be the first to read?" This was done in order to be consistent with our own statement that the *real* information we required was that contained in the notes and related to the way these notes had been written up (or left unwritten). To start the session by inquiring about the patient, without any reference to how the parents had gone about their assigned task or how the various members of the household had reacted to the parents' conduct, not only would have seriously discredited our own previous attitude, but also would have been a methodological error. We therefore paid careful attention to the spirit in which each of the spouses had fulfilled this task.

Very laconic notes or perfunctory, trivial ones, especially in the case of well-educated families, pointed to an attitude that was not—or was no longer—collaborative. Strangely perfunctory and fragmentary notes may have been made by only one of the spouses, or one spouse may have written nothing at all, claiming that there wasn't anything special to report or giving as a pretext that the other spouse had written about everything anyway.

This "difference that makes a difference" quite obviously lights the way for us when we probe into both the couple's starting game and recent developments in it brought on by our prescription. As for the contents of the parents' notebooks, the various, often differing reactions of everyone in both the nuclear and the extended families, as described in the reports, will suggest hypotheses concerning everyone's part in the game. These need to be controlled. Any very tame reaction, or even no reaction at all, on the part of family members is abnormal, suspicious, and must be looked into.

Many examples of all this will be found in the clinical histories included in this book.

As we have already pointed out, each parent is invited to read his/her notes aloud, and they are then clarified, enlarged on and delved into by questions from the therapist. After the readings, the notes are placed in the clinical case file. The therapist then draws up the minutes of the session, including a careful rereading of the notes, and underlines the more significant parts of these reports. This last move has had a number of surprising effects. In one case, which up to now has remained unique, the mother of a severely psychotic little boy used her notes (which she obviously hoped the therapist would later read) to vent her strong grievances and intense aversion with regard to her spouse. She had omitted reading these parts out loud during the session. In another case, the father of a 15-year-old encopretic padded his copious notes (which, however, he bravely read out loud during the session) with a long list of charges against his wife's parents and warned the therapist not to believe that his wife had really told them about the secrecy. There are also cases in which one parent, in reporting what has happened, will take the opportunity of the therapist's mediatory presence to include a few swipes at the other.

Aside from these exceptional cases, the reader will be able to see, by studying the transcripts of the parents' notes as they appear here and there in this volume, how genuine a testimonial they provide and how infinitely more convincing they are than any interpretation or *a posteriori* reconstruction.

PART TWO

Use of the Prescription and the Emergence of Recurring Phenomena

CHAPTER V

The "Imbroglio"

HOW HYPOTHESIZING AN "IMBROGLIO" REVEALS A COLLUSIVE PROCESS

THE PHENOMENON WE CAME TO CALL "imbroglio"[1] was historically the first to emerge in the course of our research. It turned up at the point of intersection between two recurring observations:

First we observed some unexpected reactions when our prescription was carried out. Far more frequently than we had expected, the parents' first "disappearance" did not so much alarm or incense the identified patient as it did a sibling or some other relative. This latter would then be the one to completely disregard the notice left well in sight by the "disappearers" and rush to phone the hospital and the police. Such behavior conveyed an implicit message to us, namely, "If *I* was not told in advance of any plans of this sort, something unforeseen and terrible must have happened." This was our clue to the fact that the person thus involved was the trusted favorite and confidant of one of the parents.

The other piece of recurring evidence was one we spotted during the session. A son or daughter showing the symptom would either be perceived by everyone in the family (or appear from our preliminary inquiry) as having enjoyed a particularly privileged rapport with one parent. However, when we observed interactions during the sessions, this special rapport proved conspicuously missing and the identified patient would, in fact, treat this supposedly most-favored parent either with studied indifference bordering on contempt or, less frequently, with the impassioned resentment of a jilted lover. After we had seen a good number of such cases, we started to work on the assumption that a behavior of this kind was the

[1]It will become clear as we proceed that the term takes on a special composite meaning here, encompassing the idea behind the English word (embroilment, entanglement, confusion) and the original Italian one denoting outright fraud.

pragmatic effect of the betrayal he or she had suffered at the hands of precisely the most beloved parent. We further hypothesized that the betrayal had hit home very shortly before the symptom set in and might actually even have been the symptom's unclenching factor.

This composite, recurring phenomenon we termed "imbroglio." As is always the case when attempting to name a new and complex notion, semantic problems arose. "Imbroglio" had been a useful part of our team's colloquial jargon: At the beginning we used it to define a specific dyadic phenomenon, namely the deceit and betrayal the identified patient senses have been perpetrated on him or her by the most-loved and trusted parent.

As our research proceeded and we took a closer look at how interactive processes tend to merge into the symptom, "imbroglio" assumed an overall, interactive meaning. We now use the term to cover the veritable maelstrom of "communicating behaviors" the members of a family exchange among themselves that is triggered by a specific move in the game, which we decide to consider the opening gambit.

Imbroglio, then, is a complex interactive process that appears to arise and develop around the specific behavior tactics one of the parents brings into play. It consists of bestowing a semblance of privilege and preference upon a dyadic transgenerational (parent-offspring) relationship, when, in reality, this professed rapport is a sham: It is not grounded in genuine affection and is nothing but a strategic device used *against* someone else — generally the other parent. An example should help make this clear.

A father openly lavishes praise and esteem on his firstborn daughter, endlessly extolling her wisdom and diligence. This behavior is implicitly aimed at his wife: He feels she is neglecting him and he uses this ploy to signal his lack of regard for her. For a tactic of this kind to work itself into an intricate game, there will have to be collusion, which, in turn, sparks reactive behavior in all the other family members, each busily working to his or her own ends.[2] Thus, the wife's reaction may not be to actively oppose this privileged father-firstborn rapport, but rather to let it ride. In the first place, she is determined not to afford her husband the satisfaction of seeing her suffer, and secondly, she is quite content to be allowed to enjoy the genuine, easygoing relationship she has with her secondborn daughter. As for the firstborn, she falls in with her father's design, mainly because she is sincerely flattered by his attentions. She takes his admiration at face value and strives to be worthy of the reward he allusively dangles before her eyes. She will also use the situation to punish her mother for the latter's envy-arousing relationship with her younger sister, in whose shoes she would so much like to be.

A quiescent equilibrium of this sort, structured around two stable and

---

[2]Members of the extended families, of course, also become collusive parties to this game.

by and large satisfied transgenerational couples, might theoretically last forever without any hint of a symptom. Disruption ensues in the wake of events that lay bare the fake nature of the privileged father-firstborn rapport. An event of this sort can be (a) the daughter's sudden or gradual awareness of how overridingly important the mother is for her husband, an idea that then forcefully brings home to the daughter that she has been used and deceived; (b) a genuine, heart-felt affection the father develops for his secondborn daughter, often coinciding with the girl's entering adolescence; at such a time, the blossoming out of her biological and psychological personality will quite normally foster a father's infatuation.

The "repertoire" of imbroglio situations we observed also comprised a number of other unsettling circumstances: For example, the secondborn daughter may undertake a seductive maneuver aimed at her father. At times, she plays her hand very skillfully, adopting an elusive, hard-to-get manner and making herself scarce psychologically in a way that cannot fail to arouse her father's interest. Such behavior reflects her longing to teach her insufferably goodie-goodie sister a proper lesson by snatching her father's much-touted affection away from under the older girl's nose. As to the mother, we often see her pretending not to notice the artful web of seduction her secondborn is weaving around the father, since she is all too happy to have this adolescent's help in keeping her spouse enthralled by what he finds at home. She may also be gratified to see her secondborn avenging the many humiliations the firstborn inflicted on her in the past. As we stated earlier, all or any of the above circumstances can cause the existing equilibrium to totter, leading to the symptomatic behavior, as soon as the pseudo-privileged firstborn girl realizes she has been used by her father, first led on and then "ditched."

At this point the firstborn daughter's position becomes untenable, for a number of reasons. First of all, and most significantly in our opinion, all that has happened heretofore and is now happening almost entirely defies verbal expression. This impossibility of putting matters into words is easily explained. An interacting family organization such as the one hypothesized in our example functions around multiple analogical levels that tend to shift and get snarled up with the passing of time. The fundamental exchanges underlying relationships such as these, and indeed all close, intimate human rapports, extend far beyond what is said. What members of a family significantly exchange are mainly behaviors, not words, and these behaviors influence each other. All really momentous exchanges take place at an analogical level where, paradoxically, there is the greatest danger of misunderstanding, denial, and disproof. Moreover, in looking back at our session records, we find that verbal communication may very likely have often been used in the family's past history to justify or whitewash not precisely immaculate behavior, so that our firstborn's mounting suspicions of having been duped and sold short appear to take shape from vague hunches and painfully mixed feelings, rather than from any clear and rational perception.

Let us now try and carry this concept further, deliberately disregarding the circumstance that the state of affairs is virtually impossible to express verbally, structured as it is around mainly analogical exchanges. Even if we neglect this factor, other stumbling blocks, very serious ones, stand firmly in the way of an outright denunciation of the double-cross. Let us look at them.

A transgenerational entente (in our case, involving father and firstborn daughter and built up to the detriment of the mother) inevitably has an illicit aspect to it. Now, the partner in an illicit venture is by definition not overly trustworthy, so that denouncing the existing alliance is bound to meet with disavowal. Moreover, complicity in itself is a trap. The duped one is aware (quite clearheadedly, in our view) that she has in a number of ways aided and abetted moves in the allied parent's game and has thereby become entangled in the misdeed. She is conscious of the illicit nature of what has been going on and of her part as an accomplice. This, together with justified misgivings as to her ex-ally's loyalty, is more than enough to compel her to keep silent. She will resort to a covert form of retaliation — in our example, a symptom.

Consider what the one on the losing side of such a family imbroglio would have to manage in order to avoid falling into the tragic symptom trap. Briefly, in the case of our firstborn, (a) she needs to grasp and translate into words the complex interactions everyone is busily spinning at an analogical level, where they are way beyond the reach of any verbal expression; (b) in the highly unlikely case that she be able to do this, she will still have to get up enough gumption to come down squarely on the side of one parent against the other, especially as it is the latter's affection she really craves; (c) she will have to own up to her acts of connivance; (d) she will have to expose the betrayal she has been a victim of and face her former accomplice's denials and counter-charges — and not only his, either!

In a recently published article, Mara Selvini Palazzoli (1986) tells of a personal experience she had, in order to help the reader understand a predicament of this sort. Although with far less weighty consequences and roughly similar to the problem we are dealing with here only by virtue of the attending psychological circumstances, Palazzoli's experience nonetheless let her gain valuable insight into the complex nature of such imbroglios. Her "embroiled" misadventure had precisely those characteristics of "dirty" collective games that make it so difficult for the duped one to "come clean." Since he has been taken for a ride as a result of his own connivance in dealings he knows to be shady, he is in no position to press charges. His quandary parallels that of a patient just before he or she resorts to symptomatic behavior. We must, of course, keep well in mind that in a family imbroglio the matter will certainly not be as dispassionately rationalized by all concerned as was the case in the episode that follows.

Throughout all these years I have been haunted by one question: Why is it that these families give us so little help in helping them? Why do they so often keep important information carefully concealed from us, or tell us lies? . . . An episode in my personal life may provide you with the insight it gave me.

Many years ago, in the hall of a subway, a man offered me contraband cigarettes. Tobacco is a government monopoly in Italy, and to buy contraband cigarettes is an illegal although very common practice. Since at the time I had unfortunately not yet given up smoking, I bought two packets, and was so naive as to hand the man a large bill. "Sorry, no change, wait a moment," he said, and off he went, quick as lightning. I waited for quite some time, getting rather nervous. At last he reappeared, apologized, and handed me a few coins change. I started protesting. Quite unexpectedly, the fellow turned sarcastic and said with a smirk, "You can't fool me, lady, you gave me a small bill." I got very indignant and raised my voice. Quite a crowd gathered to watch what was going on, and all at once a policeman was standing before me. "What's the trouble here?" he asked. I knew this police- man by sight, a big, hefty man, usually on duty there. Quite trustingly, I told him that the man was trying to cheat me out of about fifty dollars. To my great surprise, he looked absolutely unaffected by my plight. I went on protesting at the top of my voice, only to have the policeman give me a withering look and say harshly, "There's the way out, lady," pointing his arm towards the exit, "Stop griping and get out of here at once, before I lose my patience." The people standing around seemed very amused, so he went on: "Look at this woman, will you, she's a real character, she is! She buys contra- band cigarettes and has the nerve to ask me for protection!" And again, to me: "Now you go straight home, or I'll treat you as you deserve." I went off home, of course, but all the way there I felt overwhelmed by a hurricane of emotions such as I had never imagined anyone could experience. I was furious at the rascal who had cheated me, of course, and furious at the policeman, but I was also very deeply ashamed. Above all, I was angry at myself: How could I have got myself embroiled in such a mess, with no way out? The thought was unbearable. Buying contraband cigarettes was against the law. I had been robbed, but since I myself had done something illegal, I was an accomplice of the man who had cheated me. How could I denounce him to the policeman without at the same time denouncing my own mis- deed, and how could the policeman possibly come to my rescue without at the same time faulting me for my illicit behavior? Worst of all, I was positive that the policeman was hand-in-glove with the smuggler! Still, being a party to the crime, I couldn't accuse him. So strong were my feelings — waves of anger and shame, but also of confusion and impotence kept sweeping over me — that for a long time I kept the whole story secret from my family, and it was years before I felt able to tell my husband about it. However, this experi- ence provided me with a clear notion of psychotic imbroglio. When I at- tempt to identify with the feelings of a patient showing psychotic symptoms, all I need do is recall the turmoil of my own feelings, and my own symptoms, as they were on that occasion. Try to imagine what happens to someone conniving in an imbroglio not with short-lived characters who will soon fade out of his life and be forgotten, as in my case, but with key members of his family, with whom he has to live day after day and who may play a decisive role in his very survival as a human being. When I remember how long I kept mum about my little quandary with even my closest relatives, I no longer find it difficult to understand how a psychotic can live year after year in a psychiatric institution and keep a deathlike silence, broken only now and then by explosions of uncontrollable fury. (pp. 348–349)

IMBROGLIO IN ANOREXIA NERVOSA: WE SEARCH FOR THE EVIDENCE

Once we had identified imbroglio as the peculiar interactive family process leading to a son or daughter's symptomatic behavior, we decided to check our findings systematically also in cases involving the families of anorectic patients. The idea that prompted us to undertake such an early-on exploration of the imbroglio hypothesis and its dramatic sequel of betrayal was a very specific one: We hoped to be able to effect changes in these families without having to run the gamut of prescribing. In short, we were embarking on something that theoretically held out considerable promise, namely that the wealth of information gleaned over years of constantly using our prescription would allow us to make correct assumptions about the ongoing game and thus break it up at a very early stage in therapy, bypassing the prescriptions.

In other words, we were hoping that a recursive effect of some sort would accrue to these prescriptions, making their use less mandatory as time went by. We had long been aware that we would not be able to carry on with them forever; the day was bound to come when we would have to get them into print, revealing *why* and *when* we made use of them. We knew all too well that many families, before they come to see us, read up on our methods in the books we have written. Getting our prescriptions into print would mean that their surprise element would be lost, and we considered this the very essence of their potent effect, not so much on the parents as on their entourage. The device would inevitably lose its potential for eliciting information-loaded reactions. We therefore needed to have something new ready to replace the prescriptions before they appeared in print.

In itself, controlling our imbroglio hypothesis in this new context consisted mainly of examining, case by case and very early in the proceedings, what took place in the wake of the imbroglio's disclosure. We decided that our normal procedure in cases of families with an anorectic patient would be for the therapist to devote the second session to working principally with the offspring along the following line of questioning: *Who* does the patient feel has "jilted" her, for *whom*, and *when?*

We began this systematic control with the family presented in the account that follows. This case is described not only because it was chrono-

logically the first, but mainly because of the extraordinary effect our control unlocked during the session, an effect so astounding as to exceed our
wildest expectations. We very much doubt whether any of our colleagues,
inured by years of experience to the super-circumspect, super-well-bred
families of anorectic patients, has ever witnessed a patient "spill the beans"
in front of everybody the way our patient did in this case, laying bare so
utterly "unspeakable" a secret as that of her entente with her father. This
came about after much provocation from the therapist, who used every
opening she was given to show she was already in the know about the game
and was ready to take upon herself the responsibility of its being made
public.

The C. Family

The C. family was made up of five members, a couple of middle-aged
parents and their three daughters. The patient, Carla, was 20, the secondborn, Olga, 15, and Alice, the youngest, was 6. Even before our first meeting with them the therapist and supervisor had been placed on the alert by
a phone call from Mr. C., who had been the one to supply the data for our
telephone chart. The chart showed that two years earlier Mrs. C., pregnant
for the fourth time, had decided, with her husband's consent, to have an
abortion. The husband was now calling us to entreat us not to raise the
subject of the abortion during the session, as the girls knew nothing about
it. Actually, Mr. C. went on, Carla *did* know about it, having overheard her
mother talking to a friend over the phone, but "my wife doesn't know that
Carla knows." The sticky mess the father dished out to us in his call was, if
nothing else, a strong hint of secret tête-à-têtes between Carla and her
father, with the latter being the only one to "know that Carla knew." This
was something for us to keep in mind in drawing up a model of the ongoing
game.

Our immediate concern, however, was to get the therapist untangled
from the awkward position of having to share a secret with the husband
behind the wife's back. Also, we had to allay Mrs. C.'s fears of something
about the abortion being revealed during the session. To this purpose, the
therapist phoned Mr. C. and told him she needed to clear up the secret of
the abortion personally with his wife prior to our meeting, in order to spare
her any unnecessary anxiety. She asked to be able to speak to Mrs. C. there
and then, to inform her that Carla knew about the abortion and assure her
that the subject would not be brought up during the session, as it concerned only the parents, and the daughters were to be left out of the
matter entirely. The conversation took place, and Mrs. C. sounded very
relieved and grateful.

This done, our team concentrated on fleshing out the imbroglio hypoth-

esis with the data at hand. The telephone chart indicated a culture gap
between the two parents, with the father several cuts above his wife. Also,
it showed Carla's school record as being exceptional, whereas Olga's,
scarcely adequate at best, had suffered a severe setback during the previous school year, her first in the school that had long been the scene of
Carla's triumphant scholastic career. Olga was such a misfit there that her
parents kept her at home after the first months. They enrolled her in
secretarial college for the next school year, and she settled in nicely.

Carla's anorectic behavior started roughly two years earlier, and got
worse during her last year in upper school, at the end of which she took her
finals, naturally with flying colors. She lost weight rapidly during that year,
and her condition failed to subside despite her success in school, the
summer vacation that followed, and her enrollment at the university as a
student of architecture.

With this information to go on, plus the telling disclosures in the father's
phone call, we drew up the hypothesis that Carla, in cahoots with her
father from way back, was resorting to the symptom in order to protest an
imbroglio she had recently become aware of, namely that her father admired her only on account of her brilliant scholastic accomplishments,
whereas he loved Olga, now reaching adolescence, for her own sake.

There was an embarrassing moment during the first session when we
realized that our hypothesis was widely off the mark. Carla, a pale, intelligent skeleton of a girl, staunchly asserted that her school record had never
greatly impressed either of her parents and that, quite to the contrary, she
had felt very much alone in her sincere pursuit of cultural betterment, with
no help from her father. She went on to say that both her parents, but
especially her mother, had tended to play down her quick-wittedness and
eloquence, lest all this display of talent mortify Olga. Mrs. C. made no
mystery of the fact that she had had Carla while still too young and
immature, and had always thought of Olga as her *real* daughter. She accounted for her husband's and her own lack of enthusiasm for Carla's
outstanding scholastic achievement by the fact that there were two high-
brow female relatives in the family whose private lives were a shambles.
The father was masterfully adroit at keeping his cover, echoing his wife's
worries about Carla's overriding passion for book learning. We were absolutely unable to determine *if* and *when* he had shifted his attention to
Olga. We were also at a loss to understand what the latter's appeal for him
might be. Olga was a rather common, sallow-faced brunette, affecting the
churlish manner peculiar to so many 15-year-olds. As for little Alice, she
struck us as being a somewhat dull child, who squirmed about in her chair
at every question we asked her, looking nonplussed and eyeing her parents,
waiting to be prompted.

This disappointing first session ended with our summoning the whole
family again after a month's interval. We volunteered no comment whatso-

ever on what had happened during the session, nor was any asked for. This was mid-December, and in taking leave Carla announced jauntily that the whole family would be going to Egypt for the coming Christmas holidays.

Then came the second session, which was to be momentous indeed. While preparing for it, both therapist and supervisor were determined that the father was to be flushed out of hiding this time. We were much helped during the session by a very striking worsening of Carla's physical condition. We waived aside the conventional explanations given for this, such as overexertion and the change of climate, and insisted on hearing directly from Carla how things had been during the journey in Egypt. It turned out that everyone had been in a strained mood throughout, due to the fact that Olga showed up only for meals and spent the rest of the time ignoring her family entirely. She had joined up with a roisterous gang of young folk, who were obviously having a wonderful time.

The therapist then proceeded to ask the increasingly loaded questions she had previously agreed upon with the supervisor, to wit: (a) "Who do you think was most offended by Olga's making herself scarce?" Carla's answer came quick as a flash: "Dad." (b) "When did you first notice that Dad considered you nothing but a fine, sensible girl, whereas it was Olga he was really enthralled with, even to the point of having jealous feelings about her?"

This second question was a tough nut to crack. The father kept his poker face, while Carla, clearly on the defensive, denied she had ever noticed any such thing. The therapist was not to be sidetracked. She informed Carla that it was written all over her how little she had relished having to drink tea with a bunch of old fogeys while Dad sat fuming at Olga's gallivanting about with a crowd of young people. She referred jokingly to Olga's precocious discovery of one of the oldest womanly wiles, namely, that she who plays hard-to-get will get chased. This remark abruptly altered the mood of the session. Father sat there, looking as impassive as ever, while Olga burst out in sardonic laughter. Mrs. C. chimed in to say that for two years now Olga had been playing the femme fatale, even during their vacations at their lake home: She'd go off with a whole lot of young lads no one knew anything about. And yes, her husband resented this very much.

The therapist was now in a position to turn to Carla and exclaim: "How come you haven't caught on yet to the fact that your being around all the time, and so easily available, has caused your glamour to wear thin? Familiarity breeds contempt, you know." At long last, the provocation hit home: Carla started losing her self-control to the point where she got properly angry and came out with: "Well, I *have* to stay around because of Alice, see? And Alice needs me more than ever right now." The importance of this crucial utterance escaped the therapist's notice and she mistook it for a pretext. The supervisor, however, rushed to the buzzer and called the therapist out from behind the mirror to propose a third question, one that could not fail to disclose the circumstances that Mr. C. and Carla had an understanding which excluded Mrs. C.

THERAPIST   You told me back there that Alice needs you more than ever right now. Who made you feel you should be the one to have to take care of Alice, seeing that Mom is not up to doing a proper job of it?

CARLA   (under her breath): Dad . . . but not because Mom isn't up to it, it's just that she's so nervous, she makes a lot of mistakes . . .

The father, who up to that moment hadn't opened his mouth, came out with a blunt, emphatic statement, stressing every word, "I never said anything of the kind to Carla." At this Carla reacted vehemently, as though she'd been slapped. She jumped to her feet, stood straight in front of her father and shouted, "Oh yes you did, and for years and years, too. Do you want me to repeat your exact words, here, in front of all of them? Do you? You started this when I was eight years old and Mom got sick. When I was a little girl, the two of you would squabble constantly, and I'd always take your part because you were my idol, you were God, and she was the neurotic one, and I'd always side with Dad because I'd think, 'Dad's the one who's right,' and I went on thinking Dad was right all the time, until I found out it's he who is to blame, really, more than anyone else, and that I had this idea of my mother lodged in my head because he put it there." At this point the father turned to the therapist and solemnly raised his hand asking to be heard. In formal, exaggeratedly deferential tones, he gave the following speech.

FATHER   Kindly allow me, doctor, to say that I consider it my duty now to shed proper light on the matter. My wife has always been neurotic. She is a sick woman. Her dear, departed mother knew this all too well, and she spoke to my parents about it, and her sisters know about it, too . . .

THERAPIST   Well, I must say that if I were in your wife's shoes, with everyone in the know about my predicament—my mother, my husband, my in-laws, my daughters—all of them considering me a neurotic, and my firstborn daughter enlisted by her father to patch up all the mistakes I made in Alice's bringing up—well, I wouldn't feel very comfortable, to say the least. (Throughout the whole of this discussion, including the therapist's remark, Mrs. C. sat with her head bowed, showing no reaction.)

We must at this point admit that, despite the density and breath-taking intensity of everyone's reactions in that crucial second session, which ended by our bidding farewell to the daughters, our hopes of achieving a prompt change went unfulfilled. Carla aggravated her symptoms. It took a number of sessions with her parents, with the therapist probing deeply into the matter of the abortion, to get her to relinquish them. It also took the scrupulous carrying-out by the parents of a series of ever lengthier "disappearances," which entailed overcoming the father's extreme reluctance.

What did all this laborious effort finally allow us to reconstrue? First of all, that Carla, before therapy started, had already suffered two betrayals at the hands of her father: The first was revealed by the abortion and the second by his infatuation and jealousy for Olga. However, the abortion was the chief issue. Eavesdropping on her mother's outpourings over the phone to a friend led Carla to a discovery that shook her terribly: Her father, that model of propriety, who secretly pleaded with her to stand in for her poor mother, even entrusting her with Alice's upbringing, demanded frequent, passionate lovemaking from that attractive lady and then actually encouraged her to have an abortion. The father's shifting of his attention to Olga thus seemed to us of minor importance and an outcome of the hostility Carla had begun to show towards him after discovering his two-faced nature.

In concluding, we wish to stress how our work with other families later shed much light on the extreme tactical cunning certain members will bring into play. In the case of the C. family, the father was the able tactician: With just one phone call he got us on the wrong track by preventing us from mentioning the abortion in Carla's presence.

IMBROGLIO IN SCHIZOPHRENIA

The tangled maze of relationships we venture into when we deal with families of anorectic daughters is a tidy garden path compared to the thick jungle we need to grope our way through when families of schizophrenic patients are at stake.

To quote Mara Selvini Palazzoli's article, "Towards a General Model of Psychotic Family Games,"

> We repeatedly came across skillfully concealed games and maneuvers which, in the colloquial language of our team, we came to call "dirty games"[3]. . . . A game was "dirty," in our use of the term, when the players resorted to foul means such as subtle cunning, brazen lies, relentless vindictiveness, treachery, manipulation, seduction, ambiguous promises, ambiguous betrayal, and so on. Such means appeared particularly "dirty" because their real purpose,

---

[3]To avoid misunderstandings, we should stress that our use of descriptive epithets such as "dirty," "foul," etc., merely provided us with a convenient label for situations within the domain of the game metaphor. We were not heaping abuse on *people*: They are not dirty, foul, or whatever else, but their *game*, viewed within the framework of metaphor, quite definitely is.

as far as we could make out, was masked or disavowed, never admitted, in order to attain it more easily. What was more, this type of game contrasted sharply with the kind of families we were seeing—well-educated, apparently sensitive, dedicated people. Our hypothesis was that the patient's psychotic behavior was directly linked to a dirty game. We were repeatedly able to confirm this. For instance, psychotic behavior would explode precisely at the time when the patient felt he/she had been betrayed, or at least jilted, by the very parent who had always been closest to him/her. This game we named "the imbroglio." (1986, pp. 345–346)

As time went by, we realized ever more clearly that these families were crack players, trained in a context that taught them to manipulate relationships, using set verbal ploys and crafty moves refined and added to constantly over the years. Delving into this sophisticated bag of tools, we poor, untutored beginners could only gradually recognize such tactics as simulation (falsities) or moves that were feints or warning threats.

A clearer picture of our problem comes from examining the many instruments that make up such a secret armory. We will, therefore, attempt a succinct and necessarily simplified presentation of the ploys and countermoves that entered into the interactive processes of family members who came to see us about the problem of their schizophrenic son. Incidentally, the reconstruction of family histories such as this, which was as fascinating as a saga and cost us much sweat and tears, is badly served by its presentation, which renders it fragmentary and banal. Even deciding *how* to convey such a history is a ticklish matter, since we are forced to choose a mode of presentation: If we supply a wealth of detail and tell the story as though it were a novel, we risk getting tedious in our attempts at didactic accuracy. There will be a lot of pompous pointing-out of things, such as, "this was simulation, here we have a feint, that was a warning threat," and so on, ad nauseam. On the other hand, we could devise a synthetic table, listing in one column a series of events and behaviors, and in the other our reading of them in terms of a game or of countermoves, i.e.:

MOVES IN TIME SEQUENCE

Favorite son leaves for stint with army, adjusts easily to barracks life and seldom bothers to phone home.	Son is signaling to his mother that he is breaking away from her.
Mother goes to visit son and acts dejected.	Mother is making son feel guilty through her sadness.
Son comes home for a three-day leave at Christmas. The day after Christmas, mother departs to go and visit with a married daughter,	Mother is issuing a warning threat: "If you prefer your fellow soldiers to me, I shall prefer your sister to you."

leaving son alone on his last day of
leave.

Son returns to barracks and two days later falls into a delusional crisis, whereupon his commanding officer sends him back home.	Frightened by his mother's threat and angry at her having ditched him, son must get back home in a hurry, to control what is going on between his mother and his sister.

However, this resembles an accountant's ledger, with none of the heart-fluttering, rage and anxiety that always accompany interactions such as these, and will therefore provide a poor picture. Lastly, should we choose to present a vignette, jotting down essentials and relying on the reader's experience and intuition to flesh out the story, important connections may get overlooked and the result will be a largely inadequate model. The reader will discover that we have used all three approaches in different parts of this book, and can judge their respective merits for himself.

In the case we present here we resorted to the third mode, as the inter-actions were of a highly complicated nature and several attempts to try the other two tacks went askew. Here, then, is a highly synthetic account.

The Costa Family

The family household consisted of five members. Filippo, the patient and only son, was born between an older and a younger sister. The family was very well-off. The father was head of a large industrial enterprise founded by one of his forbears. He was an educated, ancien-régime type, clinging to hide-bound traditions and values. He had married beneath his social rank and cultural level, probably, we felt, because he wanted to make sure there would be someone around to raise a fine, sheltered family and preside over the homestead with devotion and propriety. The family lived in a huge villa surrounded by park grounds, just outside the limits of the small town where the father's company was located.

The two spouses began feuding at an early stage, with the quarrels apparently pivoting around opposite viewpoints: The father idealized the concept of home but spent hardly any time there, as his work kept him away even on holidays. His wife had come to loathe the family business as though it were a rival and frequently gave vent to her hatred of her husband's work, while obviously enjoying the life style it provided.

Filippo, the male heir, had been in a difficult position from early child-hood on. Very quiet by nature, and meek and shy in manner, he suffered from a number of ills and pains during his late childhood and preadoles-cence, and grew up in an aura of sickliness. His mother latched onto the boy's poor health as a pretext for turning him into Mom's little helpmate: He spent the day trailing around after her in the huge mansion, keeping her company, singing and making music after the fashion of a courtier troubadour. The two girls, Ilaria and Marta, born before and after Filippo and eight years apart in age, were as dissimilar as could be. Ilaria, two years older than her brother, was a high-spirited, bubbling little extrovert, whose presence would fill the house of itself. When she came home from school or sat down to meals, her voice would be the only one heard. Marta was the other extreme: She resembled Filippo in many ways, being soft-spoken and meek like her brother, but was far more enterprising than he was, perfectly capable of looking after her own affairs. She held genuine religious convictions and was part of a parish youth group.

The family went through a very difficult period when Ilaria, at the age of 17, embarked on open rebellion. Those were the days of widespread student upheaval, and Ilaria threw herself into the fray with a vengeance. She would slam the door on the sumptious villa she lived in to go down and mingle with the mob of young people in the streets. She would whiz around on the back of motorcycles, smoke pot, and nonchalantly dabble in all kinds of erotic experiments, from which she would return in the wee hours. Her father would wait up for her, slap her around, and make endless, passionate remonstrances. He obviously suffered deeply from her behavior but was quite unable to curb it, the more so since Ilaria's mother, surprisingly and in open contrast to her husband, espoused her daughter's cause as though it were part of a crusade for women's liberation.

As for Filippo, all this was later to cause him to make the tragic choice that led to his undoing. After Ilaria's revolt, when he, too, reached the age of 17, he also decided to join the student movement. Our hypothesis concerning his decision was the following: Filippo was perfectly sure he would be able to count on his mother's fellow-feeling, since he had always been her special pet — so, nothing to fear from that quarter. His sheltered position in the family, however, had bracketed him out of his father's "male" world and Filippo was, like Faust, willing to sell his soul just to have his father rave at him, too, and to see the same angry flame in his parent's eyes that Ilaria had so often aroused.

Although he was by temperament utterly unfit for such an undertaking, still Filippo went down into the streets to fraternize with the demonstrators — who promptly hailed the "kid brother" with derisive hoots. He did the best he could to be one of the boys, but his heart was not in it, and secretly he was probably terrified by what he was getting into. There followed a long sequence of disasters. His father failed to get at all angry at him and definitely was never found waiting up for him when he came home late. In fact, it seemed as though he actually pitied his son. The really cruel blow was to come from his mother. One evening Filippo, caught up as he was in rioting with the mob, neglected to go and pick up

Marta after her meeting at the parish, so the girl waited for a long time in a dark alley. The mother, who up to that time never once commented on Filippo's zealous insurrectionary efforts, reacted to this oversight with disproportionate violence, losing her self-control and heaping scornful abuse on his revolutionary heroics. At once, it became all too obvious that she had never had any use for Filippo's rebellious aspirations. Ilaria's stance had come in handy as a feminist banner behind which to move against her husband, but by this time she had quite enough of Ilaria's shenanigans as well. Her sympathy was all for Marta now, whose religious ideals she was then beginning to share.

The morning after that scene, Filippo stayed in his room. He was later found lying motionless on his bed with a sheet pulled up over his face. He had begun a radical hunger strike, which in a short time so undermined him that he had to be taken to the hospital.

In the meantime, Ilaria had moved to the nearby big city and entered the university. On her rare visits home, she waxed as fiercely sectarian as ever and waged furious verbal battles with her father. She was living with a foreign boy and spending considerable amounts of her parents' money; however, her principles extended to insisting that Filippo should never, for any reason whatsoever, go to work in the family business, as that would have labeled him as "the boss's son." At about this time the myth got started that Filippo's ruin had come about as a result of his exaggerated infatuation with Ilaria. Had he not idolized her when they were children? Had he not followed in her footsteps and joined the rebellion? So, when the family gathered in the livingroom after dinner, and Filippo sat there despondently saying nothing, father would often turn to him as though aiming to cheer him up and say, "How about it, Filippo? Shall we give Ilaria a call?" Filippo would fail to react, whereupon father himself would go off and call his daughter.

When the family first came to our center, Filippo was 23 and had been through several periods of hospitalization for delusional crises into which he had fallen after his anorectic protest. Labeled a chronic schizophrenic by the psychiatrists, he was by that time living in total idleness and under sedation in the huge family villa. Relational events concerning him had taken another turn.

However, we do not wish to dwell on the period described above, which served merely as the background for our reflections on the imbroglio Filippo came to find himself in (and actually brought upon himself). Over the long years, his mother had always made a show of the tender relationship and special affinity that bound her to him, in order to retaliate covertly against her husband for never being home. Filippo, feeling secure and flattered, had fallen in with her designs. His uneasy bewilderment started when Ilaria, reaching adolescence, gave herself over body and soul to the student movement. To be sure, Filippo had trouble understanding how so respectable a woman as his mother could back her daughter in such disreputable activities, but he was far more puzzled by the attitude of his father. Up to that time, his distant and prestigious father had paid only cursory attention to anything "the kids" did. Now he suddenly was passionately interested in Ilaria's affairs, waiting up for her night after night and staging the most formidable rows. Was this the same man who showed such deep respect for Marta and praised her modesty and sagacity? The crunch came when Filippo, bravely venturing forth in Ilaria's footsteps, was confronted with his mother's scathing sarcasm. At that precise moment his position became untenable. He was wedged in between a mother who heaped admiration on Ilaria but was secretly in love with Marta and a father who extolled Marta's virtues but was secretly in love with Ilaria. This last secret was such a terrible one that it required such snide maneuvers as pretending it was Filippo who wanted to speak to his sister on the phone, when it was her father in fact who yearned for the sound of her voice.

The relational modes this family of expert players adopted in their time-honored tactical manipulations appeared to obey one main caveat, roughly the following: In matters involving one's affections, it is best never to show how things really stand and far more advisable to show exactly the reverse.

Another family with a chronic schizophrenic son afforded us the rare opportunity of registering an explicit verbal enunciation of such a caveat by the parents, who owned up to the simulation each of them had brought into play—with the noblest intentions—in their relationship with their three sons. Here, the intricate web was made even more Kafkaesque by the fact that the family also had two adopted daughters, who immediately corrected their parents' statement, showing that the imbroglio was even *more* embroiled! We have kept the videotape of this session as a precious historical relic and may some day get around to transcribing it verbatim; we provide a summary here.

The R. family featured the parents, aged 50 plus, who had been separated for eight years and formally divorced for two. Neither had remarried. They had three sons: Gino, 33, Massimo, 31 (the patient), and Franco, 24. They also had two younger daughters by adoption, aged 22 and 18. Franco was the only one who lived with his mother. Gino was married and had a child of his own. The two girls worked and lived independently, whereas Massimo, when he wasn't in the psychiatric ward, lived in a dingy little room his father bought for him and worked in a desultory fashion in his mother's antique shop.

At the start of the second session, the therapist asked the routine questions centering on the type and evolution of each parent's relationship with their offspring. The therapist's attention was drawn mainly to the firstborn, Gino, who was parenting, to the extent of having been the one to call us and request therapy. The mother claimed her husband had always had a special relationship with Gino, whereupon the father denied this adamant-

ly, stating that he had always had a weak spot for Massimo but had carefully concealed it in order not to hurt Gino. The sisters both insisted that
their father's real favorite was — and always had been — Franco. At a later
point during the session, the two adopted daughters accused their mother
of giving Franco far too much leeway, spoiling him atrociously and making
a swelled head out of him. Franco was, in fact, a fine-looking boy with a
very self-important air about him, who boasted about building a sailboat
with his own hands. He hoped to be a skipper some day, and went on about
his hobby as though he were getting ready to launch a fleet. While he was
showing off, the mother suddenly leaned over towards the therapist and
whispered confidentially, "I must be frank with you, doctor: I always really
did prefer the girls. I wanted a daughter so much that I adopted two! I
never wanted to show my true feelings in front of the boys, so that they
would not be hurt." "What?! Really, now," the younger of the girls burst out,
"do you mean to say you pretend to dote on Franco because it's really the
two of us you prefer?"

Gregory Bateson had this to say:

> It seems that the discourse of unverbal communication is precisely con-
> cerned with matters of relationship — love, hate, respect, fear, dependency,
> etc. — between self and vis-à-vis or between self and environment and that
> the nature of human society is such that falsification of this discourse rapidly
> becomes pathogenic. From an adaptive point of view, it is therefore impor-
> tant that the discourse be carried on by techniques which are relatively
> unconscious and only imperfectly subject to voluntary control. (1972, pp.
> 418–419)

This opens up vistas of staggering complexity: What can be the outcome of much eager, conscious falsifying of relationships on the part of
one of the players in an interactive game, all the significant tactical moves
of which consist of rapidly exchanged behaviors largely beyond the pale of
verbal expression?

IMBROGLIO AND THE
SINGLE-PARENT FAMILY

Morawetz and Walker (1984), in a detailed and enlightening work on the
subject, examine the many problems that beset the single-parent family in
the course of its history. By far the greater part of the single-parent families
who consulted us for the problem of an anorectic or psychotic child had
suffered the loss of the other parent through death, and only a very few
were single-parent families as the outcome of a divorce. We shall therefore
not deal here with single-parent families who are such from the onset, as in
the case of an unwed mother.

Widowhood

Several pathogenic games may get underway in a family with a widowed parent. We will discuss here only the most severely damaging of these, i.e., the relational imbroglio we find almost every time we are called upon by a single-parent family to deal with very serious symptoms — anorectic, psychotic or schizophrenic — shown by a member of the youngest generation.

There is a fundamental concept that should be mentioned here immediately. Widowhood is obviously in itself a critical event in the history of a family. However, the baneful consequences we shall now examine will be found *only* if an "embroiled" relational organization had already taken over *before* the death of one of the parents: In this case, the surviving parent may easily behave in such a way as to provoke competitive strife among the offspring, or between the offspring and some member(s) of the extended family, in a process we posit as metaphorically equivalent to a "war of succession."[4]

Widowhood engenders the need for interactional reorganization — a key issue. To whom will the bereaved parent turn for solace and support? Whose advice will she/he value most? Who will be chosen to fill the gap left by the spouse and comfort him/her in loneliness? It will be clear at once that such questions will not cause particular harm if the parent behaves openly and coherently and shows unequivocally whom he or she intends to turn to for support. One of two diverging attitudes has it that an "inside" choice (i.e., within the nuclear family) is to be preferred, since it will not subject the offspring to close contact with a stranger, while the other considers the "outside" choice to be the more sound, since by recomposing the couple it will help along the offspring's emancipation. We feel very strongly that no organizational choice, so long as it is made perfectly explicit, is harmful in itself. In the many cases we were called upon to treat, it was invariably persistently suspended judgment on the part of the widowed parent on the matter of who was to succeed to the deceased that laid the scene for a veritable, albeit undeclared, "war of succession."

How can such a phenomenon be brought to light? In contrast to what we advocate in Chapter IX, where we tend to assign a clarifying role to modelizing the psychotic process by taking the parental couple's game as our point of departure, in the specific case we are now discussing we find it more expedient to start from a different stage in the proceedings. Since the couple has dissolved as such prior to the outbreak of symptomatic behavior in the child, we consider it necessary to reconstrue the several steps by which relational reorganization proceeded in the wake of the parent's death (although, of course, it may at times be possible to make out, a

---

[4]There were two cases in which we discovered such a war had been going on prior to the parent's death — and one in which it had broken out after a fatal outcome had been prognosticated but failed to materialize!

posteriori, that the couple had previously been locked in a stalemate conducive to a later "imbroglio" configuration). We were sometimes able to
grasp the particular type of game, which was almost always one involving a
tangled rapport with members of the extended family.[5]

With regard to the interaction shifts that come in the wake of a parent's
death, we believe that reducing the whole problem to how mourning is
experienced oversimplifies the issue, since such a point of view considers
only the impact of the stressful event on the patient's psyche, to the
exclusion of all else. The idea of leading from problems connected with the
"succession," by contrast, was an inspiring one, in that it allowed us to
correctly date the process and trace the embroiled relational configurations
back through the family's past history. We believe one must pay special
attention to the covert strategies of those widows/widowers who, in apparently random fashion, deal out to their several offspring allusive blandish-
ments and equally allusive frustrations, thus continually creating and fuel-
ing a tantalizing ambiance of uncertainty and fierce competition.

A parent will act in this manner because it is coherent with the rules of
his/her personal learning context: In the game of reciprocal provocation
previously engaged in with the deceased spouse, he or she will already have
attempted to enlist allies on his/her side against his/her partner. With
widowhood, the strategies of such a parent will obey more immediate
motivations, such as fear of being forsaken if the children should leave
home or the desire to get a game going on some other "board"—usually
that of the extended family. This stands in sharp contradiction, of course,
to what the parent openly professes, which is exclusive concern for the
children. Be that as it may, the immediate and most significant phenomenon (provided one suspects that it is there somewhere and takes the trouble to go looking for it) is the following: The widowed parent is the principal initiator of a series of confusing moves that tend to keep him or her at the
center of his or her children's interest and concern. This is the common
denominator we perceive in the three cases we shall now briefly describe.

(1) Andrea Sarto lost his father when he and his (slightly older) sister
Mariella were small children. In those first years after their father's death,
Andrea seemed to take it for granted that his mother should rely on the

---

[5]For an interesting debate on the subject of widowhood, see Stierlin et al. (1987).
These are the proceedings of the 1985 Heidelberg conference: On pages 163–205
there is a transcript of the discussion various therapists joined into after viewing a
videotape. The tape presented the first session with a family in which the
youngest child, age 15, manifested symptoms of paranoid schizophrenia that had
set in shortly after his father's death. From this transcript one gets a vivid picture,
among other things, of two widely differing conceptual and theoretical viewpoints: that of Norman Paul, who stresses the issue of how mourning is managed,
and that of Mara Selvini Palazzoli, who proposes the paramount importance of
"imbroglio" and a "war of succession" involving the siblings.

somewhat older child for support and comfort. However, as the two of them reached adolescence, and the well-behaved, highly praised Mariella left home for college, Andrea's mother led him to believe that his turn as chief comforter and advisor had finally come. The harsh facts soon countermanded this promise and dashed his hopes. Andrea's rightful place, which he had so longed to take, was occupied first by a maternal uncle, then by Mariella's fiancé, then by a friend of the family, and finally—the supreme insult—by his mother's very old mother, who had always been considered slightly unhinged. This old lady was now brought into their home and given full status, so that even she ranked higher in the family hierarchy than poor Andrea. Within a few months, his body weight plummeted from 72 to 36 kilos!

(2) Lia Cella was brought to us for consultation for anorexia that had become chronic despite a lengthy individual therapy. Her condition had taken a sharp turn for the worse of late, and the girl had quit her studies although she was very near to getting her degree. With Lia, to this first session, came her mother, Eva, who had lost her husband many years earlier, her brother, Lorenzo, a brilliant college student, her mother's unmarried sister, Grazia, and Lia's maternal grandmother. Here is how we traced back the process that had culminated in Lia's symptoms:

Eva had lived her whole life in a small town. She had worked as a seamstress in her home after she married, having had to give up her job in a workshop as her husband disapproved of her working outside the home. Her husband not only was extremely possessive, but also inflicted upon her the presence in their home of his two aging parents, whose only son he was. The grandparents died soon after the couple's children were born. Lia, who resembled her father and took after him in character, besides being especially close to him, soon started to mimic his controlling ways: She would do everything she could to prevent her mother from so much as chatting with her clients. Besides her work as seamstress, Eva also countered her husband's bossiness by keeping up her close ties with her sister Grazia, who had chosen not to marry and lived the life of a successful career woman in a big city; Grazia visited very often at her sister's home and was very fond of her only niece and nephew.

When Eva's husband died, she turned to this brilliant, emancipated sister for support and put her in charge of a number of practical matters that Eva's children were still too young to manage. Just when the children had reached an age when they could qualify as full members of the household, their mother's father died and Eva decided it was her duty, not Grazia's, to take in her elderly mother, even though Grazia had just retired. Eva said she felt Grazia and her mother couldn't live together on their own, as they had always quarreled incessantly about everything. So Grazia moved in with Eva to help care for Grandma. She gave Lia and her brother the use of her city apartment, which came in very handy when they needed somewhere to stay while attending college.

Eva's confusing maneuver consisted of ostensibly professing that she was very upset by this invasion of relatives, so that Lia, who had always yearned to be her mother's support and comfort, found she couldn't feel resentful towards Eva but had to vent her disappointment on these relatives. Meals became the scene of continuous infighting, first between Aunt Grazia and Grandma, then between Lia and either of these two, with Eva desperately trying to keep the peace and Lorenzo sitting in splended male isolation in front of the television set. And that was not all—to offset the fact that her children had the use of Grazia's apartment, Eva refrained from countering her sister when Grazia intruded blatantly in Lia's love life. Furthermore, in order to keep Grandma and Grazia from feuding, Eva had her sister sleep with her in the double bed she had shared with her husband.

Despite all of this, Eva masked her satisfaction over these arrangements behind a lot of deep sighing, which perpetuated the ambiguous image of a mother totally devoted to her children who, through no fault of her own, had not been able to spare them this serious upset in their home life. Lia, thoroughly mixed up and furiously hostile, started her anorectic fasting as a protest against Grazia's triumphant usurpation and her mother's covert, treacherous obsequiousness.

(3) In the case of Lieta Mariani, whose mother sought our help, being alert to the issue of "succession" guided our inquiry during the entire first session. Lieta's father had died ten years earlier, when his children Dorian and Lieta were 15 and 7. The family had always shared living quarters with the father's family, and they all worked together in the family concern. Relationships within the two families were fiercely contentious.

Lieta's clinical record told us she had started exhibiting phobic behavior (school phobia) at roughly the age of 10. Two years before we met her, however—she was 17 at the time—her condition had taken a sharp turn for the worse. She had abandoned her studies and all social ties entirely, and was going through manic and depressive stages with manifest paranoid behavior.

Lieta's brother, Dorian started out right after his father's death, on a deviant career that soon culminated in drug addiction. Our investigation, using the "war of succession" metaphor to guide us, yielded the following information: After his father's death Dorian had not, as might logically have been expected, been instated as his father's successor. Even before the sad event Dorian, then in a phase of rebellion, had been set up against his mother by his father's parents; he had also been intensely jealous of his sister, who was considered a paragon and was very close to their mother. It was Lieta who, when their father died, was appointed to the role of comforter to a depressed and ailing mother. Dorian, spurned and looked down upon, soon adopted the depressed and suicidal option of heroin. At this point his mother rallied and decided she absolutely had to save her son, at all costs. She enlisted Lieta, too, in her effort to control Dorian, who by this time had taken to beating people up, stealing and getting admitted to hospitals and community centers from which he regularly escaped after only a few days.

Lieta fulfilled all the duties towards Dorian that her mother had entrusted to her with meticulous care, but started on a phobic withdrawal. Her mother had apparently managed to impress upon her a terrifying picture of the world outside the family walls. After a few years of total warfare, Dorian suddenly and unexpectedly came to his senses: He got a job, started making plans, and requested his mother's financial aid to start a business venture of his own. His mother discovered he was far more pleasant company than Lieta, who was promptly dethroned. However, as we kept probing for more detail, we found that Dorian wasn't really all that well: He was subject to bouts of agitation and despondency, and he would occasionally act ill-advisedly on an impulse.

The team centered its inquiry on the problems of the mother's relationship with her own mother. The unbelievably profound, rankling resentment she felt toward her mother came to light. The older woman, it appeared, had always behaved like a spoiled, irresponsible schoolgirl and was now making a point of showing how much she preferred her two other children to this daughter. It also turned out that this grandmother had been widowed at a very young age! Thus, the "war of succession" theme apparently ran like a thread from one generation to the other, with its tragic attending sequel of distress and conflict.

Divorce

The relational tangles we find in families in which one of the parents has died also occur frequently when parents divorce. They do not necessarily center around the spouse who has custody of the children, but may involve either of them. If a parent views the separation as incomprehensible and unjust, he may fall into a deep depression that complicates the issue of reorganizing family relationships as far as the offspring are concerned. Such complications can become the source of much anguish if this parent, fearful of being abandoned, entices the children into a subtle game of confusing moves that constantly fluctuates between delusions and dashed hopes and creates jealous and competitive feelings among them. So, just as it does in the case of a widowed parent, the dysfunctional phenomenon we have metaphorically dubbed "war of succession" may also beset relational reorganization in the case of divorced parents.

Divorce, as opposed to widowhood, will, however, in itself entail a greater likelihood of relational quicksands. Let us start with the simplest of these dangers, that which threatens the estranged couple. One often observes that two parents, although they have dissolved their partnership, cling to exactly the same contentious relational pattern and raw emotional tension that made it impossible for them to go on living together. This will have no pathogenic effects on the children, however, so long as the latter are not (or do not get themselves) involved in the parental couple's game. Pathology will flare up whenever a child is involved, or gets himself involved, in a relational imbroglio.

In our extensive records of families treated for a child's anorexia there have only been three cases of severe anorectic symptomatology erupting in the wake of the parents' divorce, and we were able in all three, despite specific variables, to ascertain that one and the same relational imbroglio was at the root of the problem, to wit: The patient, prior to her parents' divorce, had not only been hoodwinked by one of her parents into thinking she enjoyed a privileged rapport with him but had also been enticed by seductive promises dangled before her eyes. In other words, she had been given to understand, "Once we're out of this hellish mess, you'll see how wonderful things will be—you and me together, just the two of us who understand each other so well that we don't even need words. . . . "

Then, when the divorce is final, the treachery stands revealed in all its cruelty. The future patient has been brutally brought face to face with the bitter fact that she always has been, and in all likelihood always will be, nothing but a sympathetic ear into which her pseudo-ally could pour all his resentment against the spouse from whom he professed to have broken away. The girl's hunger strike will begin when she finds that the fundamental premise of her affective and cognitive universe has come crashing down around her.

Now we come to the baneful games that may get underway when one of the divorced parents remarries. The relational imbroglio can reach an incredible degree of entanglement in such cases. Take the example of a reestablished couple, in which the husband marries a young woman whose first marriage this is. This husband has not yet severed his convulsed ties with his first wife and may therefore entice his young spouse into joining him in a game of perverse alliance that has the ex-wife as its target. A game of this sort will have devastating effects if it involves "using" the children.

We remember one case in which a divorced mother called on us for help. She was living with her four children, aged 12 to 20. Her ex-husband, an artist, had married one of his young pupils three years earlier. We managed to ascertain that the new wife, with her husband's tacit approval and connivance, was implicitly instigating the children against their mother. Their father, who in the past had never bothered about his children, had suddenly conceived passionately tender feelings for them and wanted them around all the time. The youngsters thus found themselves exposed to the strong contrast between a home inhabited by a glum, overworked mother and the cheerful, welcoming new ambience their father and his wife had created for themselves. They were torn between a tendency to blame their mother for having failed to understand this gifted, imaginative man and keep him at her side and, deep within their hearts, their guilt feelings towards her. These conflicting feelings clashed continuously, as is inevitable in a situation of this kind.

Harmful games of this sort will be found to involve members of both the remarried couple and that which has broken up; if they also involve the children, and this is frequently the case, they must very definitely not be overlooked, as their pathogenic potential is enormous. One must examine the possibility that such games are going on, and probe into them, whenever children of divorced parents show symptomatic behavior. These games almost always also involve members of the extended family, especially grandparents.

There is a further relational imbroglio connected with divorce and remarriage, to which we will refer briefly in conclusion. This is the case of a child who becomes the object of flattery, enticement, or outright seduction on the part of the divorced parent's new spouse. Here, too, we never start by taking such amorous attention at face value, but always train our sights on the couple's game. It is a matter of looking into and unraveling the motivation and purpose that prompt the new spouse to enact a move of this kind in his/her game with the divorced parent. Does it perhaps conceal a threat, or the attempt to enlist an ally, or is it a retaliatory move for having been made to feel less important than these children, or than this particular child, or could it be one of any number of other things? The motivation and purpose behind such a move can, in any case, be made manifest only by starting from the proper assumption, namely that it is *a strategic move made in the couple's game, which involves "using" the child.*

CHAPTER VI
Instigation

Concise Oxford Dictionary
Instigate: urge on, incite, (person *to* action, *to* do usually something evil); bring about (revolt, murder, etc.) by persuasion. So *instigation*.

Vocabolario Devoto e Oli
Istigazione (arcaico *instigazione*): persuasione al male, protratta con assiduità consapevole e dichiaratamente fraudolenta (a delinquere, alla ribellione ecc.)

Dictionnaire Robert
Instigation: action de pousser quelqu'un à faire quelque chose.

INSTIGATION AS A PROCESS

ADOPTING THE GAME METAPHOR meant resolutely heading our research project in the direction of complexity. Linguistically, such a move clashes with an everyday use of certain terms that is firmly rooted in a pattern of cause and effect. "Instigation," as is clearly seen from the several definitions cited above, is one of these terms. It engenders serious misunderstandings, especially due to its moralistic connotation. While well aware of this, we have nonetheless required a word to cover an idea and have yet to find or invent one that suits our purpose better. We hope that our use of the word will become clear as we take our readers along the winding path we ourselves followed when we first attempted to define the *concept*— starting, ironically enough, from precisely the moral value judgment normally implicit in the word *instigation*.

In an unpublished paper, Mara Selvini Palazzoli described how the first intuitive inklings eventually led to her giving this particular name to a special process:

> The first time I ever even used the word was in the spring of 1981, in a moment of utter exasperation. My colleague Giuliana Prata and I were nearing the end of a series of extremely taxing sessions with the family of a 21-year-old chronic anorectic-bulimic, whom I shall call Giusi. G. Prata was

behind the mirror. The case had been referred to us by a psychoanalyst who was a friend of the family. He had told us quite frankly that he considered it practically hopeless. Several previous attempts at treatment had failed, including psychoanalytically-oriented family therapy. Giusi, by now a chronic case, had been an exceptionally attractive girl, the only daughter of well-to-do parents, both successful in their respective professions.

As the therapist, I worked for several sessions with the parents alone, and they faithfully carried out the invariant set of tasks I prescribed. Giusi showed considerable improvement, although she had not yet entirely shed her symptomatic behavior. She still tended to act in a provocative manner, mostly toward her mother. This had me perplexed.

At the end of the eighth session, just as she was leaving, Giusi's mother told me in a highly distressed tone of voice that the girl, during these past weeks, had once again succeeded in giving her mother sleepless nights. She recounted that Giusi had received a letter written in French. Claiming that it was difficult for her to understand, she took it to her mother's office for help in translating it. It was a note of only a very few lines, written by a young Frenchman with whom, Giusi explained to her mother, she had had a brief affair a few days earlier. He was writing to tell her that he had just discovered he had syphilis.

This behavior seemed to me so incredibly harsh an attack on the mother that I was absolutely aghast — so much so that, as soon as the parents had left, I ran to my colleague in a state of great excitement, exclaiming: "We've missed something here, can't you see? There's something we haven't been able to ferret out! In order to contrive such an extravagant plan merely for the sake of torturing her mother, someone must have put Giusi up to this. Now, who was it? We must succeed in finding out who it was, and in the very next session, too, as otherwise we shall have to abandon these poor people in midstream."[1]

So, we had to be on the lookout for instigation and find a method to bring it out into the open.

This quest for the proper procedure — that is, the one we finally adopted — was in itself a trial-and-error business. First, we probed in the direction of the extended families, but we soon ruled out, as not particularly important, any pathogenic power to "instigate" wielded by family members who are not blood relatives, i.e., in-laws and the like. Any interference from these relatives is seen as part of an established cultural pattern, and therefore is not confusing. It will not particularly upset a child to notice that her paternal grandmother disapproves of her mother, especially in view of the fact that she clearly sees that the opposite situation also applies.

Next, we turned our attention to the blood relatives. There might be a

---

[1]Instigation is as pathogenic as it is *inconspicuous*. Like a malignant tumor in an inner organ, it works unnoticed and sets the scene for disaster. When I review our past caseload for instances in which we failed to succeed, I see now what I was unable to see at the time, namely, the many clues pointing to the fact that our ignorance of this phenomenon was behind a good many such failures.

maternal grandmother, for instance, jealous of her own daughter, who in a lot of verbal and nonverbal ways was trying to replace the real mother in the eyes of her grandchild. In the session with parents which we held after this intuition struck us, we first investigated the role of the paternal grandmother, who had died several years before. This person turned out to be not at all significant, since she had been openly jealous and aggressive toward her beautiful young daughter-in-law.

Next we focused on Bianca, Giusi's maternal aunt, a woman suffering from bouts of depression. Bianca, who was getting on by now, had always clearly shown how envious she was of her younger sister's charm and successful career.

Finally, it dawned on us that the place to look was within the parental couple's rapport. In the following session, therefore, the therapist continued to concentrate on the issue of the envy this fascinating spouse might be arousing by her beauty, vivacity, good breeding and elegance, not to mention her professional success. The therapist asked the husband what he thought about this. Very reluctantly, he admitted that he felt irritated now and again, for instance, at parties, when his wife would act in what he considered an exaggeratedly showy manner.

Here, the therapist realized, she had finally touched the core of the matter: The beautifully serene lady lost all control. She raged at her husband for always having been secretly jealous of her success and popularity, her many friends, her social grace and the articulate conversation she was able to make at parties, her skill at playing the guitar and singing and dancing. . . . Oh, not that he'd ever actually reproached her for such behavior, but she'd always seen him sunk in an armchair somewhere in a corner, sulking or staring straight ahead as though he were oblivious to all that was going on. Maybe, she went on, this was what so often brought on her bouts of discouragement and frustrating anguish. What on earth for? What fault of hers was it if her husband chose to behave like a mummy whenever they went out somewhere, and was she to blame if he constantly played second fiddle in his career?

The session laid bare a paradoxical fact. The husband had grown to detest precisely those traits in his wife's personality that once had attracted him and made him fall in love with her. Another and far more important issue was raised: How did all this come to happen? What exactly had the wife been overdoing for the problem to have reached such an advanced stage? In other words, was it really his wife's social manner in itself that irritated the husband, or was it, rather, his sensing that it was enacted in order to humiliate him? We explored the wife's provocative behavior very patiently, in great detail, and were able to pinpoint several instances of it. But we went further. We discovered another important fact. The husband always responded to such provocative behavior on the part of his wife in one and the same way: He would remain utterly impassive. His wife could grasp that he was furious only because his poker face would get very pale.

This session helped us construe the following interactional pattern for this couple:

camouflaged provocation $\rightleftarrows$ camouflaged rage

in which the provoking party was never able to get the provoked one to explode, and the provoked party's behavior would set off more provocation, and so forth, ad nauseam. This much was clear to us. But where did Giusi come into this dyadic game? Which parent had set her up? We first hypothesized a natural congeniality between a jealous husband and an envious daughter. However, we soon realized that certain bits of behavior enacted by the wife, which were equivalent to flaunting her superiority, might have nettled not only her husband but also her young daughter. Also, Giusi was almost certain to have seen the rancor she herself felt for her mother reflected on her father's face, and might well have wondered why her father was so faint-hearted as to stand for his wife's social pyrotechnics without reacting in any way. Likewise, Giusi's father could not have failed to notice the same bitter vexation that rankled in him on his daughter's face. Therefore, he must have behaved towards the girl in an indirectly seductive manner, signaling: "I'm so terribly unhappy, and I'd be so much better off if I had a nice, soothing person like you for a wife. . . . "

This patient reconstruction eventually led us to assume, for a while, that the onset of Giusi's symptom, given that particular family's pattern, was the result of Giusi's conviction that her mother had far too much of everything, compared to herself and to her father: She was far too beautiful, far too attractive, too charming, too intelligent, too cultured, too successful professionally — why, she even had a beautiful daughter to show off! This last item on the list was the only one within Giusi's power to take from her mother. When the family first came to us, Giusi had been an anorectic for years. She was losing her teeth and her hair, and her mother was ashamed of the way her daughter looked.

This was all very well as a hypothesis. However, if it were true, why was Giusi so cold toward her father, too? Why was she making *him* suffer? Why did she seem to delight in upsetting him by her behavior? We hit upon the explanation later on, when we realized that this father, who had prompted her behavior and enacted a lot of seductive maneuvers aimed at her, had not been able to go on indefinitely keeping secret the real object of his desires, namely, his wife. At that point, Giusi realized at last that her mother, although she had lost her beautiful daughter, was more than ever in possession of her husband. Her father was a traitor. Giusi was the one who had ended up all alone. So, forlorn and forsaken, Giusi went on acting out her silent protest against both her mother's triumphant exhibitionism and her father's cowardly submission.

How did it all end? This is a tale worth telling: There was an extraordinary epilogue.

During two sessions these issues were adequately brought to light. These were followed by the summer recess, during which these highly intelligent parents decided to impose on themselves a series of ingenious but very formidable "prescriptions," such as I, as their therapist, would never have dared even to suggest. The mother "went into depression," and took a six-months' leave of absence. During that time she stayed home, wearing a dressing gown, lazing about on a couch, slovenly and whiny and certainly not acting in a way to arouse anyone's envy. She felt that only by becoming a sick, unattractive woman would she be able to really "get through to" her daughter. Her husband kept on tirelessly with his work, but whenever possible he would be at his wife's side, encouraging her and pleading with her not to give up hope. No one was paying the slightest attention to Giusi anymore. She tried one last, extreme show of strength and made another suicide attempt, a very dangerous one. She was saved miraculously in an intensive care ward, where she was then kept for several weeks.

Meanwhile, her parents had made a crucial decision: When Giusi got back from the hospital, she found she no longer had a room to live in. What had been her room was an empty space. Her father took it upon himself to break the news: "I've taken an apartment for you on X street and had all your stuff moved there. You'll find a checkbook there for an account with sufficient funds in it to tide you over for three months; after that you'll have to support yourself. Your mother and I have decided to give you back responsibility for yourself in every way—and that includes your decision either to live or to die."

Faced with such a clear, unambiguous message, Giusi said not a single word. She made an about-face, went to her new home, and did not commit suicide. She carried out a few more manipulatory maneuvers aimed at her parents, but soon discovered they didn't work. A few months later, she had found herself a job and was quite well. When the parents told me all this they admitted that they had been on very strong sedatives for weeks, in order to keep their anguish at bay and to sleep nights. But they did it! Giusi's mother was back at work, as beautiful and successful as ever, even though she couldn't manage to be quite as socially brilliant as she had been.

Let us now go back, hopefully having made things clearer, to the knotty issue of what meaning to ascribe to the word *instigation*. In everyday usage, as we see from our dictionary definitions, the term takes on a dyadic linear-causal dimension: Someone sets someone else up, and someone is set up by someone else, i.e., one party acts and the other is acted upon. Things are not that simple, however. The conceptual model we adopted is based on the hypothesis that "someone's instigating someone else" implies *at least* a triadic level: In fact, someone will instigate someone else *against* a third party. The triadic perspective, as we all know, automatically carries with it an exponential increase in complexity. Unfortunately, however, our investigation, like our descriptive language, cannot escape the mandatory constructions of summation and analytic complication if it is to move towards greater complexity. In other words, our research must *per force* explore segments of circuits and deliberately resort to arbitrary punctuation: Why has the instigator chosen to instigate that particular person and not someone else? What was the previous relationship between the "instigated one" and the third party? And what had the "instigated" one conveyed back to the instigator? In what way might the "instigated one" in turn reinstigate the instigator?

In the case discussed above, for example, if we punctuated the story by assigning to Giusi's father the role of originally setting the ball rolling, we also needed to get to the bottom of whatever it was that had caused him to draw closer to the girl. A shared feeling of having been abandoned, perhaps? We also needed to understand in what way Giusi's mother was provoking her husband and whether, and in what way, Giusi was signaling to her father that she deeply resented her mother's provocations—thereby instigating him all over again! All this would go on until resorting to the symptoms—easily interpreted as Giusi's extreme "j'accuse" directed at her mother—might have the paramount instigatory effect on her father, i.e.: "It's my wife's fault if my daughter is in such a miserable state."

At this point it became quite clear, despite the facts that all our punctuation had been arbitrary, and the feedback reactions had considered only the triad, that there was no sharp boundary between who does the instigating and who is affected by it. The instigated one is at the same time an instigator, and the reverse is true, whereas the third party—to whom we assign the role of the principal "agent provocateur," the one who sets the whole process in motion—is made to pay a heavy penalty.

We are perfectly aware, of course, that, despite our efforts to describe the subject's complexity, we have resorted to a good deal of simplifying. In actual fact, the situation we are liable to encounter will be far more complicated and involve any number of parties instead of only the three we have presented in Giusi's case. Still, we hope to have shed more light on the meaning we ascribe to the term "instigation": *Instigation, in our use of the word, is not simply an act, or a sequence of acts, but an ongoing interactional process.* It is in the very nature of such a process to head silently and relentlessly towards a dramatic climax, no matter what historical background has engendered it or what greater or lesser contributions each of the actors may have made to it. It is a silent process, one rarely or not at all entrusted to explicit verbalization. The scenario does not foresee Iago's perverse monologues, nor his pouring mendacious revelations into Othello's eager ears, nor Desdemona's innocent doom. The tragedies played out by most of our families will have nothing to show the spectator, when the curtain rises, except a squalid succession of symptomatic behaviors.

Indeed, for the therapist, this is where the curtain rises — on an epilogue every bit as silent as the process to which, in a certain sense, it is putting an end. Our task is to provide the process with a sound track, to endow it with a voice and a vocabulary, to track down its original premise and bring to light its essential meaning.

INSTIGATION PRIOR TO THE SYMPTOM

The felicitous outcome of the case involving Giusi's family inspired us to use the intuition it had provided in order to start systematically from the hypothesis that instigation might be at work in all cases where we sensed its presence and so we needed to be on the look-out for it. Although we were as yet a long way from having drawn up a proper model, at least we had come to recognize the role of the parental couple and the fact that the couple's relationship was strongly linked to the patient's symptom. *What led us to pursue this line of inquiry was what had already struck us while we were studying Giusi's family, namely, the relentless persecution of one parent in particular.*

We decided to concentrate our efforts on the hypothesis that the patient had taken on the role of a go-between in relaying "searing" messages from one parent to the other, messages that the sender failed to express on his own. We guessed that we would be very likely to find that this phenomenon had also conditioned behavior patterns preceding those that had unleashed the symptom. We therefore wondered whether tracking it down and revealing it at an early stage might not prevent years and years of misery. In other words, we hoped that, being aware of the phenomenon itself and of the pressing need to ferret it out in good time, all we required now was an appropriate strategy for tracking it down and nipping it in the bud and we would have a valuable means of prevention at our disposal. So, we eagerly awaited the chance to test the effect of such an intervention early in the proceedings. Unfortunately, the psychiatric establishment ranks our center as a last resort for desperate cases so that it is not exactly the place where such a hope is most likely to be fulfilled. Someone up there must like us, however, because our prayers were finally answered.

The following case was the very first in time we were called upon to deal with, and we consider it of special interest for two reasons: (1) It shows how we arrived at the hypothesis of instigation during our presession discussion, and (2) it shows how the therapist conducted the session in such a manner as to bring the phenomenon to light.

In order to make ourselves understood, we shall now attempt the difficult task of synthesizing the zig-zag course of a family therapy session by providing a storyboard with fragments of crucial dialogue and sketching in of bits of behavior. The story developed along the lines we had foreseen in our presession: It was a *first* family therapy session that, as we shall see, also turned out to be the *last*.

The Baldi Family

To introduce the family, we shall start from our first contact, that is, the chart filled out on the telephone.

The mother is the one to contact our Center, for help with the problem of the elder of two daughters, Alma, age 12. She tells us the child badly lacks self-confidence and has great difficulty relating to anyone, but especially to her mother. The Baldi family, as we shall call them, was referred to us by their pediatrician, who has known us for years. It is made up of four members: Sante, the father, age 43, is a chemistry graduate who works for a small private company. Miriam, the mother, two years older than her husband, holds a degree in accounting and is sales representative of several large wholesale clothing manufacturers. She sells to retailers and her job often takes her out of town. Alma, the eldest, is doing well in her second year of junior high school, and Eva, age 10, is in fifth grade. As for the extended families, a few interesting things appear on the telephone chart: Until her death a year ago, the maternal grandmother always helped look after the girls, since their mother never quit her job. After the grandmother was widowed, she came to spend what were to be the last three years of her life in the Baldi home. There is also a maiden aunt, Rosi, 36, Miriam's sister, who gave up her profession as a beauty consultant to become her sister's partner in business. Rosi lives in her own little flat but is very often at the Baldis' for dinner and also goes with them on holidays.

As we fill out the telephone chart, we become intrigued by the very vague references the mother makes to Alma's predicament, despite the therapist's efforts to go into the matter more deeply: "She's always been such a difficult child. . . . When she was little, she'd cry for hours on end. . . . She has these sudden changes of mood that she can't explain. . . . She's terribly sensitive. . . . She demands constant attention. . . . She needs to feel sure that she is loved. . . . " There is nothing vague, however, about Mrs. Baldi's anxious and woeful tone of voice on the phone. It seems totally unwarranted by the very minor inconveniences to which she is referring.

When we inquire how Alma's father feels about his daughter's difficulties, and whether he is motivated to take part in a joint session at our center, Mrs. Baldi hems and haws in a confused manner, contradicting herself in every other sentence. She vouches for her husband's genuine desire to help Alma, then immediately gets sidetracked into telling us that he is somehow passive, in a way she cannot quite explain. She adds that her husband is very much like Alma. The mother's evident anguish, although unaccountable, arouses the therapist's curiosity, and it is all we have to go on when we give them an appointment, to which all four members of the family plus Aunt Rosi are summoned.

On the day before their appointment the secretary gets another call from the mother: She would like to have a further word with the therapist she spoke to previously on the phone, as there is something else she wants to tell him. He is not in at the time, so that the secretary merely registers that the call was made and nothing more comes of it.

The team gets together half an hour before the session is due to begin, in order to read through the notes on the chart, draw up any hypotheses that come to mind, and prepare a strategy for their verification. Everyone is impressed by how very vague Alma's problems appear from her mother's description. There is only one really important fact: The mother is far more anguished than is called for by the situation she has related. The phone call made a day before the appointment is also a sign of mounting anxiety. Besides, Alma's mother has clearly notified us that her daughter finds it difficult to relate to her and needs constant reassurance that her mother is nearby and available — not an easy thing to manage, given the mother's job!

Mara Selvini Palazzoli, who will act as therapist, submits the idea that Alma may be a past master at making people feel guilty. It is probably she who has got her mother into such a state, by her constant whining. But, has she done this on her own account or has she acted in lieu of someone else? In the latter case, who is she standing in for? There is a strong suspicion that it is Alma's father, especially since the data on the telephone chart point to the fact that he seems to be less successful in his profession than his wife.

This first hypothesis is followed by a second and a third, all of which need to be tested by the therapist.

The second idea concerns the role that the maternal grandmother played with regard to her daughter and granddaughters, especially Alma. The old lady may have disapproved of her daughter's career and competed with her for the children's affection by volunteering as a more suitable mother.

The third hypothesis has to do with Aunt Rosi, whose daily on-the-job contact with her sister and frequent visits to the Baldi home may have made someone irascible or jealous.

Next we draw up a plan for testing the validity of our three hypotheses, appointing a different member of the family as our principal source of information for each of them. Lastly, we decide that the therapist, once the conventional greetings have been attended to, will work with the father first of all. The following is the account of the most important exchanges that took place within the framework of the session as set up by the therapist.

THERAPIST   (To the father) I would like to hear your point of view with regard to Alma's problems with her mother.

FATHER   Alma needs her mother, and my wife has this very demanding job . . .

THERAPIST   Do you who suffer most from your wife's demanding work, or does Alma?

FATHER   Alma! It would be quite unthinkable for my wife not to work on her own, it's part of her character . . . but Alma has now reached the age when she needs her mother more than she does her father.

THERAPIST   (Laughing) Oh, that's one of those typical truisms books on psychology are always propounding . . . but, quite concretely, how do these difficulties Alma has with her mother really make themselves manifest?

(The father goes off on a long-winded digression. He is utterly unable to explain what kind of difficulties Alma has with her mother.)

THERAPIST   (To the mother) Do you notice any difficulty in Alma's relationship with her *father*?

MOTHER   None whatsoever. They understand each other without even speaking, and my husband will often explain to me what it is Alma wants me to know. . . . The two of them are on the same wavelength.

THERAPIST   (To Aunt Rosi) Aunt Rosi, not being a member of the nuclear family, you are perhaps in a better position to help me understand what the trouble is between Alma and her mother?

(Aunt Rosi rambles on at length about the difference in their characters.)

THERAPIST   (Interrupting her) Never mind their characters! I need to know about things that really happen. Just tell me the facts.

AUNT ROSI   Ah, well, in that case, here's a typical one for you! (She gives a detailed account of how she and her sister, when they are on holidays at the seaside, will seek out secluded corners and sunbathe topless. Whenever they do this, Alma will pull a long face and hold a grudge for days, refusing even to speak.)

THERAPIST   But who gets irritated by this topless sunbathing, Alma or her father?

AUNT ROSI   Oh, Alma. He has great respect for everyone's wishes.

THERAPIST   Well, but could Alma perhaps have appointed herself as her father's mouthpiece, on matters she knows her father disapproves of . . . even though he never actually says so?

MOTHER   (Bursts out laughing, looks greatly amused and keeps saying over and over again) Oh, really now! That's a good one, that is!

THERAPIST   Are there any other occasions when Alma interprets her father's feelings and conveys them so effectively to her mother?

(The mother wipes the smile off her face and looks puzzled. She says her husband is always very respectful of everything she does. In her work, too, he encourages her when she gets depressed about things — because she *does* get depressed about things, now and again . . .)

THERAPIST   (To Eva) What's your opinion about the trouble Alma has with Mom's job? Don't you have any trouble of this kind?

EVA   No, I don't, but Alma hates Mom's job. She'd like to have Mom around all the time, she's so old-fashioned . . .

THERAPIST   Old-fashioned, the way your Grandma was? Tell me how things were when your Grandma was living with you.

(Her answer to this inquiry about the grandmother shows that the hypothesis we had made was off the mark, and we drop the subject.)

THERAPIST   Now that Aunt Rosi has started working with Mom, she gets to be with Mom a lot more than you do, doesn't she? Which of you three feels most disadvantaged with respect to Aunt Rosi?

(Eva denies that Aunt Rosi is a problem, and so do Alma and the father. They supply convincing evidence for this, without exhibiting the slightest tension or expressing conflicting analogical communications.)

THERAPIST   (To the mother) Well, at this point I really would like to know why it is we are here *today*, why we didn't get together, say, six months ago, or six months from now . . .

(The mother tells us that what prompted her to call us was a violent argument between Alma and their French au pair girl, who was fired as a result. Alma hated her. But the real problem is that Alma is unhappy and has been so for a long time now.)

THERAPIST   You mean, she *is* unhappy, or she *acts* unhappy?

MOTHER   She says she's unhappy . . . she's even gone so far as to say she wishes she'd never been born. . . . Only yesterday she said, "I'm terrified of everything." So I asked her, "Is there any way I can help you?" and she answered, "I don't know . . . "

(At this point, in order to help the mother out, the therapist lapses into a long didactic rigmarole about the problems of adolescence, playing down abrupt changes of mood and groundless fears as typical of that age group. After a few moments of this, the therapist is called out by one of the team. The team feels that what she is doing is not therapeutic, since the minor grievances the mother has brought up are quite certainly not the real reason for her anxious behavior. We will have to try another tack, if we are to get the really inflammatory issues to surface. Why, they suggest, doesn't she ask the mother what it was she wanted to talk about on the phone when she called up?)

THERAPIST   Recently, you phoned to tell the secretary there was something you wanted to add to the information you provided for our chart. What was it?

MOTHER   (Suddenly stiffening, very pale and anguished) Well . . . some time ago Alma took some money from my purse, first 10,000 lira, then 20,000 . . . and she wasn't able to explain why she'd done it. . . . It upset me terribly. . . . I asked myself, where did we go wrong?

(The therapist silently notices that the father, in contrast to his wife, remains perfectly calm and relaxed. She asks him to tell her in detail what happened. This allows her to observe that he speaks of the matter without the slightest tension and even smiles as he does so. At one point he winks at Alma. This prompts the therapist to hypothesize that his wife's anxiety suits this husband to a T. So, she decides to pick Aunt Rosi as her next interlocutor.)

THERAPIST   (To Aunt Rosi) Your sister really got upset, didn't she? Now tell me, who do you think has the stronger personality, your sister or your brother-in-law?

(This time Aunt Rosi comes out loud and clear and gives a very eloquent answer: Her sister, she says, has a special knack for dealing with all practical matters. She is so self-assured, enterprising, a real go-getter; she's not afraid to plunge in and she usually comes up a winner. She, Rosi, has always admired her sister for these traits and been enthralled by her ever since they were children. . . . As for her brother-in-law? No, he isn't all that sure of himself, actually . . . but there are other things he feels very strongly about, spiritual values . . . whereas her sister is the one to fly high in practical things. . . .)

THERAPIST   A little too high for comfort, maybe? Dad can't help being frightened by this, I'm sure. . . . And you, Alma, (here the therapist's tone is not in the least dramatic; it is affectionate and almost joking) have taken it upon yourself to tack a bit of ballast on to your Mom . . . furnishing her with just a wee bit of anxiety by telling her you're unhappy, and by pilfering, so as to make her fear she hasn't brought you up properly. . . . You're clipping your Mom's wings a bit, for Dad's sake, because he sometimes gets frightened when Mom takes off like a jet plane . . .

ALMA   I don't really plan these things . . . there's nothing in it for me . . . and Mom is liable to suffer . . .

THERAPIST   Yes, of course, we've seen that here today, haven't we? Still, Dad feels reassured . . . I'm not saying that Dad is happy to see Mom get all worried and upset, as of course he isn't . . . but he'd be a lot more scared and suffer a lot more if Mom were to take off and fly too high. . . . So you, Alma, will go on acting as Mom's ballast, for as long as you feel that Dad is afraid of Mom's flying too high. . . . In fact, your hanging in there as ballast shows that Dad is still afraid. Mom was quite right when she said you and your Dad have a perfect understanding.

(The therapist's remarks call forth very significant nonverbal behavior, to wit: Aunt Rosi sits listening carefully, her eyes fixed on the floor, and then starts nodding her head very slowly and emphatically in agreement when the therapist mentions Dad's fears. She looks like someone in whose brain odd, hitherto uncomprehensible bits of behavior and events are suddenly falling into their proper place, as in a jigsaw puzzle. The mother stares at the therapist with a stunned expression, then looks inquiringly from her daughter to her husband. He sits motionless, his face set and inscrutable. Unlike Alma, he does not attempt to contradict what has been said, nor does he offer any justification. Only at the moment of leavetaking, when the therapist tells them she does not consider any further meetings in order for the time being, does he suddenly rouse himself from his lethargy. He stops his wife, who is about to settle the fee, takes out his checkbook and says very firmly: "This is something *I'm* going to pay for.")

We have chosen this as the first case to present in order to tackle the problem at its easiest level, one not overly fraught with difficulties: For one thing, the patient here was definitely not psychotic. However, a number of important points need close attention. The first is the perverse nature of the father-daughter coalition, covert yet so potent as to generate in the mother a state of anguish resembling that of someone having needles thrust into her from all sides by a hidden enemy. The second point was the gradual crescendo in Alma's disturbing behaviors, which presaged their burgeoning out into open symptomatology, either in Alma herself or in her mother.

More than anything else, however, we wish to stress the extraordinary thrust given to the session by our having hypothesized a game based on instigation. Had this not been done, given the vague nature of the facts the mother had submitted (she had not informed us at first about the petty thievery, almost as though she were afraid to hurt her oversensitive child's feelings), there would have been great danger of getting bogged down in a morass of psychopedagogical considerations. Indeed, the therapist almost did sink into this and was rescued just in time by the team's throwing her a lifeline.

We must emphasize, however, that the model presiding over this session was as yet a defective one. It featured the mother as nothing but a victim, whereas a game played by a couple is never one-sided or kept going by one spouse alone. In the case of the Baldis, if there was a husband secretly jealous of his wife or envious of her professional success, there also had to be a wife surreptitiously provoking him. Such a wife's provocative behavior, when examined closely, will show itself to be subtle but unrelenting. Not only will she flaunt her professional success at her husband, but—and this, to our mind, is the most refinedly cruel aspect of such a provocation—she will also show how deeply *involved* she is in her career, thereby implicitly banishing him from everything that *really* interests her. Another behavior ploy typical of these "show-offish" provokers is frequently exhibited depression. At such times the envious spouse, in order not to reveal his envy, will make it his duty to perform an energizing job. Thus, Alma's mother says she suffers from bouts of despondency, "during which my husband always helps me so much."

Another important point to be considered is that this whole game, with the alternating moves it involves, is played out basically on an analogical level (by bits of behavior, gestures, tone of voice, display of moods, etc.). Very little shows up on a verbal level. The fact that the game proceeds solely along an analogical track might seem to exempt it both from intentionality and from the players' "rational" control. In the case presented above, this may be evinced from the mother's genuinely amused and flattered expression on hearing the therapist suggest that it could be her husband, not Alma, who suffers when she bares her breasts. Equally heartfelt in its intensity, though strictly controlled where its verbal expression might give rise to dangerous admissions, is Alma's reaction to the therapist's closing intervention, namely, "I don't really plan these things . . . there's nothing in it for me . . . and Mom is liable to suffer." The father is absolutely unsoundable, even though his silence and the fact that he makes no attempt to clear himself would seem to indicate the very real shock of someone brought face to face with a revelation that is not only unexpected but also *indisputable.*

If we single out the patient's response from among the three principal characters' reactions, we find her looking bewildered and offering, as her justification, the fact that she acts unconsciously, without premeditation, and does not stand to benefit by making her mother suffer. This brings us to the following question: What has Alma discovered about the game her parents are playing? What has prompted her to become her father's "mouthpiece"?

We feel that Alma must for quite some time now have been aware, on the analogical level, both of the provocative character of much of her mother's conduct and of what is behind her father's passivity and stubborn silence. However, Alma has given this latter aspect a linear reading. She has interpreted her father's conduct not as what it probably really is, i.e., counter-provocative feedback, but rather as genuine weakness, lack of authority, and a tendency to submit. She has probably noticed her father's doleful expression, how he repeatedly looks at his watch, how he throws down his newspaper when the clock strikes eight, their dinner is drying out in the oven . . . and *she* still hasn't appeared. Alma watches as *he* tries to manage a smile when *she* at last turns up, flings her fur coat on a chair, fixes her hair in the mirror, and starts recounting how she has managed to persuade this rich American to buy a lot of impossible dresses. No reaction whatsoever from Dad — why? Why does he just sit there like a moon-calf? What's wrong with him? Is he afraid?

Well, she, Alma, isn't at all afraid. It's high time for Mom to stop doing as she pleases with no regard for anyone else, coming back at all hours of the night. Alma knows quite well what *she* can do to drive a little fear of God into her mother, to get her to worry and pay through the nose for chiselling her family out of all that time and care. All she has to do is shut up like a clam, wear a mysterious air, act unhappy, make her understand that she pines for affection, and feels lonely and neglected. Little by little, Alma edges into the game that has absorbed her parents.

When we first see the family, escalation is well under way. Mom had better not try to clear her conscience by finding a substitute to take over her duties (the French au pair) because Alma will immediately start such fearful rows that the girl will have to leave. And, should the need arise, Alma is quite capable of resorting to a few acts of pilfering in order to strike another well-aimed blow at her mother, thus letting her know that time is running out and she'd better quit her job and take up her proper place in the household. Alma has been thoroughly drawn into the game at this point.

One dilemma that remains and is difficult to solve concerns Alma's intentional design: In what way might her behavior be intentional? Could she be trying to help her father? Or has she started to compete with him as well — does she want to succeed where he has failed? Might she, too, sincerely and desperately be craving this elusive mother who escapes her clutching hold like quicksilver? Another question the team discussed at great length was: How might this case have evolved spontaneously, had it been left to itself? To judge by the many examples witnessed over the years, evolution could have taken any one of several directions. There might have been a crescendo in Alma's provocatory maneuvers. The "pathological power" of the girl's behavior, at first covertly encouraged by her father, might have swollen to formidable proportions. She could have gone on from petty thievery to ever more undesirable behaviors, which at that stage would have been utterly beyond either parent's control. Or evolution might have followed a different pattern, enhancing the mother's depressive symptomatology. This would have placed Eva in a pivotal position. If Eva, as she grew up, had sided very openly with her mother, such depression would not have been likely, whereas if Eva, too, had abandoned her mother it would probably have been inevitable.

A third and most ominous evolution might have seen Alma developing frankly psychotic behavior. The starting point for this would have been the girl's suspicion that her father was betraying her. We have examined this issue in detail in Chapter V.

All that has been said here clearly underlines the importance assigned to what we have called "instigation." It also shows how hypothesizing such a phenomenon, correctly appraising it as a covert presence, and elaborating adequate strategy for revealing and excising it early on amount to a powerful tool for prevention.

This is why every case in which instigation might conceivably be at the root of the trouble should be carefully probed into. In itself such an inquiry will be of benefit due to the informative lode it carries with it. We very frequently see how the family member at the receiving end of the instigation will tend to be inordinately upset and anxious, though unable to give a reasonable explanation for all this worrying. The therapist will need to carry out a stringent, very explicit probe, as was seen from the way the session with the Baldis was conducted and will also apply in a number of cases we shall discuss later. The therapist must keep a tight rein on the proceedings and block all attempts at escaping or deviating. Nevertheless, the tone will never be dramatic or overwhelming, except in very rare instances. The normal attitude will be kind and humorous, devoid of any reproach or accusation. If tension builds up, a burst of laughter will help relieve it. As stated earlier, the information-giving effect of testing for instigation can be therapeutic in itself. However, one should not rely on this too much. The information will generally need to be elaborated and transformed into an intervention. Take the intervention enacted in our first (and last) session with the Baldis: Nowadays we would no longer close the session in that same way.[2] At the time, however (November 1982), we relied

---

[2]The first session would now be conducted as described here, but no explicit intervention would be made at the end of it. We would simply dismiss the aunt from any further encounters and summon only the nuclear family to the following session. On this second occasion we would go deeply into the wife's (provocative) part in the family game. We would also work at length with the two daughters, in order to obtain sufficient information about the extent to which each of them is involved in the parents' problems. We would then decide whether to simply move to disentangle the girls from their parents' game or to plan such an intervention followed by further work with the couple alone. In Part Four we describe in detail our present way of working.

on the therapeutic effect of merely breaking up and rendering impossible the father's negated coalition with Alma.

INSTIGATION IN PSYCHOSIS

In some families of patients exhibiting severe psychotic conduct, we were inevitably late in ferreting out instigation. These families were already in the midst of therapy when we gained our first intuitive insight into the phenomenon (1981). We therefore started probing for it, in an advanced phase of therapy, when no satisfactory changes were forthcoming, although the parents had carried out our prescriptions. *We were still a long way from imagining such a phenomenon to be an intrinsic component of "psychotic games."*

We will now illustrate one of those first cases, in which probing was undertaken belatedly. It was a very serious and difficult case, and the reader will notice at once how it differs from the Baldi case in the extreme reticence of both parents, but especially the father.

We had fortunately already learned not to be put out by the reticence of such families. We had (at last!) come to understand that reticence was due not so much to a desire to outwit the therapist as to the spirit of the game! Both spouses firmly believe that one should never show one's hand, and that even simply answering certain of the therapist's questions would be tantamount to laying one's cards on the table and thereby losing out.

In the case that follows, the inquiry undertaken to discover the roots of Giorgio's anger in some facet of the couple's game shows the wife fitfully dodging the issue in every possible way, primarily by trivializing, whereas her husband (whose posture as he sits crouching on his chair in itself speaks volumes) is tight-lipped except for a few inarticulate mutterings. Drawing on her experience with Giusi's parents, the therapist here, too, leads off her inquiry from the key question: *Who* is it Giorgio most relishes nailing to the cross?

The Galli Family

There are four members in this household: The parents, Tonio and Mina, both in their early forties, who are white-collar workers; their son, Giorgio, age 15, who has been a psychotic from the age of nine; and the maternal grandmother, age 67, who lost her husband ten years ago and has lived with the Gallis ever since.

The explosion of Giorgio's psychotic behavior was foreshadowed by an abrupt change a few months earlier, affecting only his conduct at school. Giorgio, who had been a bright and dedicated pupil in first and second grade, suddenly became iron-willed about refusing to do any homework or prepare his lessons. His father, who returned from work before his mother, would plead with him as best he could, but it was an uphill struggle every time. At the end of that school year, his mother decided to send Giorgio off to a summer camp run by the company his father worked for. As soon as he got there, Giorgio started exhibiting acute psychotic symptoms of a perse- cutory nature, and ever since, despite a year's internment in a specialized institution, he had steadily worsened.

Giorgio developed formidable blocks, even in the most elementary be- haviors. It would take him two hours to get through a meal and he would sit on the toilet for hours. His mother would have to drag him off the toilet seat, wash him and put his underpants and socks back on him. An exhaust- ing ritual obliged his parents, in turn, to dress him in the morning, take him to the toilet, and undress him at night. His father, who was by nature a very patient man, would occasionally lose his temper with the boy and slap his face.

In the team discussion prior to the seventh session with only the par- ents, Mara Selvini Palazzoli, who was the acting therapist, decided to carry out an investigation aimed at discovering whether instigation might be going on. She sensed that, although both parents appeared very strongly committed to therapy, something was holding things back and obstructing a favorable course. Some of the symptoms, such as the feeding block, had disappeared, but the exasperating, clearly provocative, slow-motion behav- ior was still going on. Although the therapist resolved to undertake the probe in the session at hand, she chose not to work according to a set plan but rather to be free to jump at any chance offered her.

The session starts with the wife reading her notes. These contain details of Giorgio's intolerable conduct—just the opening the therapist has been waiting for.

THERAPIST   (Interrupting) *Mrs. Galli, which of you three, in your opinion, does Giorgio most enjoy nailing to the cross—your husband, his grand- mother, or you?*

WIFE   (At once points to herself) Why me, of course. No question about that, oh yes, yes, yes—he always passes him (her husband) over when he wants something especially absurd. It's always me he turns to.

THERAPIST   Why should Giorgio hold such a grudge against you? Why are you the one he wants to destroy?

WIFE   . . . I don't know. (She starts off on a long spiel about what some psychologist told her years ago. The therapist raises her hand to stop her.)

THERAPIST   Giorgio has been going on this way for years now, he's abso- lutely dead set on getting his way. It's as though he were saying to himself: "You've simply *got* to lick her."

WIFE   Yes, yes!

HUSBAND   (Bites his lip)

WIFE   But Giorgio isn't always like that with me. (She explains that there are also times when Giorgio will seek her out, "times when the two of us attempt to find each other, not to lose each other.")

THERAPIST   (Interrupting) *Mina, try to think of things that may never have been mentioned, but that he (husband) might find fault with, in you. Things you do . . . your way of doing them . . . that you feel he resents.*

(After giving the matter some thought, she says her husband definitely objects to her going to bed late. The therapist follows this track for a while, but it leads nowhere.)

THERAPIST   There could be other things that make your husband angry — think carefully.

WIFE   (Chatters on about her habit of not turning off the lights in the house.)

THERAPIST   (Interrupts her sternly) No! I'm talking about important things that you do, or used to do, that Giorgio might feel made his father angry.

WIFE   I don't know . . .

THERAPIST   (Heatedly) *I don't believe Giorgio has only this personal grudge. Mina, tell me whether Giorgio is acting as a loudspeaker mostly on account of some grievance of your husband's, or mostly some grievance your mother has against you?* You see, in our work here with families, we see children who carry other people's messages, who convey messages, that other people don't dare utter. . . . At Giorgio's age he ought to be leading a life of his own. Why should he bother to torture his Mom when it's other people who are angry at you? (Very positively) *Well, he does this because he can see someone looking peeved at you, someone who doesn't speak up.* Who is it that looks the more peeved, then, your husband or your mother? Who is it that's more annoyed with you?

WIFE   I don't know . . .

THERAPIST   I'm sure, I'm quite sure that there's . . . that there has been something (looking at the husband) that your wife used to do . . . something that made you suffer and got you very angry . . . (pleading, leaning forward toward the husband, who squirms around on his chair, stony-faced). Can't you help me, Tonio? Won't you please do me this favor?

WIFE   Well, maybe . . . at the time when the company I work for had its premises just opposite our house. . . . I'd neglect my family for the office . . . I'd come home late, 8 o'clock, sometimes even 8:30. . . . You know (she brightens up and laughs), you know, my son doesn't really trust me all that much. . . . He was always suspicious . . . he'd keep on asking who those people were he could see me with . . . through the window . . .

THERAPIST   Does your husband trust you blindly?
WIFE   Yes, I think he does.
THERAPIST   *No. No, no, no! He felt that your work was more important to you than he was!* (To the husband) *Isn't that so?*
HUSBAND   (Glum) Well, it *did* seem nice for her to be home at a reasonable hour.

(Wife says husband may be a bit jealous—he disapproves of her using makeup. "Yes, I know, you say it's bad for my skin, but the truth is, you don't like it." And Giorgio, too, keeps asking her, "Why? Why do you do it?")

THERAPIST   When you'd come home late in the evening, whose side would your mother be on?
WIFE   Their side!
THERAPIST   Ah, so the little threesome would line up against you. You were the traitor . . . and you've got to do penance all your life . . . and it's Giorgio who is making you pay for all your acts of disloyalty! You were the most important person for all three of *them,* but you kept signaling that your work was more important than *they* were . . . so Giorgio now wants you to atone for that, for the rest of your life . . .
WIFE   I certainly hope not . . . (she tells how exacting her job always was, and how important it is now that she's become head of personnel).
THERAPIST   (Laughs) Even when you're at home you keep on letting them know you're thinking about what's happening out there . . .
WIFE   (Joins in the laughter) Oh no, I learned to keep things to myself. Nobody ever listened.
THERAPIST   But maybe they can see from your expression that you're still thinking about . . .

(Wife starts on an explanation of the difficult times the company is facing at present.)

THERAPIST   (Interrupts and goes resolutely back to the red-hot issue) *Who would let off steam at you when you came home late? Would your husband be the one to let off steam that way?*
WIFE   No, never.
THERAPIST   (To husband) Tell me how things would go, on an evening like that . . .
HUSBAND   (Tells how the three of them, Grandma, Giorgio and he, would sit around waiting, grumbling. . . . Occasionally he had phoned her, to tell her to hurry up . . . but he stopped doing this, in time. . . . His mother-in-law took it on herself to phone . . .
WIFE   Yes, *I* was the one who told them to phone.

THERAPIST   *So, Giorgio felt it was his duty to call you back to your home, where you had a husband . . .*

(While the therapist says this, the husband nods repeatedly.)

THERAPIST   Let's go back to reading your notes, Mrs. Galli.

(The wife goes on reading. There are frequent interruptions from the therapist, who asks questions that elicit explanations. This is followed by the husband's reading his notes. Winding-up time is drawing near, but the therapist wants to finish testing her outgoing hypothesis, to wit: At this stage of the game (of instigation), Mina's provocatory behavior towards her husband has surfaced very clearly: constantly assigning priority to her work rather than to him, obstinately staying up nights after dinner instead of joining him in their bedroom — all this was quite evident. But what about him? In what way was this husband instigating his wife's provocatory behavior? The therapist got the idea that the husband might be responding to provocation with a provocation of his own, by skillfully dissembling his anger. She decided to explore along this track.)

THERAPIST   Mrs. Galli, let's go back to the matter of your staying at work. We have seen that not only Giorgio, but your mother, too, would act on your husband's behalf. Your husband called a few times and then left off, and then your mother would be the one to call, to urge you to come back, saying it was late. Then Giorgio joined in the act, refusing to do his homework with Grandma or his father. He tried to get *you* to come home and do his homework with him, but he failed. So, tell me, *why was it your husband found it so difficult to say things to you like,* "Either you come home by 7 or I'll let you have it?" Anyone who keeps mum like this has a volcano seething deep down inside. Someone else, or perhaps several other people, will catch on to the fact that this volcano is raging and decide to convey the message! Had you realized how jealous your husband was of you? Did he try to conceal this? Was he jealous of your women acquaintances, too?

(Wife goes off at a tangent about her women friends and how patiently her husband always behaved.)

THERAPIST   (Interrupting her, to husband) When your wife came home late and made you so furious by keeping you waiting until 8 or 8:30, *why didn't you simply fly at her, and tell her straight out that this would have to stop?*

HUSBAND   Well, there would be a little griping . . . just a few words . . . but, things being what they were, that was all.

THERAPIST   (Confidentially) Has your wife always been this pig-headed? Have you ever been able to get her to do anything at all? . . . You can't get her to go to bed at a reasonable hour or come home early . . . what else? What did you ever succeed in getting her to do? Only Giorgio has managed to curb her obstinacy, to bring her to her knees and keep her confined for hours on end to the bathroom, pulling his pants off and on.

WIFE   Yes, that's true. Only Giorgio . . . but he (husband) never ever let me know about all this suffering of his . . . he never let me see it. . . .

THERAPIST   But it was there, all the same, for Giorgio and Grandma to read quite plainly on his face. They got the idea there might be some cheating going on, so Grandma started phoning . . .

WIFE   But I was the one who told them to phone when I was late in arriving . . .

THERAPIST   (To husband) Didn't your mother-in-law ever say, "Why don't you stand up for your rights, why don't you put your foot down?"

HUSBAND   No. We just groused, all of us.

THERAPIST   Well, Giorgio *did* succeed in bringing her to heel—even though he had to act crazy to do it!

The reader will notice that here, too, inquiry into a possible instigation process leads to the parental couple. Unlike the first case we reported, which involved presymptomatic instigation, this family featured a member of the extended family, i.e., the grandmother seemingly taking sides openly with her son-in-law and her grandson against her daughter's obsession with her career. (However, although this wasn't proved, she might in her heart of hearts actually have despised this ineffectual son-in-law so much so as to take it upon herself to call Mina on the phone.)

As for the couple's game, each case we dealt with at that time seemed to throw the motto "never give in" into sharper relief as a recurring feature. A standing rule barred one spouse from ever fulfilling any implicit, reasonable expectation that the other might harbor pertaining to the simple sphere of everyday existence. Thus, Mina had never done any of the little things Tonio so badly wanted her to do, and Tonio had never satisfied Mina's longing to hear him say how much he wanted them and how he suffered from being denied them. These, however, were only the outward signs of a drama the true essence of which still remained beyond our grasp.

INSTIGATION BY MEMBERS OF THE
EXTENDED FAMILIES

The possibility of instigation by someone in the extended families should be investigated whenever symptomatic behavior appears during childhood or adolescence.

Our clinical experience has shown that such pressure on the patient by someone in the extended families will take priority even over marital strife in bringing on the adolescent syndromes that *DSM-III* (American Psychiatric Association, 1980) classifies as Major Depression.

We quote:

> In adolescents, negativistic or frankly antisocial behavior and use of alcohol or illicit drugs may be present and justify the additional diagnoses of Oppositional Defiant Disorder, Conduct Disorder, or Psychoactive Substance Abuse or Dependence. Feelings of wanting to leave home or of not being understood and approved of, restlessness, grouchiness, and aggression are common. Sulkiness, a reluctance to cooperate in family ventures, and withdrawal from social activities, with retreat to one's room, are frequent. School difficulties are likely. There may be inattention to personal appearance and increased emotionality, with particular sensitivity to rejection in love relationships. (p. 232)

Our own case histories falling into this group show that families will contact us for help when the patient, boy or girl, is somewhere between 17 and 21 years old, or perhaps slightly older. Such youngsters will often have been overprotected during childhood, due to a physical illness, rehabilitation for some minor handicap, the advice of some psychologist to "enfold them with affection," etc. All these situations, one can argue, will tend to make them accustomed to feel they are special, and certainly relieve them of much responsibility. Sometimes they will be only children, and our inquiry will reveal that they are surrounded by a flock of grandparents, doting uncles and maiden aunts, all unfailingly loving, who have always treated them with the greatest affection.

By the time the family shows up for treatment, the patient will generally have chalked up a hopeless school record, or even an adamant refusal to attend school at all, on the grounds that he is too anguished and unable to concentrate properly. If the patient has already had to face the choice between more education or a job, he will have managed to get out of any possible commitment to work by claiming that he is beset by ill-defined fears or by insisting on someone else's finding him just the type of job no one is ever likely to offer him.

Still, such apparent "loafers" lead anything but pleasant lives. They spend most of their time cloistered up at home, with their social contacts limited mainly to their relatives. They will often have a prominent part in fierce domestic rows, the very thought of which is enough to keep their parents subdued, as they dread complaints from the neighbors. Frequent visits to psychiatrists and any number of attempted cures have landed them on heavy medication, the sole effect of which has been to prolong their sleep into the late morning hours. Still, during the family sessions these patients will exhibit no delirious behavior, and their use of language is perfectly appropriate. They will complain that they have been, and still are, neglected and misunderstood and will stubbornly insist on their absurd grievances, claiming that their parents are duty-bound to grant them anything they wish. As for the parents, they usually look harassed and at the end of their tether. Also, they are bewildered by waves of contradictory advice coming at them from all sides. Grandparents, uncles and aunts will gang up and endlessly repeat that "the poor child must be humored."

As is well known, cases of this type do not respond to individual therapy, which either produces an early dropout or drags on indefinitely without the slightest improvement.

Having failed in our attempts to apply family therapy to the few cases of this sort referred to us before 1979, inventing the prescription came as a welcome shot in the arm and restored our optimism and self-confidence. However, in the first two cases of this sort treated with the prescription, a brief period of improvement was again followed by failure. This was especially disheartening, as we were unable to figure out where the error lay.

A lot of time was to pass before we discovered that we had committed a sin of omission. We had neglected to give due consideration to the flock of grandparents and aunts and look into whether they might have set the child up against one or both of the parents. Once we became aware of our oversight, we explored this hypothesis (which also proved a valuable source of elucidatory information) in all likely cases and realized how naïve we had been.

It became instinctive for us hereafter to link the patient's grievances, his absurd chip-on-the-shoulder attitude, to the likelihood of someone's putting ideas into his head by, on the one hand, enticing him with a lot of small favors and, on the other, getting him to see himself as a poor, deprived creature, unloved by those whose duty it was to provide affection. The arrogance with which such a patient would air his grievances, as well as his brazenly defiant stance, could only mean that he was persuaded that someone was backing him up.

A telling case in point is that of our work with the family of an 18-year-old son, whose predicament was typical. Gianni was the elder of the two sons of a family with a modest income. The mother had had to quit her job on account of the constant care and long rehabilitation programs Gianni had required during infancy and early childhood. His health was very poor and his vision impaired.

Gianni was the oldest grandchild and the great favorite of both his paternal grandmother and a maiden aunt. These two had openly shown him, and not simply inferred, that they pitied him for having such a hard, tense, unfeeling mother—a view unfortunately shared by the maternal grandmother, who catered to the child's every whim.

When we first saw the family, Gianni had decided a year earlier to refuse both school and a job. Due to heavy medication, he would sleep until late into the morning. He would leave his isolation only for an occasional visit to one of his grandmothers or a car ride with the maiden aunt, who regularly supplied him with music tapes. During the session, having flatly declared that his family was utterly incapable of understanding him, he stated that he was thinking of leaving home but couldn't carry out his plan because his parents refused to hand over the gold coins his relatives had given him on various occasions. This money would have made it possible for him to go off on his own, find a job, and live wherever he chose. His parents, of course, were sure that he would simply squander the money, and therefore refused to let him have it.

In the third session, to which we summoned only the parents, the team agreed with the therapist that the latter would have to come out and explicitly inform the parents that it was wrong for them to worry about Gianni's squandering his little nestegg. Since the boy was already of age, what really mattered was to avoid losing any more time; they should take up the challenge and give Gianni a chance to prove his mettle. There was, of course, little chance of Gianni's attempt being successful, and the odds were all in favor of his returning empty-handed after a couple of weeks' vacation. Should this be the case, however, his pretexts for continuing a life of leisure would stand disproved, and they would be able to put the screws on him, even to the extent of denying him readmission to the family home.

All this the therapist stated very forcefully, with a twofold purpose in mind: (1) to observe the parents' immediate reaction, i.e., how willing each of them was to take a tough stance; (2) to ask to see Gianni's cards, as in a poker game. He wanted to find out if Gianni was simply shooting his mouth off, like a boastful child, and would quickly retreat when it came to the crunch, or whether he was the persevering type who would go all the way. While the therapist was making his speech, careful attention was paid to how the parents reacted. The father seemed to fall in very readily with what was being said and nodded his approval of what the therapist was suggesting, whereas the mother sat there stiffly, with her head bowed, looking perplexed and almost hostile.

The therapist left the couple, in order to discuss matters with his team. They were in a difficult position. This was the third session, which is usually the one in which the secret prescription is issued. But what could they prescribe, in response to Gianni's open challenge? Further to prescribing secrecy, might some sort of pedagogical instructions also be in order? There was danger of causing confusion. Also, it was essential to give proper consideration to the fact that each parent had reacted very differently to the therapist's statement. Quite possibly, the mother was feeling apprehensive about the way the grandmothers were likely to take all this.

We finally made a decision that seemed very wise: *There was to be only one prescription, namely contracting (and keeping) the secrecy compact.* As to what to do about Gianni, this the therapist would leave to the parents to decide, on the basis of what they felt up to doing. Actually, the therapist would add, he had already told them what was required, theoretically at least, to get Gianni out of his impasse, but he fully realized that he was not *they*, since he did not feel fatherly towards the boy or find himself beleaguered by a flock of relatives and well-meaning neighborhood busybodies, sure to be outraged at the idea of such a tough stance. Moreover, he would go on to say, there was the danger that Gianni, faced by such a tough response, would increase his provocation and start an escalation. Thus, the therapist decided, he was leaving it to them to work out a proper course of action with regard to Gianni, one that they would both have to agree on, based on how much stamina they could manage between them. Should one of them have the strength to carry out the plan, on no account was he or she to impose any decisions on the one who didn't feel up to it — although taking up the boy's gauntlet was now the only way of saving him from a wretched existence.

The session followed the pattern as foreseen, and at its conclusion the parents committed themselves to keeping the secret. They resolved that all further action would need to be discussed between them. The wife no longer appeared hostile. The rest of this therapy, quite a dramatic one, led to a successful outcome: Gianni rose to his parents' challenge, foolishly squandered his little treasure, attempted a return as the prodigal son, got a cold reception, and thereupon agreed to bargain with his parents about his role in the family. Meanwhile, the parents stood up heroically to a barrage of finger-wagging by grandmothers, aunts and righteous citizens of the small town where they lived.

Let us pause here a moment and consider a point that is especially important in dealing with cases requiring urgent decisions. We feel dutybound to respond to such urgency. Whenever we have failed to do so, concentrating solely on issuing the prescription, we have forfeited credibility and the family's trust. The important thing is to draw a sharp line between what is *prescribed* and mandatory (secrecy, the disappearances) and what is *counseled*: The latter is for the two parents to accept and carry out as best they can, according to their joint potential.

Now, back to the main topic of this chapter. The notion that a member of the extended families may be "instigating" is one that we probe for in virtually all the families we undertake to treat. However, there are certain families we feel are especially at risk. These are families in which the father, having achieved economic and professional distinction, lords it over his family of origin. A casebook featuring such families would provide wonderful background material for an essay on *envy* as feedback to *provocative ostentation*. It was only by keeping all this in mind that we were able, in the course of our work, to unravel a large number of truly amazing situations.

For instance, in treating the family of Celina, a 17-year-old depressed, Optalidon-addicted, suicidal girl, we were able to ferret out the following incredible convolution: The patient's father, in his early forties, was a brilliant, self-important professional. The mother, who came from a modest family, had a younger brother whose business venture had ended in bankruptcy. This man's wife, Aunt Veronica, was an attractive young woman, intensely jealous of her brother-in-law's success and very resentful of the latter's disdain and refusal to help them. She managed to bring about the following instigation maneuver on several fronts: (a) She set her sister-in-law up against her stingy, heartless husband; (b) she seduced her brother-in-law, took him to bed, and set him up against his wife; and (c) she latched on to the couple's little girl (the patient-to-be), taking her for walks every afternoon, stuffing her with ice cream and constantly telling her how unfortunate she was to have such parents.

When we meet a family we consider at risk, we use a quick check we have elaborated for revealing telltale signs. It consists of several queries:

1. Has the husband been conspicuously successful in his career, in such a way as to raise him above the status of his relatives?
2. Has the husband a tendency to flaunt his superior status?
3. Have his relatives, as a result, become envious of his success?
4. Has envy given rise to critical comment about him?
5. Has the husband denied financial help to his relatives when they needed it?
6. Has the wife become influenced by all this criticizing of her husband (split in the couple)?
7. Was the child (patient) present when this issue was being argued, or has he in some way been made a party to this controversy?

As may be seen, danger will wind its devious course through a series of escalating interactions with the extended families, and may even reach the ultimate liability, namely the situation in which one spouse plots against the other, possibly involving the child in the couple's breakup.

Finally, we should say here that another situation in which the possibility of instigation on the part of members of the extended families is always considered and probed into is that of the child of divorced patients who exhibits disturbed behavior. Being referred to by grandparents as "that poor little thing," exposed to much deep sighing and sympathetic tut-tutting, as well as caustic remarks on *who* it is who is unwilling to make a sacrifice for the sake of the family — all this, especially in a child, can induce a self-pity that will soon show results. The best-known and most common of these is total failure in scholastic achievement. It is as though the child, riding this wave of collective compassion, were communicating to his parents: "Now that you've ruined my life by depriving me of a proper family, you're going to have to get busy extricating me from the mess I'm in."

We might call this a sort of "indemnity neurosis." It is far more common than one might think and has the unfortunate effect of reinforcing the grandparents' pernicious tendency to champion the cause of these "pitiful" children: "How can anyone expect him to study properly in a household like that?" This is why studies into the harm caused to children by a divorce should always include scanning the field for the possible presence and special pattern of an instigatory maneuver sparked by one or several relatives.

INSTIGATION HAS A
BOOMERANG EFFECT

Our work at the Center initially allowed us to observe only small segments of the instigation circuit. As our research proceeded, however, we were gradually able to trace feedback loops, which enabled us to observe a highly interesting phenomenon: Instigation will tend to backfire on the one who has presumably set it going. We called this "the boomerang effect." Becoming aware of this helped us discard a linear notion of instigation and move towards viewing it correctly as a process. Unmistakable examples of this "boomerang effect" were found in the notes the parents wrote and brought to the session. Here we were dealing with plain facts, recounted by people who had lived through these events, and there was little room for our prejudices or interpretations to influence their wording.

These chronicled processes would turn up in the notebook of one of the parents at a certain given stage in the proceedings, namely once the couple had succeeded in joining forces. This was when we would hear tales of how one parent would indignantly reject a child's attempt to set him up against the other. The very fact that the child would make such an attempt would immediately lead us to infer that this type of maneuver had always been part of the family pattern. It would be extremely difficult for a child to dare to speak in a certain way about his father to his mother, or vice versa, if he hadn't previously been allowed or invited to do so. This showed us how the parent, whose attitude towards his/her spouse had changed as a result of therapy, would emphatically spurn the child's efforts to stick to the old pattern. Indeed, not only would this parent refuse to play along, but he would come out openly on the side of the accused.

Here is an extract, quoted verbatim, from the notebook of the mother of Filippo, a schizophrenic, in which one can clearly see how Ilaria, his sister, tries time after time to rouse her mother against her father. The notebook was brought to the eighth session, where its contents were read out loud by the mother.

Another row with Ilaria after lunch today. We are sitting together, smoking. The others aren't around. She starts talking about her difficulty in finding a room in the students' hostel at her university. She hasn't been able to find one. She tells me what she thinks are the reasons for not finding one, and I find them totally unreasonable, but don't feel like getting into an argument—into the umpteenth argument, that is. She insists, and goes on complaining as usual about her Dad not understanding her and keeping her on a tight rein by giving her so little money. At this point I cut her short and tell her he's the one she should talk to about it. But she stubbornly goes right on with the same old tirade about money. After shrugging off the argument a few more times, I decide I'd better give her an answer. I tell her her father is probably very disappointed by the way she behaves, and that a relationship is based on give and take, and can't be all take. . . . She says it's hard for her to ask her Dad for money because he always makes her crawl for it. I remark that it doesn't look that way to me, seeing that right after her holidays in Sicily she had come along asking for more funds for a vacation in the mountains . . . and so it goes, until she bursts out and says she feels everybody in the house considers her a scrounger who gets everything she wants and doesn't care about anyone else. I reply that she herself has made the diagnosis. She goes on grumbling about how Dad always argues about money with me, too, and gets insolent. I tell her those are matters that concern only her father and me, and she should keep out of them. I try to avoid the argument, but Ilaria simply won't stop provoking. At last I tell her I don't think she knows what she wants. She bursts out crying and yells at me, saying she has no self-confidence because we make her feel insecure and that I should know all about that, since I see the psychologists at the Center all the time. I retort very calmly that I don't want to talk about the Center, because of the secret. She yells that she doesn't want to know anything, but that I *must* tell them at the Center that I am the one who deprives her of her self-confidence. She goes on like this, in a terrible state, until I finally lose my temper and raise my voice. I say that if anyone around here has been stifling everyone else, and is overdoing it in every possible way, that is she, and she alone. At this point Filippo appears: He comes down from his bedroom, very calmly, and says to me: "If you two must fight, please do it outside," but he isn't at all angry.

Quite clearly, the boomerang has come a full circle here: However, she who originally sent it flying is no longer willing to catch it and toss it back. The daughter's obstinate insistence reveals she is in a state of extreme tension that equals her amazement at finding herself face to face with a mother changed out of all recognition—an amazement that clearly hints at how very different things were in the past.

INSTIGATION WITHIN THE INSTITUTION: THE CIRCUIT CLOSES AND THE PATIENT CEASES TO BE ANYONE'S CONCERN

It was extending our experience to an institution that enabled us to piece together arcs of circuits, add on and probe into collateral loops, and put the whole circuit together. Here, too, we will make ourselves more clearly understood by taking our readers with us step by step up the path we struggled along to get to the composite views we now hold, instead of simply setting it out before them as though we had come upon it full-blown.

Our first significant experience with instigation as it occurs in an institution was at the District Psychiatric Service at Corsico, near Milan. We were working on a research project involving elderly chronic patients (Covini et al., 1984) who had all spent many years in an insane asylum. The project entailed working very closely with our four nurses, who were the ones to gather as much accurate and detailed information as possible about any relationships our patients had kept up with members of their family of origin still alive at the time.

One patient in particular, among these chronic long-time inmates, held our attention for quite some time. Her name was Lina. One of our senior nurses knew her very well from the time when she was still in the local mental hospital, which had since been dismantled in the wake of a 1978 law reforming psychiatry in Italy. When the group working in Corsico began planning Lina's rehabilitation she was already 70 and had for several months been living in an old folks' home. Her presence there was causing problems, however, as she had frequent bouts of acutely agitated behavior which required her to go to the hospital for a few days. The staff at the home had asked us to rid them of the burden of Lina's presence, which did not fit into the general atmosphere. While we were discussing the possible reasons for these outbursts of agitated behavior, the senior nurse came up with the information that, way back when Lina was still at the mental hospital, the staff had been positive that it was her sister's visits that upset her. *The staff at the old folks' home, she said, had by now come to the same conclusion.*

Inquiry about this sister yielded the following information: Anna, age 64, was the youngest of Lina's four sisters. Born to a family of poor parents, she was the only one who had managed to get an education and marry a respectable employee, who had died a few years earlier. A widow with no children, she took great pains to appear refined. She drew an adequate pension, dressed nicely, and alternated active membership in a host of charities with pilgrimages to holy sites and vacations at a hotel. Ever since Lina had landed, in her early thirties, in a mental hospital, Anna had been the only one to visit her regularly. What was more, after Anna lost her husband, she consented to have Lina come and stay with her over the main holiday periods. The staff at the mental hospital had recommended this.

We then learned about the way these regular visits of Anna's took place: She would show up every Sunday morning. The moment she arrived, she'd get busy overhauling her sister. She'd take Lina to the bathroom, scrub her thoroughly from head to foot, change her underwear, comb her hair and trim her fingernails, strongly suggesting by her behavior that the nurses were a lazy bunch who neglected the inmates. She would complain about the food, about how dirty the rooms were, about the medical treatment offered. She would address all members of the staff, regardless of rank, in a haughty, demanding tone, as though she were ordering about the personnel of a luxury clinic. As our senior nurse was quick to point out, this behavior was exactly the same Anna had shown while Lina was in the mental hospital, where it had also deeply irritated the staff. At that time, she recalled, the nurses would remark that if "the countess" was all that fault-finding and fastidious, she ought to be keeping her sister at home with her.

At this point, we were starting to get a better picture of things: *It was clear* that the nature of Anna's visits to her sister had had a provocative effect first on the staff of the mental hospital and later on that of the old folks' home. The entire staff, from the chief psychiatrist down to the lowliest assistant nurse, thoroughly disliked this person. So, every time Anna left after her irritating visit, the personnel would take it out on Lina. One can easily imagine the criticism and sarcastic comments that were bandied about: "What does that woman expect, in a nursing home like this? If she has all that money and feels entitled to a whole lot of things, why doesn't she take care of you herself? Why doesn't she hire a private nurse?" The pragmatic effect on Anna's behavior was unwittingly to instigate Lina against her sister. In the end, Lina, caught in the crossfire between her sister and the staff, would break out in confused and uncontrollable fury and land in the hospital. Even the staff's urging "the countess" to take Lina to stay with her over the holidays must have smacked of a veiled, spiteful reprimand, i.e., "With all your airs and graces, how can you possibly leave your sister in hospital over Christmas?"

After we had collected this information, we drew up a working policy. Since Lina needed to be taken out of the old folks' home, we had to try and settle her permanently in Anna's home. This required one of our therapist's inviting both sisters to the Corsico center, in order to find out what Lina really wanted. For once, we told ourselves, Lina would not be treated like a mail packet and freighted off somewhere without even having been consulted. If Lina proved willing, we would undertake to persuade Anna, by showing that we had nothing but praise for her. Far from criticizing her for having sent her sister to a home, we would lavish praise on her for her unflagging solicitude. In order to convince her to take in Lina, we would guarantee the assistance of our two nurses.

During our first encounters Lina kept pretty much to herself: She seemed inclined to leave the decision to the practitioners. As for Anna, gratified by the praise bestowed on her and reassured by the fact that the nurses would be standing by, she agreed to take in her sister. For almost two months, to our great satisfaction, everything worked like a charm. Our nurses reported that Lina, normally passive and taciturn, had unexpectedly become very talkative with them, and would even crack jokes about how trying it was to live with someone like Anna. This unusual behavior of Lina's, when we heard of it during our team meetings, gave us the encouraging feeling that her attitude towards our nurses was improving.

Then, suddenly, Lina suffered such a severe crisis that she had to be rushed to the hospital. Our nurses, who hastened to Anna's home to make arrangements for Lina's admittance, found her in a state of intense agitation: She was foaming at the mouth, screaming and gnashing her teeth like a rabid animal. An elderly woman was hovering near by, someone our nurses had never seen before. She introduced herself as the eldest sister. Two younger women there with her turned out to be nieces.

While the nurses were soothing Lina and dressing her, with the ambulance on its way, this little group of relatives started expostulating against Anna. As they saw it, Lina's crisis had been brought on by Anna's refusal to take her to Venice to attend the funeral of a brother-in-law. Anna had left the day before, dressed to the hilt, having announced that her attendance at the funeral would suffice to represent all the sisters. They were left in charge of Lina. One of the nieces, especially, was very outspoken in stating how they all disapproved of Anna, of her holier-than-thou attitude and the way she always wanted to be conspicuous, to act high and mighty, and boss everyone around. A tangled family conglomerate was thus brought to light, a fine patchwork of envy and rancor, of which the Anna-plus-Lina twosome was but a small part. Worse, our nurses, too, had got enmeshed in the web: Frustrated by Lina's unexpected relapse, they had vigorously joined in the chorus of recriminations against Anna.

As for Anna, when she got home and found Lina had been taken to the hospital, she sent our Center a doctor's certificate stating that she suffered from a cardiac condition and was therefore no longer able to house a serious psychopath at her home. We had lost all hope by this time, and it was only in order to try to understand where we had gone wrong that we summoned the sisters, the nieces, and Lina to the Center. Lina was brought in from the hospital. We witnessed an unbelievable changeover: Anna talked of her heart condition and said she was demoralized by the inordinate expectations and demands the team at the Center had made on her. She stressed the serious nature of Lina's crisis and declared that another solution for her sister was urgently needed. The several sisters and nieces had all come full circle and swung round to Anna's side, obviously fearing the Center would attempt to palm Lina off on them. They chimed in to support Anna's contention, saying she was so kind and generous. Everyone agreed that it was high time the Center found an institution for chronic cases in which Lina could be put away.

The meeting ended on a very sad note. Lina, perfectly clear-headed, turned to the therapist and, in a touching tone, said softly, "You see how it is, doctor, I don't belong to anyone." At the end of this session, the team did a lot of painful soul-searching. They had to admit they had blundered badly. Instead of freeing Lina from the instigation game of which she was the victim, they had spurred it on to new vigor.

They felt they were now able to reconstruct Lina's history as an inmate as follows: Lina was admitted to hospital and started establishing some kind of rapport with the staff. Whenever Anna came to visit her, she would try to bias Lina against the staff by criticizing everything. The staff members, thoroughly irritated by Anna's high and mighty attitude and her slyly derogatory manner, would vent their feelings on Lina and say how much they pitied her for having such a sister. We were forced to the conclusion that our plan had entirely failed to change this setup. We had only "pretended" to give Anna credit: In actual fact, we had gone on regarding her as a big nuisance and conveyed these sentiments all too clearly to Lina. We had behaved towards Lina exactly the same way her sisters had, losing sight as we did so (and this was disastrous) of the fact that only Anna stood between Lina and her confinement to an institution for chronic cases.

While the team was doing its bitter post-mortem, the prevailing opinion was that the analysis reported above was final, and there was nothing to add. We had not yet discovered that a key figure had been left out in piecing together the instigation circuit — namely Lina, whom we had placed in it only as a victim, not as an active agent in her own right.[3]

THE VICTIM AS AGENT

It was the institutional record of a boy of 10, Nando, that finally led us to complete the loop, to see the victim as agent as well.

Nando's case history featured a diagnosis of autism, made shortly before his third birthday. A few months after this diagnosis was made, Nando's father, a policeman, was killed in a shoot-out. His widow stayed on in their apartment, which adjoined the home of her parents, with Nando and his sister, who was eight at the time.

The case was referred to our private Center when Nando reached the age of 10, by the consulting psychologist of a rehabilitation center for handicapped children in which Nando was a boarder from Mondays through Saturdays. The psychologist advised the mother to undertake

---

[3]Happily, after this smarting debacle, and despite Lina's considerable age, the Corsico team did not give up on her. They managed to wangle the city council into providing a little one-room apartment in which Lina, who accepted eagerly this time, went to live. At the same time the team made a compact with the sisters, and especially with Anna: They were not to interfere in any way with Lina's newfound independence. Ever since that time Lina has enjoyed life in her little home, which she keeps spotlessly clean and tidy. Every now and then, but not all too often, she invites Anna to lunch. Most important of all, for four years now she has not had a single relapse.

family therapy because Nando, whenever he was sent home for the week-end, changed into a veritable demon. The main victim of his bites, pinches and swift kicks was his mother, who often had to enlist the aid of her parents and of an uncle who had lately moved into an apartment in the same building, in order to avoid matters taking a tragic turn.

On Monday mornings, when Nando left to go back to his care center, the apartment was a shambles. Nando's behavior at home was the exact opposite of that he showed at the institute. The psychologist's report stressed how willing he was, and how he was making small but constant progress in learning, how he socialized with his companions and took an active part in group therapy.

Our files show that Nando, his mother, his sister Maria, and the mater-nal grandparents were summoned to the first session. After we had read the telephone chart, for which the mother had supplied the data, we drew up the hypothesis that an escalation was under way, involving, on the one hand, the institution, which insisted on Nando's spending the weekend with his family, and on the other, the mother, who had by now reached the end of her tether. We felt it would be important to look into how Maria and the grandparents fit into this picture. The telephone chart also reported that the mother had warned: "You'll see, Nando will behave properly during the session, but that's not the way he is at home, believe me."

Instead, Nando was a perfect terror during the session, so much so that the therapist, after a quarter of an hour, begged the grandparents to take him home, whereupon the child kicked up a terrible row, weeping and howling. His grandparents said they couldn't possibly take him home on their own, and his uncle had to be called on the phone to come and get them.

In the midst of all this, the therapist managed to notice several things, namely: that the grandparents were firmly entrenched on the side of the mother, so much so that, as they were leaving, they kissed the therapist's hand, begging her to free them all from this terrible scourge; that Nando, tall and slender, had a beautiful face and a very alert and vivacious manner; that Maria had kept regally aloof throughout, in splendid isolation from everything that went on around her (the telephone chart said that her mother had informed us that Maria went to stay with friends whenever her brother came home on weekends).

Once the therapist found herself alone with the child's mother and Maria, she realized that since the escalation involving the institution and Nando's family had reached such an extreme, there was no point in under-taking family therapy. Nando's mother, in fact, behaved towards the thera-pist as though the latter were part of the institution: Looking distraught, all she did was weep and pull up her sleeves and skirt to show all her bruises and bites. There was nothing we could do right away except send the referring psychologist a note certifying that Nando's weekends at home had to cease immediately. Once the vicious circle involving violent, mutual rejection had been broken, we could discuss what was to be done.

A chance encounter, a few days later, shed a lot of light on the case. The therapist happened to meet a colleague who worked at the center Nando attends. She asked her if she knew Nando. The very mention of the name caused this colleague's face to light up. She smiled with such affectionate interest that the therapist, at first, thought there must be a case of mistaken identity. But no — it really was Nando, our Nando. The colleague went on about how charming he was, how willing and cooperative . . . so much so that no one could understand why he behaved so violently at home! At this point, the therapist made a mental line-up, as in a photomontage, of two faces — the distraught face of Nando's mother and the loving expression of her colleague — and suddenly saw the light: Nando must be a highly accomplished actor! He must have seduced the staff at the institution, and he must have done so to set them up against his mother. Thus, he was acting the part of a helpful, willing little marvel, who behaved so nicely towards everyone, charming them by thinking up clever little things to do and say, and was eager to gradually learn what they were teaching him — *leading them to understand that he was doing all this because they were good to him.* Implicitly, however, by his ingratiating behavior towards the people at the care center, Nando was turning the staff there against his mother, who had sent him off to an institution because she couldn't stand having him around! In return, the staff members, instigated by Nando, fanned his resentment against his mother ("every time you get back from your visits home it takes time for you to calm down and be yourself again, you poor child"), *and* they egged on his mother's resentment against the child ("he behaves so wonderfully when he's here with us — how can he possibly be such a nuisance at home?").

When all this has been said, what can a mother do with a child who is "impossible" only with her? All she can do is hand him over to the staff at the institution, as though saying: "You're so good and clever, well, you can have him, he's all yours." But the staff at the institute doesn't want to be saddled with Nando. . . . So, the circle closes, and Nando is no longer anyone's concern.

Thus, in order to tie in all the circular elements of the sequential segments that make up the phenomenon we have come to call instigation, we have had to go all the way back to the patient. To get there, we have had to blend into a single person two aspects only seemingly in contrast — namely the instigation's victim and its perpetrator. This fusion of opposites was something we became aware of once we discovered the very potent and refined means the patient would resort to in order to implement instigation. We have classified these stratagems under the loose heading of seduction.

Seduction, here, applies to a vast repertoire of sophisticated bits of behavior, *all of which are basically a maneuver to ingratiate oneself to some-*

one one wants to set up against someone else. Thus, the psychotic patient's behavioral bag of tricks includes a formidable capacity for picking the right behavior for each occasion and modulating his conduct accordingly. In this respect, Nando's case was especially revealing, because it was so extreme. Like Dr. Jekyll and Mr. Hyde, Nando would wear two diametrically different faces, one *for* the staff at the center and the other *for* his mother. Almost always, however, such maneuvers will be subtler and less obvious. Only by being aware of their existence, and therefore prepared to seek them out, will we be able to "see them coming" in good time and avoid being ambushed by them.

CHAPTER VII

The Parental Couple's Game and the Patient's Involvement Therein are Made Manifest

FIRST ATTEMPTS TO DISCOVER
THE PARENTS' GAME
AND LINK IT TO THE
SON/DAUGHTER'S SYMPTOM

WHAT FOLLOWS WILL, we hope, provide a clear picture of our initial efforts to make out the games the parental couple was playing and link them to the child's symptom. This entailed an incredible amount of very hard work. Perhaps we will be more successful in sharing this experience with our readers if we present a few cases which, at the time, we found particularly challenging.

What we mainly hope to convey is the formidable difficulty we faced when trying to unearth desperately needed information in order to draw up plausible and therapeutically effectual hypotheses. This task kept us under an unflagging, almost obsessive pressure and taxed our powers of intuition so greatly that the strain at times threatened to become unbearable. We stress this because, by recounting these case histories in a way to make them less tedious for the reader, we run the risk of glossing over our bumpy moments and conveying the idea that everything was relatively smooth and simple. The reader might be led to think we were dealing here with self-aware, cooperative subjects eager to come clean and volunteer the information we needed.

The therapeutic rationale that governed the proceedings we are about to relate no longer satisfies us very much. It has a number of flaws and leaves too many issues open to doubt. However, we present it, as there is no better way for us to give an idea of how we started out and our point of departure. The title we have tagged onto each case is a metaphorical hint at the special way the patient entered into his or her parents' game.

The Counterespionage Agent

When his family first contacts us, Mauro, the patient, is 12. He is the oldest of three children. Enzo and Amelia, his parents, are nurses and work at the same city hospital. They are each out of the house roughly eight hours a day and often work different shifts. The family lives in one of four small flats housed in a modest villa. Various members of Enzo's family occupy the rest of the house. His mother lives across the landing from them and his two brothers, both married and with children of their own, live in the two upstairs flats.

The family has come to us for help with Mauro, who has already been examined at the district psychosocial center, which referred him to us with a diagnosis of "psychotic behavior in a mentally retarded subject." Mauro enacts this undesirable behavior to an alarming degree, mainly at school. At home he is not particularly obnoxious. He stays mainly in his room, drawing pictures and thinking up solitary games to play. He hardly ever goes into the backyard to play with the other children. At school, however, he is a perfect terror. Not only does he fail to show any interest whatsoever in class activity and refuse to pay attention, but he flares up suddenly and starts exhibiting bizarre and unacceptable behavior, whereupon, in what by now has become a routine, the principal phones his home and asks someone to come and get him. His latest exploit was by far the most spectacular: The superintendent looked up to see him doing a balancing act on the school roof.

In our first meeting with the family we seemed to be heading for a total flop. We had asked the paternal grandmother to attend, along with the nuclear family. For what seemed an endless length of time the therapist, despite all her experience and skill, was unable to bring the situation under control. The three kids acted like a bunch of excited monkeys, noisily chattering and giggling. The grandmother looked hostile and the parents acted helpless and reticent.

Finally the therapist wormed a crucial admission out of the father: Mauro's school principal had forced him to contact the Center by telling him he was no longer willing to keep Mauro in school unless the family undertook some sort of therapy. This was how the therapist came to know that the family was there under duress. This eye-opening bit of information also prompted her to make a lightning hypothesis: Mauro, who lives in a house overrun by relatives, just might be getting himself sent home from school in order to fulfill some self-assigned duty. Acting on a hunch, she turned to Mauro and said, "Well, Mauro, you can't fool *me*. You're not crazy, and you're not even retarded. I'm sure you get yourself sent home on purpose, by doing all those weird things like dancing around on rooftops. And I'm also positive that the reason you get the principal to send you home is because there's something you feel you have to do at home — something you consider very important. You're worried that something might be going on at home and you want to be there to stop it. Well, what is it you are trying to prevent?"[1]

Everyone's immediate reaction to this daring piece of guesswork was sensational: This unruly, giggling group suddenly froze in mid-motion, the way a film will freeze on a single frame. The hubbub ceased instantly and there was a long tense silence. Predictably, no one volunteered, either then or later, to answer the therapist's question. This very eloquent reaction, however, pointed clearly to where the core of the matter lay.

Despite this initial clue, we were well into the fifth session with this family, and seeing only the parents, before we managed to ferret out information enabling us to understand Mauro's reason for getting himself sent home: He was acting to stop his grandmother from stealing into their flat while his mother was at work, poking her nose into his mother's things and rummaging through her drawers.

We cannot even begin to describe the perseverance and exhausting effort of the imagination we had to bring to bear on the case before we could obtain a clear picture of this couple's game. Enzo kept up a steady stream of talk, most of it irrelevant, while his wife played the perfect sphynx, sitting up straight as a ramrod, queenly and aloof, uttering only a few syllables now and then after much meditating. Here is what finally came to light:

The father, a glib, rather snappish sort, was a twisty double-dealer. He would argue vociferously with his mother over trifles and insult her copiously in the process, but wouldn't raise a finger to stop her constant interfering in family matters and supervising their every move. His mother was a habitual intruder, who would come snooping around at all hours of the day, peering into every corner and even examining the contents of the pots boiling on the stove. The most important thing, however, was that Enzo had given her a key to his flat, on the excuse that she didn't have a telephone and might have to use theirs in an emergency.

The revealing bit of intelligence about the mother's key was mentioned quite casually during the session, while Enzo was telling us of his reluctance to go on the prescribed "disappearances": He feared that his mother, who kept a constant vigil at her window, might take it into her head to cross over to their flat late at night, wake up the children and ask them where he

---

[1]The therapist, in making this statement, was obviously leading from the premise that there is always a logic behind any "psychotic" behavior that produces such clear-cut results: In this case, it involved being sent home from school.

and Amelia had gone. Even more astonishing was the fact that Amelia, too, had entirely neglected to mention that her mother-in-law had free access to the premises. Only when the therapist pounced on the subject and prodded her did Amelia admit that she often found signs of her mother-in-law's trespassing—some of her things would be out of place and her papers messed with. Also, her drawers were clearly undergoing regular inspection. Despite all this, which must have infuriated her to no end, Amelia had never said a word to her husband; he was now hearing of it for the first time in this, their fifth, session.

The seventh session, in which we planned to test how effectual we had been in breaking up the absurd game involving Enzo's active provocation and Amelia's stony silence, was one for the books. Enzo had already told us in the sixth session that he had had the lock changed on his front door and told his mother to use one of his brothers' phones if need be. He gave her no explanation for this change, but she obviously got the message. She went no further into the matter and from that day on stopped dropping in on the family at all hours.

In the seventh session, Amelia stole the show. This silent, forbearing woman did something no one else had ever done before or ever was to do in the future, for as long as we kept on working with the prescriptions: She used her written notes, which she knew she would have to read aloud to the therapist, to address a strong and heartfelt appeal to her husband. For the first time, protected by the mediating presence of the therapist, she let herself go and disclosed how deeply this man had made her suffer in the past. She invited him to join her in setting up a new, honest, unambiguous relationship. But this was not all. Her notes also recounted a highly dramatic incident. One morning, while she was home, she got a call from the superintendent of Mauro's school, asking her to come and collect Mauro, who was up to his tricks again. In Amelia's own words:

> I got in the car and drove to the school. I was perfectly calm and kept thinking how much I loved my son and that there would simply have to be a stop to this. I found Mauro in the superintendent's lodge, all flushed and sweaty. The staff members were eager to tell me what had happened, but I cut them short: "I'd rather hear about it from Mauro, if you don't mind. Let him be the one to tell me." So Mauro told me he'd got into a fistfight with one of his schoolmates, who had made fun of him. He'd bloodied this boy's nose and then, to escape retaliation, had taken refuge in a broom closet. The superintendent had dragged him out of there, and here he was. As Mauro was finishing his story, another attendant came along with Mauro's coat, so that he could put it on and leave for home. I gave this man back the coat and said: "No, I'm not going to take Mauro home. I don't want to. Mauro is going to go right back to his classroom now and behave like a sensible boy." I took my son's face in my hands, looked him straight in the eye, and said very firmly and gently: "Your place is here, Mauro, this is where you belong and where I want you to be—with your school friends, with boys your own age. Do you understand?" He nodded, and I left.

As Amelia read her notes, the therapist felt her eyes getting moist. She sensed she was witnessing, for the first time ever and at first hand, a very important event, namely, the dissolution of a secret mother/son coalition. Her feeling was confirmed by Mauro's sudden change of behavior at school. He became a willing, well-behaved scholar. Although his schoolwork remained below par, the psychotic behavior as well as the dramatic phone calls from the principal, became a thing of the past.

This case illustrates how we were obliged to work our way up to the seventh session before finding a convincing explanation for what was going on and unraveling the remaining enigma. How, for example, were we to account for the whole group keeping silent in answer to the question addressed to Mauro in the first session? Amelia's attitude was simple enough to understand: Her silence was not really directed towards the therapist. She was only getting on with her game, which consisted of denying her mother-in-law (and her husband) the satisfaction of so much as letting on that she knew the house searches were taking place. And it was logical, too, for Mauro and his father to keep mum in that session, Grandma's presence being a source of great embarrassment to everyone.

Surely, the team thought, in the following session, with Grandma out of the way, much useful information would be supplied by the nuclear family. No such luck. The only thing that had changed, by the time our second session took place, was that everyone's rambunctious and disqualifying attitude towards the therapist had disappeared—it had probably been the effect of the old lady's very noticeable hostility towards the very idea of therapy. Why, then, was everyone still obstinately refusing to divulge what it was Mauro was trying to prevent by getting sent home? Why was no one willing to let us know how things really stood, even though they were all here together because one of them was in serious trouble? No one, not even the child's mother, dared take the initiative and be the first to make a move that threatened to upset the game. When the spouses were summoned alone to the third and fourth session, they failed to budge from this position, and it was only in our fifth meeting that the information suddenly popped out, quite by chance.

The Vice-Squad

Very often, the veiled threat[2] running through the spouses' exchange of provocations will feature sex as a strong bugaboo. If the true nature of the menace does involve sex, the actors will under no circumstances volunteer

---

[2]*Threat* is a frequent variation on the general theme of tactics basic to the spouses' skirmishing. It is one of the most primitive and best-known ploys used in interactional games, and can also be attributed to the behavior of the higher mammals.

to talk about it, and the therapist can only guess, from certain signs, that sex is a part of the ongoing game.

This will be easier to detect if the wife is the one actively provoking and strikes us as being "sexy" in some way. However, to complicate matters, this is not always a useful clue. There are times when a wife we had immediately classified as unattractive proves to be remarkably skillful at keeping her husband on tenterhooks by subtly hinting at an affair she just might be contemplating. So, we can't rely on our own sense of aesthetics to guide us, and this is another reminder of the fact that nothing is impossible where psychotic games are concerned.

The case that follows was, in all respects, remarkable. The actors were a couple in their forties, who had come for help with their only son, a boy of 18. Dario had been discharged a few months earlier from the psychiatric ward, where he had been admitted in an acutely delirious state. Even before this episode, the boy had quit school, given up all his friends and his very active involvement in sports. He was now spending all his time shadowing his parents. His mother, especially, would find him clinging to her like a leech.

Dario's parents owned and operated a company selling office supplies. They were both good-looking, but the wife was by far the more alluring of the two. Not only did she look nothing near her age, but she dressed and did her hair in the style of a somewhat brazen teenager, without looking at all ridiculous. There was an aura of sinful eroticism about her that was difficult to pin down exactly but that the male members of the team felt distinctly, even through the mirror.

This observation, however, did not at the time help us reconstrue the ongoing game. Only when we got to the stage of prescribing evening outings did any significant clue turn up. To our surprise, since we were dealing with a sophisticated couple who led an active social life, the husband raised a stream of endless objections when the disappearances were prescribed. This led us to assume (a) that he was afraid the disappearances with his wife would displease Dario, and (b) more significantly, that this omnipresent, watchful son suited him perfectly.

The hypothesis we drew up then was that this husband, instead of coming straight out and insisting that his wife dress and act more modestly, was resorting to a covert maneuver to further his ends. Following this lead, we first discovered that the husband had hired one of his wife's sisters and two of her aunts as warehouse supervisor and saleswomen in the family business—a veritable guard corps. Unfortunately, not even this squad of vigilantes was enough to reassure him, so that Dario, his only son, was needed as well. But, how?

By zeroing in on what had gone on before the psychotic crisis and gradually overcoming a lot of hedging and sidetracking, we reconstructed the following series of events. Dario's psychotic explosion had come in the wake of a pathetic episode. His best friend, a boy his own age who had often been a guest at Dario's home, had developed a serious crush on Dario's mother. Soon thereafter, Dario's father had suffered a heart attack. It struck us that this husband might have nagging doubts about his wife's indifference to this handsome young adolescent.

This lovely woman's fascination lay precisely in the air of seductive mystery that surrounded her. None of the spies enlisted to keep tabs on her could ever make out exactly what went on under that beautiful mass of hair and behind those deep, dark eyes. Was she in love? Was she completely impassive? Was she amenable to a fling, or even hankering for one? *Had* she sinned?

Dario, after a brief phase of unusual behavior (he tried to upset his mother by hanging out with a gang of hooligans) decided to take it upon himself, via "psychotic" behavior, to control the "red-light" aspects of his home life. In his role as a "psychotic," Dario proved a formidable body-guard. This became his daily routine: He would get up the moment his parents did, have breakfast with them and then trail after them to their place of work. A little desk had been placed for him alongside his mother's: There he sat the whole day, doing absolutely nothing, he eyes riveted on his mother. All attempts to get him to go out and meet his friends, or to send him to the movies, or to involve him in any of the many sports he had previously enjoyed, were to no avail. If he was alone at home with his mother for any length of time, he would walk around her in circles, as though it were his job to check on everything she did. Twice he had walked slowly across her room, stark naked and with a conspicuous erection. This latter move made us think that Dario, too, was having trouble figuring out what his mysterious mother's true feelings for him were, and that this conduct was his way of asking her to define them. But his mother, as is proper in such cases, simply pretended not to notice.

This and other incidents like it eventually led us to hypothesize that a spouses' game based on sexual threats was under way in all cases when a child was going about in the nude, making erotic advances, or hopping in and out of sundry beds. Such threats, as we knew from the time *Paradox and Counterparadox* was being written, signal that an erotic rival in the family, usually a son or a daughter, is being preferred to the established partner. This involves sending out messages that hint at desire, arousal, and attraction so obvious and intermittent that they jar openly with the con-text: The recipient cannot but feel anguished and confused by them. This, in turn, induces the appointed rival, once he or she has come to wield "psychotic" power, to "psychotically" demand a showdown.

The most spectacular case of its kind to come our way, and one that ended in a particularly elegant and amusing fashion, was that of Daphne and her family. Daphne was a pretty girl of 22, the second of three daugh-ters. Her parents belonged to the upper-middle class. Four and a half years

before we met them, she had started exhibiting delirious "psychotic" behavior. This had continued, albeit intermittently, so that by now she no
longer had a scholastic career or a proper social life. She was an expert
skier, and her only remaining solace was the occasional trip to the family's
mountain chalet with her father.

Daphne ushered in her erotic behavior, as well as her traipsing about in
the nude, when her parents, after strenuous objecting and endless procrastinating (mainly by the father), finally went on the prescribed weekend
disappearances. Soon after the first of these, Daphne began her erotic
posturing, which she flaunted with cunning bisexual impartiality at both
her father and her mother. When she was alone with her mother (a big hulk
of a woman, as frazzled and unkempt as her husband was clean-cut and
athletic), Daphne would rush to embrace her and press her mouth to her
mother's in a long, passionate kiss. And this was not all. Her most embarrassing and disconcerting performance consisted of stripping off all her
clothes. This she was capable of doing in two seconds flat—all of a sudden
she would be standing there, drawn up to her full height, her clothes lying
around her in a heap on the floor. She even did this on the street once,
when her mother dragged her out against her will, on the grounds that the
girl simply had to get some fresh air. This was quite definitely the last time
anyone ever tried to get Daphne to go out when she didn't want to! The
most intriguing thing was that the girl had also twice done her nudist act
while alone with her father in the study.

Her parents reported these upsetting new traits in Daphne's behavior to
the therapist during the session that followed the weekend disappearance.
The first thing the therapist wanted to know was what the parents had
done. It turned out that they had both reacted in much the same manner.
The mother had looked the other way with an embarrassed little laugh and
the father, too, had averted his gaze, remarking that he didn't really think
the weather was hot enough for that sort of thing. . . .

This unforgettable session ended with the therapist's issuing a prescription and suggesting a choice of behaviors. The prescription, of course,
concerned more disappearances, of both the evening and the weekend
variety. The choice of behavior, on the other hand, consisted of three set
suggestions, similar for both parents. To the mother: "If Daphne should
kiss you on the mouth again, I can suggest three ways to react: the first, to
kiss her back, every bit as passionately; the second, to do what you've done
up to now, namely shy away from her and act embarrassed; the third, to
slap her across the mouth as hard as you can." To the father: "If Daphne
appears in the nude again, when you two are alone, I suggest you do one of
the following: one, take her in your arms, lay her down on the sofa and
mime erotic behavior—if the girl really seems willing, don't hesitate to have
proper sex with her; two, do what you've been doing, that is, pretend not to
notice; three, take off one of your shoes and wallop her with it, with all your

might." To both: "The next time we meet, each of you will as usual bring along the notes you've made on everyone's reactions to your disappearing. As to which line of conduct you chose, if Daphne has given you occasion to do so, you will tell me next time which of my suggestions you decided to follow."

When the next session rolled around, it turned out that Daphne's mother had not been obliged to choose: She had strenuously avoided ever being alone with her daughter. The father, on the other hand, had been "trapped" by Daphne. Early one Saturday morning, as he was loading his things into the car for a trip he was planning to make to the mountains alone, Daphne came out to the car, cold and silent like a statue, carrying her things. She put them in the car and climbed in. The poor man felt his heart sink: That night threatened to be a rough one — and so it was. Shortly after he had gone to bed, Daphne came gliding into his room in her nightgown, acting as though she were sleepwalking. She took off her nightgown and got in under the covers. However, she didn't touch him or sidle up to him. What did the father do? The therapist might have known this consummate player would not have deigned to adopt one of *her* suggestions: He chose a fourth alternative, one more in keeping with his own way of doing things, and it worked like a charm. With polished sarcasm, he said, "I suppose you want me to think you haven't worked out your Oedipus complex properly yet. I don't go for any of that nonsense, and I think you're simply having a whale of a time making me look foolish." This said, he pointed to the door. The girl took a flying leap out of bed and through the door, and disappeared into her room.

The catharsis came next morning. The father, while he was getting dressed, could hear coming from the kitchen a low, cheerful humming that he hadn't heard in years, together with the delicious smell of freshly made coffee. Daphne had made a wonderful breakfast and loaded the table with all sorts of good things. She poured his coffee and then sat down opposite her father. As she was pulling her chair up to the table, she looked straight at him and said, with a brilliant smile: "The time has come to be honest with you, Dad. Physically, I've always found you utterly repulsive." After this lucid two-way showdown, all erotic sparring between father and daughter was over, forever. Daphne made no further advances to anyone, including her mother, and thus had more time to devote to her own problems. Gradually she began to solve them all, and in time she became a ski instructor and became engaged to a nice, suitable boy.

The Family Auditor

Contrary to what our ingrained cultural values might lead us to suppose, money, as such, is rarely a paramount issue in schizophrenic games: These games are interactional tangles so thoroughly laced with long-standing covert and secret rancor that they rule out any itemized accounting or submitting of bills for services rendered. We learned in time that families of this kind never open their accounts for inspection. Outstanding debts are liable to be claimed (or so the claimant thinks) by the creditor's taking to bed for years, or waxing delirious in a hospital. . . .

We now come to the case of an absolutely fascinating family, straight out of Thomas Hardy. They were village blacksmiths, as their forbears had been, who generations ago had settled in the same part of Lombardy. The mother was a lean, wiry little woman, unbelievably energetic. Next to her four strapping menfolk she looked even tinier than she was, yet she worked alongside them at the forge whenever she was needed, besides running the household, tending a vegetable garden, and raising all kinds of farmyard animals.

Giano, the patient, was 22. Four years ago he had been diagnosed as a schizophrenic. He was a young giant, whose impressive height and bulk contrasted sharply with his meek expression. Ten years younger than his brothers Augusto and Cesare (both in their thirties, married, with children), Giano was quite definitely the family pet.

What we read on the telephone chart made us envision the family logistics as an ideal breeding-ground for psychosis. Four years before we met the family, the father and his three sons, working like galley slaves, had built with their own hands the large shed that housed their forge and the workshop. Then, in one corner of the piece of land they had bought on mortgage from the local council, they had also built four little terrace houses, the last of which, left unfinished, was to be Giano's if ever he should marry.

When the family came to us, Giano, once strong as an ox, tireless on the job and easily able to do the work of two men, was regarded as being a chronic invalid. He had been through numerous bouts of delirious behavior and in and out of the hospital on countless occasions. At the time, he was spending his days lying in bed in his room, where his mother would join him every afternoon. She would take along her knitting and sit there, keeping him company. He was an empty shell of a man. The family had been referred to us by a cousin on the mother's side, a social worker, who had heard our Center spoken of as "a last resort."

Even as we read through the telephone chart, we started hypothesizing. This young man, who for years now had stayed cloistered in his room, from which he could see, through the window, the furnace where his father and brothers were toiling away, must be "striking" against some injustice *committed against him* (an assumption that proved too simplistic, naturally, as no one turns schizophrenic for any so linear, clear-cut and obvious a reason).

During both the first session, to which we also invited the referring cousin, and the second, with the nuclear family alone, the therapist made every effort to find out just what Giano's grievance might be. Although she stuck strictly to the factual context, impressing the family with her apt inquiries, worthy of a tax consultant, concerning what everybody was earning, how profits were shared, whose names were on the property deeds, etc., she met with a solid wall of trivializing and contradictions. Nothing of any help came to light.

Starting with the third session, only the parental couple was summoned. The information we obtained, and the reactions elicited by the couple's scrupulous carrying out of the prescriptions, allowed us to reconstrue a fascinating family saga.

Gina, the wife, that tiny, hyperactive woman, had gone to live with her husband's family when she married. This latter was a clan of 25 people, all living together in one big farmhouse. The forge, at which her husband worked together with a whole squad of cousins, was also close by. Everyone worked under the strict supervision of an uncle on the father's side, Ario, who ruled the clan with an iron hand.

Gina suffered terribly from this subservience, and for very down-to-earth reasons. Any purchase she wanted to make that was not specifically for her family's immediate needs had to be approved by Uncle Ario, who would either give or withhold the money as he thought best. Her greatest disappointment came when the uncle vetoed the idea that Augusto, Gina's firstborn, should go on to get a higher education. Augusto was a very bright boy, and his teachers had all encouraged him to go on studying. Instead, Uncle Ario decreed that Augusto was a strong, healthy boy and therefore useful in the family forge. Instead of Augusto, the uncle sent one of his granddaughters to college. Gina's husband, afraid to cause strife in the family, said not a word and forbade his wife to complain or protest.

Gina racked her brains for years to find a way out of bondage. At last she heard that a bank was building a branch office in their village and was offering lodgings and a salary to a janitor. She went after the job and landed it by offering to clean the building at night. At last she had a home for herself and her family that she could call her own, and they were all free from the tyrannical uncle's tutelage. Unfortunately, the family forge was still where it had always been and was the clan's common property.

Augusto took the next step. He decided he would be the one to *get nasty* with Uncle Ario, and left him to go and work on his own. He rented a warehouse in the village, where the two older brothers, with their father, installed their own forge. Giano was still at school at the time. His mother had her heart set on his getting a technical school certificate. Three years later, the family made their great leap forward: By skimping and scraping, with financing from the bank and long-term loans from the authorities, they managed to build the large shed and the little houses on virtually nothing but their own effort and determination. Giano worked much harder than anyone else. He quit school to be able to spend every single day, from morn to night, on the building site. His mother would urge him on, saying, "Come on, Giano, one last effort and we'll have it made — think how happy we'll be then!"

The first signs of Giano's unusual behavior came a few months after the family had moved into the newly built house near the workshop. This sober, parsimonious young man suddenly turned into a profligate spend-thrift. He'd get in the family car every evening and tear around the countryside, wasting gallons of gasoline. He'd buy a lot of useless junk and throw it in the back of a drawer, never to be looked at again. For a while his mother kept him supplied with cash with what she made by selling her rabbits and pigeons, but the crunch finally came. Giano was taken to the local hospital in a delirious state. From then on, under heavy medication, flabby and obese, he had drifted in and out of hospital at regular intervals. He had been totally idle for years now, so that Augusto and Cesare were saddled with his share of the work, too. Even their father had to pitch in occasionally. The brothers chided their mother for "spoiling" Giano, but she retorted that Giano's wages should be put in a bank account for him, because he had ruined his health by working too hard to get the shed and houses built in record time.

Since we were as yet relatively inexperienced at the time, therapy in this case became a considerable adventure and caused as much anxiety. Up to the seventh session, the results were spectacular. The spouses collaborated eagerly, and faithfully carried out the prescriptions, which included a "disappearance" of nearly a month's duration during which they left Giano at home alone. By the fifth session Giano had already started to get up out of bed in the evenings and go off to the village to meet with his friends. After the sixth session, the boy started helping out in the workshop, albeit intermittently. This fact was brought to our knowledge by the mother's triumphant announcement at the start of the seventh session, when she welcomed us by crying, "Giano is working!"

Unfortunately, that same session also brought a few other things to light. With a show of feigned contrition, the mother confessed that, on an impulse she wasn't able to explain, she had let Giano into the secret by telling him she was going on these outings reluctantly and only because the Center had ordered her to. Now, why should Gina have done that just when Giano was showing such remarkable improvement? It took long, painstaking work and an extra dose of intuition to deduce, from her sighs and half-spoken words, that Gina was severely disgruntled: The situation in the newly built workshop was beginning to look suspiciously like the one they had left behind, when they had all been enslaved to Uncle Ario. This time her two older sons were taking over, especially Cesare, the secondborn. Cesare was the family treasurer. He held the purse strings and dealt with the bank. He was the one to parcel out money to everyone else. Gina's husband wasn't good at practical matters and everything was in Cesare's hands now.

The therapist turned to the husband to see what he had to say, but this was a dismal fiasco: He equivocated shamelessly, brushing aside his wife's misgivings, and insisted that Cesare was very generous and would never do anything crooked or underhand. Through all this, his wife kept an impassive silence and stared down at the tips of her shoes.

The team debated for hours about what was to be done. Clearly, the mother felt a greater need than ever to strengthen her alliance with Giano, since her husband was siding with the two older boys. However, we couldn't let this sway us: Our contract with the parents had been perfectly straightforward, i.e., should the secret be let out, therapy would be terminated. Gina had let the secret out on purpose. For some reason, she must have feared that her Giano, once he was back at the forge again, would join forces with the rest of her menfolk.[3]

We hated the idea of giving up on this case. Now that the secret was out, we decided to make one last, desperate attempt: We ordered the parents to go home and announce to Giano and the others that therapy would now be broken off because the therapist has resolved to leave the field—*Giano's two brothers were too tough for her*. This happened in the autumn of 1981. Shortly afterwards, the therapist received three letters from Gina, at roughly two-month intervals. The first of these was dated December 18th and very dramatically depicted a totally unrecognizable Giano. He was now rebellious, quarrelsome and at war with everyone, including his mother. Gina wrote that the therapist's *proclamation*, when relayed to the boys, had upset Giano terribly. That same evening he had resumed his nightly roving around in the family car, wasting all that gas. After a few days of this, he went back to work in the family forge. He worked as he pleased, however, and would take no orders or suggestions from anyone. He kept his own hours, but when he did work, he did an excellent job. He had pointed out his brother Cesare to his pals at the bar, referring to him sarcastically as "the boss." On one occasion, he had ordered Cesare out of their house, when the latter casually sauntered in to use the toilet, in such fiery tones that Augusto's wife, present at the time, later remarked, "Where on earth has he kept all that fury hidden inside of him up to now?"

The last of Gina's letters, which we got the following spring, was a terrible one. It hit us like a clap of thunder and suddenly rent the fog we'd been floundering in for so long. For the first time, a full six months after the end of therapy, Gina was lifting the veil that shrouded her relationship with her husband. We quote the main part of her letter, and regret that the

[3]As we see things today, we would not simply hypothesize the mother's fear and discuss it among ourselves but voice it explicitly in the session.

poetic nuances of the original, deriving from the writer's lack of grammar and her dialectal expressions, will get altogether lost in the transcript:

> My husband is a good-for-nothing. When I first married him, he'd make me go to his Uncle Ario whenever we needed money, and now he's making me go ask his sons. Only God knows how it makes me feel to have to do that, and I get to thinking, this is the way it's always going to be, and Giano won't ever get well, either. Giano has been locked up in his room, in the dark, for days now. Please, doctor, write to my older sons and tell them what to do, before it's too late. . . . but don't tell them I asked you to. . . .

After all this time, once we had read this letter, we were able to see more clearly into the case. Giano had gotten enmeshed in the couple's game in early childhood and had been held in fealty to his mother. At the age of 18, he had decided to quit school and throw himself body and soul into the family building enterprise. This was probably his way of applying for admission to the male coterie. Unfortunately, he was turned down. His brothers weren't about to share their seniority privileges with him. As for his father, although he acted the boss the way Uncle Ario had, deep down, as always, he must have felt quite content to be left out of the fray and delegate the two older boys *to keep his wife in check.*

So Gina, after fighting so long and so hard, found herself back where she had started from 20 years earlier—stuck with a husband who set no store by keeping accounts and forced her to go to Cesare, hat in hand, just as she'd had to go to Uncle Ario. Gina, who had toiled at the bank day and night for years in order to provide her family with a home of their own, was now receiving no salary or share of the profits, and had to fall back on the sale of her rabbits and pigeons if she wanted a little money of her own that she needn't account for to "the boss."

As for Giano, he must have felt everyone had let him down: His mother was totally absorbed in her own grievances and his father and brothers had rejected him. This had made him decide to go it alone and to claim his rights. He had forced "the grown-ups" to do his share of working and sweating as well as their own, while he stayed snugly in bed and let himself be catered to. Giano had set himself up as the family auditor and was squaring the accounts.

The team discussed this letter at length and then decided the therapist would neither answer it nor, of course, write to the older boys as Gina asked her to do: The struggle for change seemed to have now come out into the open, the therapist having unleashed hidden antagonistic tendencies, in both Giano and his mother, of the kind that can bring on a new, different organization.

Follow-up. On June 2, 1985, the therapist phoned the referring person and asked about the family. This was the answer: "Giano is just fine. I have only very positive things to report about him. He hasn't been taking any medicine for three years now. His brothers, however, have had to acknowledge that they'd been exploiting him, treating him like a baby and never letting him have his say or decide anything for himself. Well, now he's on an equal footing with the others, even though he's had to fight hard for it. He has a girl friend and he's crazy about her. He's lost weight and looks wonderful—you should see how handsome he is now! I saw Gina some time ago and she told me you folks had worked a miracle, but that she was ashamed to call you up—she said she felt guilty towards you, but she didn't say why. . . . "

WHEN THE PRESCRIPTION GETS SWALLOWED UP INTO THE COUPLE'S GAME

It took the salty wit of Lido, a true-bred Tuscan "man of the people," to make us realize for the first time that there are cases when we can expect the prescriptions to be carried out only if we find a way to entirely rule out any notion of pleasure or amusement accruing to the outings—only thus can a "real" man comply with it and not lose face!

The case in point involved an elderly couple, who had married late in life. Their only son was a chronic schizophrenic. Nelia, the mother, was the more motivated of the two with regard to therapy, as her life was severely conditioned by the child's pathology. Our inquiry revealed that she had been quite a fetching young girl, who had spent her youth in the frivolous ambience of a fashionable boutique, working as a dressmaker. She had finally given in and married this commonplace, unattractive man, on the rebound, after one of her many unhappy love affairs. The two of them had left the city where they had been living up to then and settled down in a country town on the Arno river, where the husband had been born, and where he worked at the local tannery. Nelia had insisted on working as a seamstress in her new home.

The couple's history hinted strongly at a covert struggle between this attractive, sociable woman, always ready to sit down and have a nice, long chat in one of the shops, and her unsightly, jealous husband, who would have liked nothing better than to have her all to himself, cloistered away at home under lock and key.

The evening disappearances were duly prescribed. When the spouses brought in their notes, we learned of the impossible place Lido had chosen for them to disappear to, namely a derelict chicken farm with a garage built onto it, a few miles outside town! This was how Lido described their evening outings:

We'd fix a thermos of hot coffee and some sandwiches, take along two blankets and a box of candles, and off we'd go. After a couple of miles we'd leave the main road, drive along this little country lane and pop into the garage. We could really be sure no one would ever find us *there*. Nelia, poor thing, though she was worried to death about leaving Duccio at home alone, would have loved to go to a restaurant. She's been complaining for years that I never take her anywhere. But I explained that when you people prescribe something, it's to be taken like medicine. It's not something to be enjoyed. However, when we'd get back and Duccio would be there, staring at us with his mouth wide open, we'd act as though we were in a wonderful mood and had had a whale of a time.

Lido had gone to all this trouble to organize these unlikely picnics just to thwart his wife's wish to be taken out for an evening of fun! For the team, this was a revelation. It was as though a spotlight had been trained on the willful stubbornness and tactical scheming that run covertly through the tangled relationships of couples such as this. Once we were made aware of this, we were sometimes able to forestall and fence off, without further questioning, the obvious displeasure a husband was likely to show on being issued the prescription. We would throw out a feeler. "You don't *have* to take out your wife to give her a good time," we would chance, "the only thing that matters is that the two of you agree, for the sake of your child, to make him/her *think* you've been enjoying yourselves. I'm aware that this may be embarrassing and humiliating for you, and we can't promise that your in-laws won't laugh behind your back, saying, 'Just look at that grumpy old fogey, suddenly taking his wife out for a fling, like a young Lothario . . . he must be off his rocker. . . .'"

By acting on a hunch, and turning up the cards presumably involved in the game in an easygoing, humorous fashion, we are sometimes able to defuse age-old conflicts that have turned stiff and unyielding from having been kept silent so long. However, we will sometimes run into a case where complying with our prescription lays bare some special circumstance, making it inadvisable to pursue this course of action. This happens when the prescription, once it was introduced into the couple's game, had been artfully used by one of the spouses to further his/her own ends. The following is a typical case.

The father of a 16-year-old girl with a diagnosis of major depression turned up at the session after a weekend disappearance wearing a thoroughly disgruntled expression and acting hostile and vexed. The therapist empathically insisted on hearing what the trouble was. This brought forth a sarcastic outburst:

Have you any idea, lady, how long it's been that I've known about the romantic little hotel in the Apennines where I took my wife last week? Can you guess? Twenty years! I've known about it all that time, and for years I've kept asking her to come and spend a weekend with me up there. I could never once get her to come. She'd always have some excuse handy, involving her mother. Yet this time, would you believe it, she came along, pleased as Punch, just to show me how happy she was to have to obey your prescription, doctor. For 20 years she used her mother as an excuse for not pleasing me, and now she's delighted to have the excuse of having to obey *you*.

The team talked the matter over and agreed that, under these circumstances, prescribing further outings would be inadvisable, as it would have implied siding with the wife. But what were we to do? At long last we decided not only to forgo any further use of the prescription but also to implicitly encourage the wife to enter into an alliance with her husband and stop pitting him against "the women" (not only the therapist, that is, but also their daughter, Barbara, whom she waited on like a slave).

The therapist went back in to meet with the parents after the team had decided what to do, and turned to the wife. She told her how deeply she sympathized with her for having gotten entangled anew, even though she was now such a consummate co-therapist, in the old game played by her family of origin. This game involved falling in love with women for the purpose of disconcerting men. Disappearances were therefore impossible. However, there was still a slim chance of helping Barbara out of her predicament *if* the mother could invent some prescription of her own, designed to change the girl's behavior, and resolve to carry it out, and *if* she managed to get her husband to join her in this attempt and they tackled the job together. The mother looked extremely put out, but she accepted without a murmur.

It worked. The spouses returned for their next session looking very pleased with themselves. They had thought up and enacted a very clever initiative. In cahoots with the family doctor, who was to prescribe "innocuous" medicine for her to take, Barbara's mother took to bed for 10 days, ostensibly suffering from a very painful attack of lumbago that completely immobilized her. Barbara rose to the occasion admirably. She took over the household, cooked her mother's meals, served them to her in bed and then joined her father at the dinner table. She even ran errands continuously, whenever anything was needed.

Cases such as this taught us much about the spouses' games and helped us refine our tactical skills. Other cases, however—and there were quite a few of them—would find us up flat against a stone wall as impervious as a dam. These we will go into later.

WHEN THE PARENTS VIE
FOR THE PATIENT'S FAVOR

In the course of time, our experience and skill in conducting clinical work increased, and we became ever more proficient at grasping even minor fragments of key information as they surfaced. This, in time, ena-

bled us to "map out" parts of these ongoing games, which are as malignant
as they are sophisticated. One such game is that played by two parents
vying for their child.

Here, too, reluctance to carry out the weekend disappearances and a
general worsening of the situation following the first "disappearance" stark-
ly revealed the incredible tactical farrago some families will build up. What
is more important, this information suggested ways in which we could
hope to unravel the maze. The following is a case in point.

The Malerba family consisted of four members. The father was a successful publicity copywriter and the mother taught high school. The patient, Primo, a boy of 15, was referred to us with a diagnosis of major
depression, nocturnal enuresis, and encopresis. His sister, Gaia, age 12, was
considered a healthy child.

The mother was definitely the one who acted more anguished at the
idea of the prescriptions, although the children were old enough to be left
home alone and had never behaved in such a way as to rule this out. Very
laboriously, and although their attitude remained essentially unchanged,
we reached the point when three weekend disappearances were prescribed. This announcement aroused such terror in the mother that we
were obliged to postpone the next session several times. When the parents
finally did turn up, they confessed to having been on only two of these
outings and had firmly resolved never to go on another. The mother's
attitude towards the therapist was extremely hostile.

It turned out that the disappearances had not caused particular mis-
haps: The children behaved well and proved unexpectedly resourceful in
looking after themselves. However, Primo's enuretic and encopresis symptoms got much worse and, to compound the issue, he had started neglecting his schoolwork entirely. This was not all: The couple's marital rapport
had deteriorated to such an extent that Mrs. Malerba was seriously contemplating a legal separation.

When the therapist tried to find out exactly what had happened, this
came to light: Mrs. Malerba revealed that after each weekend absence, her
husband had literally showered expensive gifts on Primo. In order to be
fair, he spent an equal amount of money on things for Gaia. However, the
more Primo's father lavished on him, the more demanding the boy became. He acted as though all this, and anything else he wanted, was his
due. It was as though his father were obliged to pay out huge sums as a sort
of compensation to his son for having been so wicked as to have preferred
his wife's company and disappeared with her. In keeping with this logic,
Mr. Malerba had also booked two seats on a costly charter flight to take his
son abroad to see a big football match. This meant there was to be a trip to
counterpoise the reprehensible weekend: This was what had made the
wife's blood boil.

And what did we discover when we probed more deeply? What was the
real reason for the mother's anger? It turned out that Mrs. Malerba was

unable to compete with her husband where money was concerned. She never missed an opportunity to flaunt her superior background—she came from an aristocratic family who had been none too pleased to see her take up with someone whose work was publicity and whom they thought of as nothing but a glorified barker—but these distinguished forbears were unfortunately penniless, so that Mrs. Malerba had only her teacher's salary to call her own. Thus, we learned that in order to even the score she would devote endless hours to Primo's homework. She would write essays and summaries for him and read pages of history into the tape recorder so that he could listen to them when he went out walking! This, of course, was her way of showing contempt for her husband's vulgar display of riches, and this was how Primo was roped into the couple's game. Each parent was outdoing the other in *begging his pardon* for having betrayed him by disappearing with his/her legally wedded spouse!

It should be noted that this tangle became visible only during the seventh session, when the disruptive effects of the two weekends had prompted the parents to make such conspicuous competitive moves. However, their separate efforts to seduce the child must have been going on long before this, even though they had been very covert and difficult to detect. Once we had made out what the game was, we were able to enact a specifically provocative intervention, which proved successful. The therapist told the parents she agreed with them on the matter of calling off the disappearance acts, since they were obviously too hard for them to carry out. She professed pity for these two woeful creatures who had fallen into a trap set by their wily son (and by their still more wily daughter who, without even having to stick her neck out, was trailing along after Primo and picking up the gold as it poured from his pockets). As she persisted in her inquiry, the many guilt-arousing maneuvers Primo had enacted towards his parents came to light. She ended by assigning them the task of putting their heads together and thinking up some little initiative to counter Primo's pathological power—although, she added, she wasn't pinning any excessive hopes on this.

This case highlights a few significant points. First of all, reluctance to go on the outings is as accurate a signal as that emitted by a Geiger counter. It shows that the parents immediately perceive such disappearances as incompatible with their game. Such a signal notifies the therapist that he must get busy and find what's behind it. There must also be an effort to distinguish between the parents' positions, although, as we have seen, their positions often merely seem to differ. Finding the reasons for their reluctance early in the proceedings may help forestall their refusal to comply with the prescription. However, we wish to stress how important it is to also see any negative effects *in the wake* of a weekend disappearance, as in the case we have just described, as a clue to the special intricacies of the ongoing game.

This is where the therapist's aplomb comes into play, as well as his skill in using the prescription. This skill will increase as the therapist ceases to use the invariant prescription as a cure in itself and tends to see it ever more — for better or for worse — as his most powerful instrument for eliciting information. Its potency, unlike that of a microscope or a telescope (which allows us, by enlarging the picture, to look more closely at a cell or a star while leaving it unchanged), is inherent in the fact that, very often, though not always,[4] it alters what we are observing and causes an outpouring of significant phenomena. If the therapist avoids the tendency to get depressed or feel hostile when the prescription appears to have miscarried, and views this incident as a guideline for further investigation, failure will become a stepping-stone to success.

There are also other cases that can prove very revealing, such as that of parents who carefully hide their fear of carrying on with their prescribed disappearances under a mantle of such utter despondency that the therapist, too, is affected by their despair. In trying to account for this all-round dejection, we often discover, under this mantle, that the patient — a consummate player in his own right — has reacted to his parents' disappearance with so brilliant a retaliatory move as to frighten them out of their wits and discourage them from ever trying again.

Consider, for example, the case of Celina, who thought up a particularly clever ploy (see p. 117). Celina was a chronic anorectic-bulimic 17-year-old, addicted to Optalidon (analgesic pills). She was an only child and both her parents were very successful in their careers. When they "disappeared," she countered by getting herself "adopted" by an elderly, childless couple who had been looking for some way to make their lives more meaningful. She dredged up from her past one of her schoolteachers and appointed her as her special confidante. With this woman and the latter's husband she would go off on Arcadian weekends, which she would refer to as perfectly delightful. Celina was warning her parents very eloquently by implying: "If you're going to go off and dump me here all alone, I'll find myself another, far more suitable, couple of parents."

Naturally, Celina's *real* parents failed to see any connection between their waning enthusiasm for therapy and the girl's threatening retaliatory move, so that the news about Celina's weekends cropped up entirely by chance, while the subject of conversation was quite another one. In fact, the therapist actually failed to notice it; it was the supervisor who grasped the importance of this casual remark and called her colleague out in order to urge him to probe into the matter. Celina's cunning countermove thus came to light. We immediately dubbed the parents "poor little orphans," and encouraged them to proceed with their outings. Discoveries such as this never fail to amaze us in terms of the intensity of these family relation-

---

[4]Viz. certain cases in which the patient is quietly engulfed into the ongoing game, as in the foregoing.

ships and the subtlety of the maneuvers and countermaneuvers that are brought into play.

Among many cases in some respects tragic and grotesque, one was especially pathetic. It concerned the couple we have already spoken about in the section headed "To keep the secret is to get married!" (Chapter III). Roughly five months after therapy was terminated, Giuseppe, the father, phoned the therapist who had worked directly with the family. The outcome in this case had been successful at the time, insofar as both parents redefined their son, Alex, as "a perfect darling." The parents had been married now for nearly a year. Giuseppe was calling to tell the therapist that Alex was gradually reverting ever more to his former provocative behavior. This was very different, however, from what it had been before therapy. Alex was irreproachable at school, where he worked hard and was highly regarded. It was only at home, with his parents, that his conduct was becoming ever more exasperating. "He plays the fool and treats us like fools as well," his father complained, "We're absolutely desperate and don't know what to do." The therapist suggested that only the parents come for an interview, and this was immediately agreed to.

In order to set the reader into the atmosphere of that session, here is a transcript of the notes the therapist jotted in the clinical file later that evening:

> I was feeling dead tired this afternoon, after a harrowing session that took all morning, and I felt sick at the thought of having to go back into that room. . . . Little did I know I was about to make a marvellous discovery, which was revealed to me bit by bit through the couple's information. Isabella burst out right away saying that their marital rapport was back to what it was before they first came for therapy: Giuseppe, she said, was again the grumpy, sulky man he once was, and was creating a gloomy atmosphere at home. Giuseppe responded to Isabella's tirade by waxing indignant: He turned to me and confided, in a shaking voice, that during these past weeks he had often thought back on what I had suggested during one of their first sessions, namely that Isabella might be setting Alex up against him and gloating over his ensuing heartache.
>
> I extricated myself with difficulty from this crossfire of accusations and at last managed to ask a blunt question: "Essentially, why were things all right between the two of you last year and what was different, exactly, about your relationship at that time?" To my amazement, they answered almost in unison, without the least doubt or hesitation: "We got along well because Alex was good to us." This synchronous reply switched on a lightbulb in my head and made me ask specific questions that caused the following fact to emerge: If Alex acts rudely, he exasperates his parents, but, above all, they build up deep resentment towards each other, as each of them blames the other for Alex's misbehavior.
>
> I am so excited by this discovery that I am able to communicate very empathically with the couple. I start by depicting them as two poor, deprived creatures who had unsatisfactory parents of their own, so that Alex, for both of them, is their sunshine, the air they breathe, their one and only love.

When Alex is a good boy, they are both happy, and they love each other. When Alex is nasty towards them, they are both unhappy, and they blame each other. But, I go on to say, Alex is an intelligent, sensitive boy who clearly senses that he is in danger of getting permanently entangled in his parents' needs and desires and of being looked to as their indulging mother. "Alex needs to go ahead and grow up, and this is why he is frustrating both of you."

My words act like a bolt of lightning. Isabella and Giuseppe go on repeating "True, true! We both depend entirely on how Alex behaves towards us." I go on to say that Alex isn't provoking them, they are provoking *him*, by making such absurd demands on him. They both nod vigorously at what I'm saying and Isabella provides the ultimate confirmation by recounting a recent episode: A few weeks ago, during carnival, Alex had taken part in the school play. All the parents had been invited, but Alex's parents hadn't shown up. Alex came home heartbroken, because he'd had a lot of applause and his parents hadn't been there to witness his triumph. "So, it's just as you say," said Isabella, "We're always tugging at him and asking to be comforted, but we never notice anything *he* might be needing, or asking us for."

I wrap up the session by telling them that enlightenment as strong as this rules out the need for any further prescriptions and that they are sure to deal adequately with the situation in their own way. Giuseppe states very solemnly that what he has learned here today will make an enormous difference in his rapport with Alex. The couple even looks different already: Every now and then they exchange glances and burst out laughing. Isabella explains that it's just too hilarious to think of themselves as pleading for Alex's love like a couple of beggars.

As they get ready to leave, I am swept by a wave of strong affection for these two. I put my arms around their shoulders, in a demonstrative gesture I never make, and act on an impulse by saying: "You're really two very nice kids, both of you." Now, as I write this, I realize that if they sense they have an understanding mother, they will be more likely to set Alex free to get on with the business of growing up.

PART THREE

Devising a Model of Psychotic Processes

CHAPTER VIII

The Game Metaphor

INTUITIVE USE OF
THE GAME METAPHOR

IN PREVIOUS WRITINGS (Selvini, 1985; Selvini Palazzoli et al., 1985), we referred to "games" more or less interchangeably in terms of both metaphor and model. This may have caused some confusion. Today we have abandoned any intention of exactly defining what we mean by the word "game," since we have neither drawn up a game theory nor adopted anyone else's. Game, to us, is a metaphor and as such will forever remain intuitive and elusive. We have quite another purpose in mind, namely to come ever closer to defining exactly the processes that lead to a subject's psychotic behavior. To this end we are attempting to devise *models* of the psychotic *processes* that develop in a family.

In common scientific parlance, a model, depending on the specific field and its language particularities, either enunciates a scientific explanation in its definitive form or renders it explicit by a demonstration. Model, in this sense, is synonymous with scientific theory. We were wrong, therefore, to speak of "game" as though referring to an overall scientific theory of human games: Our purpose, and hence our point of departure, was to construct a *local* theory, limited and temporary in scope, that could serve us better than those available in understanding, and hence dealing with, human behavior commonly defined as serious mental disorder.

The systemic model had performed this function in the past. Very gradually, however, as we report in Chapter I, dissatisfaction on clinical grounds with paradoxical methods began to coincide with our half-spoken but growing misgivings about systemic theory as a whole. We still professed allegiance to systemic doctrine, but we began to think mainly in terms of games. We did not, however, adhere to any of the game theories (as proposed in von Neumann or in bits of Bateson and Jackson), nor did we make such theories the basis of our speculation. We were even less inclined to draw up our own general theory of human games. We resorted to the game metaphor in order to convey intuitively, by using the expression "family game," that which is implied by common expressions such as *political game, power game, money game,* and the like. Our use of the word is therefore purely intuitive and informal and intends to call up associations, similes, and linguistic allusions that can render the phenomena we are studying more immediately intelligible.

A LANGUAGE FOR SPEAKING
OF HUMAN RELATIONS

The word *game,* in fact, immediately brings to mind associated notions such as *group, team, subjects* (players), *position* (leader, second-string player, attack, defense), *strategies, tactics, moves, skill, turn-taking* (i.e., a time sequence). It places at our disposal an idiom strongly resonant of interpersonal relations (exchanges of behavior, that is). Words like imbroglio, instigation, threat, feint, promise, seduction, volte-face, cooperation, winning, losing, stalemate, and so forth all serve the need to describe interhuman affairs. Moreover, these words are not peculiar to any specific jargon but are a part of everyone's vocabulary, which makes them immediately accessible also to our patients.[1]

A game consists of an exchange of concrete bits of behavior among subjects. Systemic parlance often engenders confusion here by talking of other things, such as electronic components, chemical substances, machines, heavenly bodies, mathematical formulae, or elementary biological organisms. The game metaphor conjures up a whole chain of allied metaphors. Game, for example, strongly suggests the key element of *strategy.* This, in turn, has military overtones, thereby evoking the idea of *conflict,* in which *deception* is an important issue. And so it goes. Thinking in terms of a game, therefore, helps us frame certain concepts that are basic to our field of research. One need only think of such pairs of opposite/complementary concepts as: individual/system, cooperation/conflict, autonomy/dependency, conservation/change. These are key concepts for the study of interactional processes, for which the systemic vocabulary failed to provide a clear reference.

Take the cooperation/conflict coupling, for example: It is easy to discern how the cooperative aspect of any game (sticking to the rules in order to keep on doing what both parties have agreed to do, namely, play the game) is inextricably tied in with the contentious aspect (competition). The family is a micro-organization based on cooperation towards common objec-

---

[1]One can draw a remarkable parallel on how the evolution in our use of language coincided with our abandoning a reticent attitude towards our patients (see Chapter XIV).

tives (well-being, mutual support, the upbringing of the offspring). Given each partner's physiological self-interest (egocentricity), negotiating the terms of such cooperation will inevitably entail conflict. Each partner will vie for the most favorable position, both as regards his rank in the specific group to which he belongs (the nuclear family, for instance) and in each of the several outside groups of which he is also a member (the extended family, his work environment, the context of his leisure time, etc.).

Thinking and speaking in terms of a game create a new vocabulary that intuitively correlates to a vast variety of games with which everyone is familiar. Even these conventional games, whether played by individuals or by teams, are a useful source of analogy. Obviously, the similitude must never be posited as equivalent to an identification, the difference between a family's history and a game of chess being macroscopic.

WHERE SYSTEMIC AND STRATEGIC
REASONING CONVERGE

The game metaphor has proved effective in integrating general rules governing the players' interactions (systemic-holistic thinking) with moves made by individual subjects (strategic thinking). A conventional game, in fact, has intuitively obvious features: (a) Moves must be made in turns (a game, like dialogue, is structured around alternating interventions rather than simultaneous ones)[2]; (b) all players agree as to which rules are to apply, thus reducing the likelihood of unpredictable moves; (c) within the established rules, a wide choice of available moves remains, which results in the game staying undecided. In other words, there is an opportunity for each player to use his special strategic skills and intelligence, and it is *this* that characterizes any given game. Once a game (a conventional one, that is) has been explained *generically* in terms of the equipment it requires and the rules that govern it (tennis, football, etc.), its *specific* identity will lie in the alternating sequence of the moves the individual players undertake.

The sequence of events that the game follows may be described verbally—consider the radio broadcast of a football game, for instance. A game will, therefore, always be the result of the alternating interventions made by the single players who, bent on winning the contest whether as individuals or as a team, respond to the opponent's move with one of their own. All this takes place within the framework of an explicit, agreed-upon set of rules.

Using the game metaphor in this manner helped us achieve a perspective in which individual subjects are not split off from their mutual interdependence, and interdependence is not split off from the individual subjects. The individual subject is seen as interdependent and relatively

[2]On this subject, we refer to the brilliant work of K. Kaye (1977).

unpredictable, according to his greater or lesser skill at availing himself of the range of choices his opponent's move has left open to him. And this, we repeat, takes place within a framework of accepted rules.

BREAKING FREE
OF OMINOUS DOGMATISM

Thinking in terms of games also brought us greater mental freedom. Constant coercive fealty to systems theory had become a heavy dogmatic encumbrance. There was a strong tendency to endow systemic thought with a connotation of "Truth" and to contrast it, on ingrained sectarian and ideological grounds, with "Error" (as represented by psychoanalysis and other intrapsychic theories). We had undoubtedly been influenced in this by the prophetic, almost religious bias of some of Bateson's teachings. Cutting adrift from so multivalent and systemized a body of doctrine (Ashby, 1954; Bateson, 1972; von Bertalanffy, 1968; Watzlawick et al., 1967), and replacing it with only an open metaphor concerning games, freed us to a remarkable extent from the constrictions of preconceived dictates. Today, systemic thought is still an important part of our assets, chiefly on account of its evocative images and its potential for tracing how interpersonal processes evolve.

Our use of the expression "game metaphor" also echoes the idea of game as it is found in the contemporary social sciences where, albeit with a variety of meanings, it is used to describe "reality" and interpersonal relations in psychology, sociology, economics, political science, and so forth. As Ricci so aptly puts it (1984, p. 303), this concept "renders the traditional boundaries between separate fields of the social sciences extremely tenuous and inevitably finds the research worker trespassing on territory not 'officially' his own."

REDISCOVERING THE INDIVIDUAL
AND GOING BEYOND HOLISM

More specifically, thinking in terms of a game prevented us from persisting in a typical fallacy inherent to systemic thought, namely, ignoring the individual subject. Individual moves and strategies suddenly came boldly to the forefront. One very helpful idea that headed us in the right direction was *organization* or, rather, comparing the family to an organization. An organization has its own organizational chart, on which individual members are positioned in hierarchical order. Organization, therefore, is not a holistic concept. Comparing how an organized structure operates in actuality to the official structural chart is in itself an object lesson on individual subjects and their strategies (Selvini Palazzoli et al., 1987).

Systemic teaching, notably Don Jackson's, always included the idea of games but concentrated exclusively on the *rules* as they appear in the here and now, without considering a time dimension or distinguishing among the strategies enacted by single subjects (remember the famous example about the Martians who watch a game of bridge [Jackson, 1965]). This kept everything well entrenched in systemic holism, and the simplification it entailed gradually caused systemic holism to be judged inadequate.

Systemic analogy involving aggregates whose components lack subjectivity (cells, telephones) entirely disregards the individual dimension. Systemic holism takes only such variables into account as fit the idea of the family as a whole, i.e., communication, myth, rules, and the like.

CONFUSION ABOUT RULES

As regards the specific issues of rules, by reassigning proper attention to the individual and his strategies we realized how systemic terminology had always wavered confusedly between two different definitions:

1. A rule is the outcome of negotiations between two players, or their mutual agreement on some previously established norm. This meaning surfaces whenever the family is likened to a state with a constitution made up of articles (rules), both explicit and implicit.
2. A rule is something that the observer infers—it is useful for describing, from the outside, certain recurring bits of behavior. These behaviors go on repeating themselves due precisely to the players' inability to negotiate effectively about rules.

In this latter case, then, the rule is an entirely external construct: From the players' point of view, there will simply be a repetitive series of moves (or tactics) that allows for no negotiating, whether explicit or implicit. In fact, such stable patterns of moves are repetitive precisely because the players are unable to negotiate about some issue or other. An example of how this second definition of "rule" applies is the impossibility of defining a relationship (commonly believed to be typical of a family in which transactions are schizophrenic) or rejection (a communicational modality often found in anorectic families). One can readily explain the great interest and attention afforded the topic of rules in classical systemic literature (Haley, 1959; Selvini Palazzoli, 1972) if one recalls that everyone was firmly anchored to the holistic point of view in those days.

Rules were useful conceptual devices for *describing* a system that lacked substantial inner differentiation: One simply gave up trying to understand how the system functioned in terms of individual strategies, and only kept a sharp lookout for redundancies. Then, with a nice bit of non sequitur, these recurrences were set up as the system's repertoire of rules. Today, if we consider Watzlawick's example of the chess game (Watzlawick et al., 1967, p. 37), we see how absurd it is to denote as a rule both the moves each single piece can make on the board (within limits that all players agree on) *and* the fact that a game between two players of equal ability often ends in a draw. This latter may be a recurring event, but it is certainly not a *rule* agreed upon by both parties, although it may well seem that way to a Martian who cannot make out the players' strategies. For all practical purposes, and in order to avoid confusion, we now find it expedient to limit our use of the word "rule" to the first of these definitions. Thus, the spouses' stalemate, in a psychotic family, is not a rule but merely the combined effect of two countervailing strategies.

FUNCTIONALISM

The holistic idea is closely tied in with that of functionalism. Functionalism considers the behavior of all subsystems *subservient* to the survival and cohesion of the whole. In clinical work, this supports the assumption that the patient's symptom benefits the other members of his family and that he is sacrificing himself for their good. Bogdan (1986, p. 30) gives a good definition of functionalism as it characterizes the *systemic* view of family therapy:

> Why do families develop problems, and why are these problems often so hard to resolve? Ask a family therapist this question and chances are you will get something like the following answer: troubled families need, at least temporarily, to have a problem, even when they say they want to solve it. If they didn't have *that* problem, they would suffer from something even worse. If the school-phobic child were not staying home, his mother would become anxious about being alone during the day. If the delinquent teenager were not worrying and upsetting his parents, they would fight with each other and end up getting a divorce. In other words, the I.P.'s problem protects, or serves a function for, the family.

Bogdan says quite rightly that functionalism met with success because it posited a link between the individual symptom and the family, thereby justifying the very existence of family therapy. In the course of our research, however, we gradually abandoned the functionalist tenet[3] in theorizing about the connection between the symptom and the family.

[3]Functionalism has long played a role in the social sciences, from Durkheim to Parsons by way of Malinowski, Spencer (organicism), Saussure (linguistics), Radcliffe-Brown and so on. At the core of the current anti-functionalist polemics in sociology lies the contention that the model does not account for evolution, for history, or for change. It is interesting to note that we followed this same itinerary in our "local" research on psychosis: We discarded "synchronic" functionalism and moved on to focus on *process*, a concept that entirely rejects the organismic idea of function.

During the functionalist era it was a matter of dogma that we should seek not the *cause* of a certain behavior but its *effect* (never ask "why"; always ask "to what purpose"). Time was when we would always strive to pinpoint the useful impact on the other family members of the patient's symptom in the here and now dimension. We remarked in Chapter I on an illogical linking of the symptom's pragmatic effects (such as managing to keep a sibling effectively tied down at home) to a hypothesis assigning intentionality to such a symptom. *Clinical experience, we maintain, belies the tautologic functionalist premise according to which the system is its own best explanation.* In our clinical practice, as we have shown, this notion was systematically put to use, but only as an expedient: By introducing the paradox, a rhetorical device, we provoked the patient's angry response by setting him up as a saint devoted to his family, when in actual fact we felt sure he bitterly resented all the other family members.

When we use the game metaphor today we are mindful of the experience acquired during our years as functionalists and "true believers" in systems doctrine. They trained us to explore links between individual behavior and family relationships. We have, however, discarded the communicational and biological stereotypes that would have us see this connection as functional, positive and sacrificial. The connection is a spiraling process of moves and countermoves. It obeys the strategies of more or less skilled participants (on the individual level), is conditioned by the opponent's moves (on the micro-systemic level), and by sociocultural rules (on the macro-systemic level), and is also influenced by unforeseeable events.[4]

The symptom is at one and the same time influenced by others (by the moves others make) *and* planned by the patient as a part of his strategy. Taking our clue from the game metaphor taught us to see that any individual strategy must first of all be egocentric. Even when we observe ostensibly altruistic behavior, such as that of one spouse protecting the other, we will always assume that this conduct is part of some self-serving strategy, presumably enacted for a specific tactical purpose.

INDIVIDUAL DIFFERENCES AND THE SUBJECT AS STRATEGIST

As far as we are concerned, cognitive holism was the last stronghold of holism. Focus, at the time, was entirely on a family's basic articles of faith (i.e., its rules, myths, *Weltanschauung*, lineal epistemology) and on the connection between these beliefs and the patient's symptom. This is by far the most sophisticated theoretical premise of holism. Yet even it has a fundamental shortcoming. It fails to adequately model either the subject

---

[4]See the concluding remarks of Chapter XII on the complex genesis of the symptom.

or the evolutional processes in a family. If we think in terms of a family epistemology that is inadequate for solving a crisis in the family's life cycle, this forestalls research into the peculiarities of each member of a family group. This is, however, precisely the factor that will respond, at long last, to our probing when we reason in terms of the game metaphor. Obviously, no player in a game ever has unidirectional power over the whole group of players. It is wrong, however, to carry this statement to extremes. To contend that power does not exist, that it is merely intrinsic to the rules of the game, leads us to neglect the strategic subject's "freedom."

In fact, there will be important differences in the degree of power (or freedom) possessed by each member of any group-with-history. These differences can be defined at several levels:

1. *The hierarchical level.* This is determined by the subject's place on the organizational chart of the group to which he belongs.
2. *The cultural level.* This relates to the law of the land and to firmly entrenched customs and beliefs, such as, for example, the legal differences concerning the hereditary rights of a spouse and of the offspring.
3. *The subcultural level.* This concerns the way a certain social group has adapted to prevailing cultural norms. For instance, nowadays a woman belonging to the upwardly mobile social classes will follow the trend and aspire to personal and professional fulfillment.
4. *The level of the intrafamilial game.* The member who enjoys more prestige in the family will also yield more power than he who occupies an abject, underrated position.
5. *The individual level.* A subject's personal qualities and merits (such as beauty, physical strength, intelligence, wealth) affect his choice of possible moves in the game.

Complex overlapping and interwining of these several peculiarities deals out specific cards to each individual, consequently determining his or her potential for influencing other members of the family. If we equate *power* (or freedom) with an individual's potential for making others do what he or she wants or, conversely, for *not* having to do what others want him/her to, this will also define his/her range of choices and decisions and therewith his/her capacity to influence others. If this is true, power is not simply an intrinsic part of the rules of the game but is strongly tied in with the special qualities listed above that accrue to every individual.

The male partner in a couple, for example, depending on such factors as his professional status and the subculture in which he lives, may carry out certain bits of behavior (i.e., certain moves) that are barred to the woman. If this were not so, how could we account for the statistical fact that Italian men, after a divorce, remarry so much more often than Italian women?

Our culture encourages the woman to stay on alone with the offspring and the man to remarry. It also encourages a man to marry a woman who has not previously been married (or at least one who has no children), whereas a woman will be under social pressure to "make do" even with a divorced man, if this will rescue her from being an old maid.

Such cultural rules are important systemic binds in family games. We doubt whether it is still appropriate to use the hackneyed word "power" in referring, for example, to the "power" that a man has to get a divorce and then remarry. Nonetheless, it is essential to be aware of individual traits (those culturally conditioned, those induced by the game itself and by the game's history, namely the prestige bestowed on one of the siblings, etc., and those intrinsic to each individual—beauty, etc.). They must all be taken into account if one is to go beyond the facile oversimplifications of systemic holism.

FROM AN ATEMPORAL CONCEPT OF CIRCULARITY TO ONE ENTAILING A PROCESS

The game metaphor also served us well, once we had superseded holism, by helping us retrieve a *historical* dimension in our findings.

An interactive, intrafamilial process is the outcome of the collusion, in a time sequence, of the diverse strategies enacted by the individuals involved therein. Equifinality, a dogmatic tenet of systemic thought, had always cautioned us to ignore the history both of individuals and of their families and concentrate solely on the here and now. Today we clearly perceive that the principle of equifinality is valid only for the simplest of biological systems. As von Bertalanffy (1968) puts it, an egg cell divided into halves will develop into two normal living organisms; a human fetus, on the other hand, if split into halves will not develop into any living thing. Similarly, the autistic child who does not experience the various stages of normal cognitive development will, as an adolescent, recuperate intellectual and linguistic skills only in part.

The model of a cybernetic system (a computer, a thermostat) strongly emphasizes negative feedback, i.e., conservative processes. Systemic organismic metaphors (biology) also point in this direction: The system's goal is its own survival. In therapeutics, this nullifies the time dimension. Only the present is considered, and the history of an individual or a family is entirely ignored.

The systemic concepts elaborated at Palo Alto (Watzlawick et al., 1967), part of which we incorporated into our thinking, were implicitly based on the model of a telephone network. This is an elementary idea of interactive circularity. All users of a telephone system are equal, and neither their individual characteristics nor their history has any importance. What matters in a telephone network are actions and reactions occurring in a brief lapse of time. The circuit of reciprocal influences is extremely rapid.

When this implicit model was applied to the sphere of family relations, it proved inadequate. Circularity in family interactions (process) requires years to reach the point at which a member becomes a patient. *So the circularity that matters to us is in the history, not in the instant.* Take a husband who beats his wife: This symptomatic behavior is the result of a complex historical process. On the systemic level of cultural rules, the groundwork for this symptom will have been provided by a certain given view of the male role in society. On the systemic level of the family's subculture, it will emerge from a background of acceptance and elaboration of the aforementioned cultural norms.

Another influential factor is the history of that particular family's game, made up of the parental couple's alliance and rifts with their families of origin and with their offspring. Nor can we overlook what one might call *intermediate variables.* These derive from systemic rules and the family game, on the one hand, and from specific behaviors, on the other. They might include the husband's allegiance to certain cultural norms and to a certain type of family game, which has led him to assume a characteristic individual stance, depending on his level of learning, his personality, his motivations and expectations. By stubbornly limiting the scope of our exploration to the here and now and inquiring, for instance, what the wife did just before her husband started beating her, we are obviously being simplistic and reductive, in quite the same way the Palo Alto approach was "minimalist" when it insisted on focusing only on the sequences of behavior that preceded and followed the symptom (and especially on the attempted solution).

It is, of course, necessary to think *also* along these lines, and to take the here and now into account; such findings, however, must be integrated in a multidimensional model. Our wife-beater has been predisposed to his behavior by a series of influences that reach far beyond whatever provocation his wife may enact just before he pitches into her.

We have very vivid memories of these past phases in our therapeutic work. At such times we would rack our brains trying to make out what *real* advantage a husband might stand to gain by his wife's depression. We were caught in the trap of functionalist biological simplification, wherein all members of the system are held to be on an equal footing and equally motivated towards preserving the system's existence and unity. The corollary to this is that the symptom *must* serve the interests of all concerned.

In concluding, we should state clearly that we have by no means abandoned a circular view of these influences: We have merely outgrown the naive constrictions of viewing the actions of all intervening parties as occurring on an equal level and within a very brief lapse of time (as in the example of the telephone network). Circularity, as we see it today, is the result of welding together arcs of the circuit by a long process over time: this process also comprises an elaboration of *intermediate* (individual) variables.

POSSIBLE MISUNDERSTANDINGS
AND RISKS INHERENT IN THE
USE OF THE GAME METAPHOR

The advantages of adopting the game metaphor were many, but there is need for caution: The game metaphor can give rise to some dangerous misunderstandings.

The first and most obvious of these is associating the word *game*, however vaguely, to entertainment. Nothing could be further from truth. As we all know from our own experience, the game our family plays touches on our very existence. It is a matter none of us can take lightly. The unbelievably violent sentiments inspiring a family game and coexisting with it are probably always decisive, whether they spark off dramatic developments or stifle a promising personality in stultifying monotony.

The most widespread and dangerous of these misunderstandings, however, is the one derived from an everyday acceptance of expressions such as "political game" and "strategy." C. Ricci (1984, p. 302) stresses how the notions of game and of strategic behavior carry with them, in our homely speech, "a strong negative connotation of premeditated and rationally conscious action—usually *against* someone or something." The analogy with intensely competitive and conflict-laden political games breeds confusion, as it obscures or even loses sight of the intrinsic solidarity that characterizes systems such as the family. Analogy with other basically competitive contexts, such as von Neumann's simulacra, partake of the same flaw— they overemphasize the notions of *decision* and *result* (Rigliano, 1988). Our research on families showed us how misleading it is to use these two parameters for interpreting and describing what goes on in families. In a family, results and decisions are very ill-defined concepts: This clearly distinguishes them from things like a company budget or an electoral contest, and makes them useless for our purpose.

One direct consequence of applying such an "economy-biased" misconstruction will be to create a false picture of the subject. As a member of a family, he will be thought to resemble a company executive or a politician. Even these latter, as a matter of fact, in their roles as members of a family will be nowhere near as rational, calculating, conscious of their objectives, clearheaded, and farsighted concerning the results of their decisions as they need to be in their professional context.

In the sphere of our intimate affective relationships—and the more so the more important these are to us — our objectives are never clearly envisioned and pursued; indeed, they are often very muddled. Also, because these ties are of vital importance to us, we will often resort to self-deception and assign the noblest of pretexts to our objectives. The covert, devious nature of psychotic games are extreme instances of such common self-deceptive mechanisms. It must be made very clear, then, that in speaking of covert strategy we are not referring to a rationally concocted scheme, coldly blueprinted in advance, by which cunning and duplicity are enlisted to get the better of one's own family. The "embroiling" parent, or the parent who "instigates" does not, in our opinion, have a clear idea of what he is doing. Only the occasional brief flash of insight lets him perceive, almost subliminally, that his conduct is blameworthy. This same line of reasoning holds for the patient's connivance.

Finally, there is a third misconstruction we often encounter. It centers on the idea that only "pathological" families play games. If we take a game as being an interactive organization evolving over time, *it is impossible not to play a game.* No group-with-history — and consequently, no family — can avoid organizing its interactions. It will depend to a great extent on the characteristics of this interactive organization and on its evolution (which are both factors virtually beyond the pale of any individual's conscious power to determine) whether the single members of the group will feel sufficiently happy or whether someone, at some given time, will resort to a symptom in order to signal that he or she is in an untenable relational malaise.

CHAPTER IX

Devising Diachronic Models

A FIRST SCHEMA OF A
SIX-STAGE PROCESS:
TOWARDS A GENERAL MODEL

W E HAVE REPEATEDLY ILLUSTRATED how the series of invariant prescriptions turned out to be an unexpectedly rewarding line of inquiry, in
that it not only enabled us to lay bare such deep-seated, subtle phenomena
as instigation and imbroglio but also led to our rediscovery both of the
individual and of individual strategies. By far the most important result,
however, was the step forward it afforded us in our effort to draw up a
model for family games. Little by little the arcs of the circuit seemed to join
into one large spiral, namely the interactive process leading to psychosis.
Even while the original team at our Center was still inventing a new
paradox or specific ritual for each family, we were already dreaming of
being able, some day, to draw a map which could help us in the psychotic
maze.

The several teams who later pursued this line of research possessed a
new instrument to help them, namely the invariant series of prescriptions.
They were therefore no longer hampered by the need to find an adequate
intervention to suit each separate case and no longer flustered by a plethora of non-essential variables pointing in potentially infinite directions
within each family configuration. This gave them the freedom to concentrate on registering the recurrences that were found when moving from
one family to another. Such recurrences, as well as the differences, were
thrown into sharper relief against the backdrop of the invariant prescriptions. So, after years of scrupulously focusing on the here and now, as per
the principle of equifinality, we were qualified, at long last, to deal with the
time dimension as a concrete, manageable entity: The arduous chore of
reconstruing and tracing the prior evolution of the game every time we met
a new family no longer loomed so formidably before us.

STAGE ONE OF THE
PSYCHOTIC PROCESS:
THE PARENTAL COUPLE'S STALEMATE

For our point of departure in analyzing the time sequence, we singled out the game played by the parental couple. This choice, as we remarked when first presenting our model, was of necessity an arbitrary one. In actual fact, we might just as well have traced the couple's malfunctioning back to some preexisting game played by one or both of them in their families of origin, a game likely to have left deep scars, influencing both their choice of a partner and their current individual strategies. If we go back Old Testament fashion from generation to generation, we can always pick a significant point in time from which to start, although it will never be the primordial instant, the zero point, at which the game first got started.

The choice of the couple's game as the first segment from which to map the process, though arbitrary, was not a random one. It hails back to the very origins of family therapy and echoes the dictum imparted several decades ago by the founding fathers, to wit: Whenever there are disturbed children there is a disturbed marriage, although all disturbed marriages do not create disturbed children (Framo, 1985, p. 154).

Having started from this fundamental intuition, we are now able to flesh out this statement with greater specification. First of all, we can now define the visible features of the marital couple's "disturbance" more precisely. Not just any kind of marital problem, we now know, will engender psychosis in one of the offspring: Violent, explosive conflict, for instance, will not do this, nor will a sequence of betrayals followed by reconciliations, nor will the rigid assignment of parental roles that deprives the couple of adequate flexibility and freezes them into a changeless, stereotyped mode of functioning. Our research has taught us that *the* disturbance with a morbid outcome is, in every case, the special game we have called the spouses' stalemate—and that game alone.

In a stalemate game the two opponents, like two chess players, seem doomed to go on challenging each other endlessly. There is no way out of their deadlock. No acute crises take place in the couple's rapport, no furious cathartic scenes clear the air, no temporary separations offer respite. One contender will now and again set off a spectacular volley of attacks or provocations and appear to be winning the day, whereupon the other, very stealthily, will pull a card out of his sleeve and neatly foil his opponent's maneuver.

For the sake of clarity we have called the first type of player "the active provoker" and the second "the passive provoker," although these terms are imprecise. The "active provoker" can usually be identified quite readily, whereas labeling the "passive" one is more difficult, since he or she may easily be mistaken for a victim cowering in the tiny corner of the board to which his opponent's pawns have apparently confined him/her. Only when we look closely at this "passive" player's unruffled, steady moving to and fro in his narrow little space, repeating his one move over and over again, do we discover his special way of provoking. A passive provoker, for example, is the husband who "does his level best" to follow his wife's advice and live up to her expectations, but simply cannot manage. It's beyond him. Again and again he fails—not for lack of trying, of course—but nevertheless he fails. Who knows, perhaps next time round, if his wife were to give him better advice, or maybe less of it, or in a different tone of voice.... Another example of the passive provoker is the wife invariably amenable to every-thing, who surrenders immediately on every issue and gives in meekly even to her partner's most absurd demands, but will never budge an inch from her little vantage ground, her own private bulwark, from the height of which she manages to endlessly frustrate her husband.

This power to keep the partner on tenterhooks, then, is the one thing the "passive" spouse will never relinquish for anything in the world. For example, a wife's one and only wish may be to have a minimum of privacy at home. Her husband, who gives in immediately in all their arguments, will steadfastly refuse to grant her this. There will never be an explicit show of force, a head-on collision, an outright quarrel or even an explanation that could unblock the stalemate: This husband, the only son of a widowed mother, simply cannot face the idea of depriving his mother of her person-al key to their apartment, lest the old lady feel left out of things. Not that he particularly relishes having his mother around at all hours, of course, but he is absolutely incapable of hurting her feelings. So, quite passively, without breaking his cover, he deploys his strategy and counters his wife's constant interfering. This goads his wife even more fiercely into the silent battle. She will never leave the field, dead set as she is on expropriating the little stronghold her husband has mapped out for himself.

Another example is the spouse who has never been heard to utter a word of praise or encouragement despite the other's desperate attempts to elicit some sign of approval. This "passive" spouse ignores the frantic sig-nals that eventually veer to disappointment. When all comes pouring out in bitter remonstrances, he/she will react with wide-eyed surprise and non-committal mumbling that will definitely take all the wind out of the other's sails.

As we stated earlier, defining a spouse's stance in the couple's stalemate as "passively" or "actively" provoking is very imprecise and derives from superficial evidence. We must always remember that a family game is an ongoing process, a sequence of behavioral thrusts and parries, occasionally dotted by life events and everyone's reactions to them. This is equally true of other forms of marital games, of course. Stalemate, however, is a special game, one that entails carefully avoiding any escalation or, even more important, any real rift. Each partner responds to the other's move by a countermove canceling out any advantage the opponent has gained, yet neither has the slightest intention of winning all down the line. Further work will be needed to understand how a married couple got enmeshed in such a tragic tussle in the first place. In Chapter XIX, dedicated to the stalemate enigma, we will present the latest development in our efforts to clarify it.

Our use of the game metaphor and of some rather truculent terminology might make the reader think that we really believe the parents of a psychotic child hate each other and are mutually intent on inflicting as much pain as they can. This is quite obviously not so. In our discussions after a session with a "stalemated" couple our team often comes to very different conclusions. In some cases we will unanimously agree that we are dealing with two implacable enemies ensnared in a game they have entered unwittingly; they are able neither to call it quits nor to yield to the other. At other times we feel that the contenders, like contestants in a heated sports event allowing them no respite, are welded together by passion. This does not allow them to budge from their respective positions; stubbornly, persistently, the stalemated contest goes on. Friends and acquaintances often see such passionate contenders as an ideal couple and they, too, may think and speak of themselves in romantic terms. As one particularly clear-sighted and very honest mother of a schizophrenic boy once told us, "We are like two rocks constantly crashing against each other, yet only this endless colliding, which neither of us is willing to give up, puts some oxygen into our lives."

It is true, of course, that one cannot expect to fully grasp from the outside how happy or distressed any given couple really is. We certainly don't claim to be able to do this. *The child who will become psychotic, however, does exactly that.* This, quite probably, lies at the root of his predicament.

STAGE TWO: THE SON/DAUGHTER'S INVOLVEMENT IN THE COUPLE'S GAME

We have already seen how difficult it is to identify a passive provoker, even at close distance. The patient-to-be makes precisely this epistemological error: he attributes faults and merits on a linear scale, mistaking the passive provoker for the victim and the active one for the victimizer.

Wynne and Thaler Singer, in their classic work on communication in families of schizophrenics (1963), already noticed that the symptom-ridden son or daughter is apparently always the one most deeply involved in the parents' private affairs. Our team has for some time now been asking the children of such families a standard question during the first or second session, in what has by now become a ritual aimed at exploring how each child perceives the parents' couple relationship. The question is: "If you should wake up tomorrow and find yourself in Dad's place in the household (in Mom's place, inverting the question), how would your behavior toward your Dad (Mom) differ from his?"

Such firm but tactful probing will often find the patient inclined to modify the behavior of the actively provoking parent, thereby revealing that he disapproves of it. His siblings, on the other hand, will usually tend to portion out blame and merit more fairly between both parents. They may sometimes even side with the "active" provoker, whom they see as having a loud bark but no bite. Other siblings occasionally share the patient's view but are never as severely upset by their parents' problems, which they do not seem to consider any special concern of theirs.

The extent to which a child is involved in his parents' marital problems was a key issue for us even at the time we were writing *Paradox and Counterparadox*. As we view the problem now, in the light of our current model, we realize that it is extremely difficult to determine, case by case, how fully a child is obeying a spontaneous impulse when he sides with the parent he considers the "loser" against the "winner." To some extent, of course, he does so on impulse, since he totally "misreads" the couple's situation.

Active moves are more spectacular than passive ones, which often go unnoticed. Also, the active provoker will probably sooner or later bring the repertoire of moves he uses against his spouse into play against his son/daughter as well, so that, for example, a father who treats his wife in a controlling manner will eventually be likely to treat his child the same way. When he does so, he unwittingly pushes the child over into his wife's camp. The mother, however, may also have been soliciting the child's allegiance actively, by a series of more or less covert seductive maneuvers (deep sighs, hints about her unhappy lot, etc.) or by encouraging such seductive behavior in the child (meaningful glances, emotional outpourings, impassioned confessions, etc.).

This particular phase of the interactive process is the one most difficult to reconstrue *a posteriori*, and it is definitely the most secret one, as it is sensed to be illicit. Our present thinking on the matter is the following: Seductive messages, conveyed on an implicit and analogical level, may safely be viewed as ambiguous promises — seduction is always that.

The patient is enticed into the game by a promise the fulfillment of which is then indefinitely postponed. When the child joins the family game in his own right, the promise so ambiguously held out will be just as ambiguously disavowed, and the typical pattern of oscillating coalitions described by Bateson and coworkers will set in. Thus, when the patient resorts to outright psychotic behavior the loser will join forces with the winner against him, whereas when the psychotic behavior is relatively under control the loser will swing back to the patient's side and start the seductive maneuvering and ambiguous promises all over again. And so it goes, on and on. This is a true "volte-face" inflicted on the patient, even though its main purpose may not be to deceive him. (M. Viaro, personal communication)

The spouse will in all cases be concentrating primarily on his/her partner and on their game.

Such a configuration differs from Haley's "perverse triangle" due to yet another aspect of coalitions of this type: they are not only undercover, transgenerational and disavowed, but they are also almost entirely expedient and instrumental, at least on the parent's part. This explains their high pathogenic potential. What is proffered here is not a compensatory incestuous relationship ("Let's you and me stick together for comfort, since 'that one' has us both suffering so much"), but a bond sought after for the sole purpose of rapping the active provoker. Throughout all this maneuvering, the passively provoking parent has his/her sights trained constantly on the other spouse, not on the child, although the child may be deceived into believing he has become a sort of vicarious spouse. We feel that this circumstance entitles us to refer to such a coalition as an imbroglio, of which the patient, at this stage in the process, is already the victim. We consider this a major difference between our model of interaction and concepts such as "denied coalition" and "perverse triangle."

There is also another more important aspect: Our model has a diachronic dimension. It is a coordinated succession of interactive behaviors. This diachronic aspect is totally missing in the concepts referred to above, in which the time factor is merely the condition by which an unvarying pathogenic pattern repeats itself. This, we feel, fails to account for the fact that psychosis sets in at one time rather than another.

Strategies entailing imbroglio and seduction (i.e., ambiguous promises), followed by the presumptive ally's unexpected volte-face, seem to provide a more adequate explanation for the psychotic tragedy. The crux of the matter is not so much that the patient has a "frail ego" (psychoanalysis) or has been systematically exposed to destructive communicative patterns (double bind): The more convincing answer would seem to be *that at some given moment the basic premise on which the patient has founded his affective and cognitive universe shows itself to be false* (M. Viaro, personal communication). The patient grasps the instrumental nature of the bond with an ally he has always considered above suspicion.

It is often true, of course, that the patient-to-be himself will feel a strong passion and yearning for the parent he considers the winner, and will go to any lengths to captivate the latter's allegiance or else prevail over him/her. However, the patient's move toward the winning parent "on the rebound" will be far less instrumental than the choice his former trusted ally made with regard to him. The former ally's volte-face, as we shall see, actually has the power to drive the patient into the vortex of psychosis.

Things are not always that simple, of course. As we probe into such interactive processes more deeply and the number and variety of the cases we examine increase, more detailed courses emerge. They seem to follow a zig-zag pattern. It is not unusual, for instance, for a patient to construe the couple's game (particularly during adolescence) by carrying out an inversion maneuver of his/her own, to coincide with a certain amount of role-swapping in the game the parents are playing. Thus, a future schizophrenic may spend his childhood firmly in his mother's camp, and his mother, in the pattern of their daily life, may appear to him and to her extended family as the victim. Should any particular event upset this situation and the mother start taking her revenge, the future patient will gradually slip over into his father's corner: His father will in some way have signaled to him how deeply he has been wounded and humiliated. All during this second phase the patient, in his heart of hearts, is secretly siding with this "losing" parent, although he never comes out openly against the other.

STAGE THREE: THE SON/DAUGHTER'S
UNUSUAL BEHAVIOR

Slowly but surely the child will have to face up to the sad fact that casting his lot with the loser has failed to spur the latter into action, and that the rules of the game have been left unchanged. The game blindly follows its usual relentless pattern. This becomes an obsession with the patient. He/she is determined to put an end once and for all to both the effrontery of the winner—who has gone on shamelessly provoking—and the passivity of the "ally"—who has gone on eating humble pie. He now throws his full weight into the scale. Up to that time his allegiance to the "loser" had taken on the form of almost imperceptible signals: From now on it will be impossible to overlook. The child embarks on an entirely new course of behavior, which, although "unusual" for him/her, is not pathological. He may, for example, start heaping violent verbal abuse on the "winning" parent or else refuse to speak to this parent at all. He may stay cloistered up in his room and refuse to come out. He may start squandering all his money and coming back late at night. He may fall back in his studies or even quit school altogether. This conduct serves a twofold purpose: It aims to challenge the "winner's" arrogance and curb his provocations ("showing him/her what's what") and to set the "loser" a good example of how one should go about rebelling.

We should say here that this stage of the process is often very difficult to reconstrue after the fact. The symptomatic behavior the child subsequently adopts often cancels out, in his parents' recollection, the "unusual" behavior that preceded it, which was strange but not pathological. The parents may also tend to label as "strange" what in itself was normal adolescent behavior, although a fractious attitude, for instance, may not have been a part of the youngster's previous repertoire. And there is more to this matter. In our experience, which despite eight years of careful research is unfortunately still limited, the "unusual" behavior preceding the explosion of the psychotic symptom may be perfectly physiological adolescent behavior, showing up for the first time and betokening the child's drift towards autonomy. However, even in the case of such physiologically normal behavior, we cannot rule out the possibility that it was brought into play as a threat. In the cases we have dealt with, behavior of this kind was perceived by one or both parents as a formidable menace. Should this be the case, the child's behavior could be a pretended move towards autonomy, whereas it is in actual fact the opening move in a psychotic game.

In order to make this clearer, here is a short profile of a specific psychotic process in which unusual behavior simply pointed in the direction of the patient-to-be's efforts at achieving autonomy. Monica was an only child, conceived out of wedlock by a young, lively, and very attractive seamstress who later married the father, a smug, controlling, and possessive businessman. Throughout her childhood and adolescence, Monica thought of her mother as a lovely little bird kept in a cage by her strict husband. Monica's father needed to have his wife at his beck and call all the time. Monica was sent off regularly to summer camp during school holidays. This yearly separation would invariably be the occasion for daily heart-rending phone calls from Monica to her mother.

When the girl turned 15, her mother needled her husband into joining an exclusive country club: The time had come, she insisted, for Monica to mix with the right crowd. This was quite obviously the mother's way of gaining a foothold in high society, and she used this ploy to fuel her husband's already lively terror of her gallivanting around and charming everyone in sight. As that particular summer drew near, Monica's mother suddenly announced to all concerned that the girl must be sent to England right away, so as to allow her mother a well-deserved holiday.

Then, an extraordinary thing happens: Monica's conduct, once she has crossed the Channel, is peculiar to say the least. She never calls home at all. If her mother wants news of her daughter, she must be the one to do the phoning. Monica is curt and indifferent; all she says is that she's having a wonderful time with her new friends.

Monica, back from her English holiday, is definitely not prepared for the shocking effects her behavior has had on her parents. Her mother meets her at the airport and launches into a string of acid comments about how fat her daughter has become. She carts her off the very next day to a doctor, who prescribes a strict diet. Her father, however, has the worst surprise in store for her—he has replaced her with a son! An 18-year-old nephew who lives in the country has been invited to come and stay with them, in order to attend school in their town. Monica hates this presumptuous cousin of hers on sight, especially since her mother delights in heaping ravioli and lasagne on the intruder's plate while Monica gets paper-thin steaks and a bowl of salad. As for her father, he very obviously enjoys spending the evenings discussing politics and finance with this newly acquired son. At this point, Monica becomes irrevocably entrapped in the family game. When we first meet her in therapy, at age 23, she is a listless psychotic living like an outcast in her own home. Her weight oscillates wildly between a mere 25 kilos (55 pounds) and gross obesity.

This case requires some comment. In our later reconstruction of this particular process we hypothesized that Monica's "unusual" behavior was due to her having crossed over to her father's side. Irritated by her mother's constant threats to throw herself body and soul into the social whirl (and having seen the effects of these threats written all over her father's face), the girl ushered in her "unusual" behavior in order to convey an urgent invitation to her father, namely: "*I'm* certainly not going to give Mom the satisfaction of calling her up every day to tell her I can't live without her, and you, Dad, would do well to take a cue from me and simply ignore all her empty boasting." Her father didn't get the message. Frightened by what he thought was his daughter's attempt to break out of the family, he quickly found himself an ersatz child. Mom's retaliation for not having been called up was something Monica could deal with, but her father's move definitely was not: Her weight oscillations had Monica swinging back and forth, like a pendulum, between two smarting rancors.[1]

STAGE FOUR: THE TRUSTED ALLY DOES A "VOLTE-FACE"

Just as not every disturbed couple necessarily has a psychotic offspring and not all children of a "stalemated" couple necessarily get deeply entangled in the "loser's" problems, so not every child who sets out to teach his "winning" parent a lesson necessarily winds up a psychotic. In fact, we shall probably never see families in our practice in which such "unusual" behavior succeeds in reestablishing at least a partial equilibrium. For instance, the winning parent might be persuaded "to think things over" and retreat, thereby showing that the lesson has struck home. The child will be out of danger. Or the "losing" parent may be the one to learn the lesson and finally raise his/her voice in defense of the child's rights, so gravely jeopardized by the other spouse's provocations, and in doing so, show that he/

[1]The tragic conclusion of this process left the question unanswered: Was Monica's unusual behavior a *real* or *pretended* autonomisation? Perhaps this question could be solved in individual treatment.

she, too, can stand up for his own rights, which up to then have been passively relinquished to the winner. Should none of these changes come about, however, the child will have failed miserably in his twofold purpose: The winner will go on provoking and the loser, instead of joining the child's attempted rebellion, will stick to his submissive role. What is more, the "loser" will simply stand by and fail to raise a finger when the other spouse starts getting back at the child. He/she will do a perfect volte-face and side with the winner in upbraiding and even punishing the young rebel. In other words, the "loser" will cross over decidedly into the camp of the very person the child had naïvely considered their common "enemy."

STAGE FIVE: PSYCHOSIS ERUPTS

Having failed to rein in the winner, and left in the lurch by his secretly appointed accomplice, the child feels forsaken by everyone. Such feelings are likely to be mixed. There will be depression due to the betrayal, and there will also be a sense of impotence, blind, destructive rage, and a violent yearning for revenge. The depressive aspect will probably prevail when the bond with the "losing" parent was more genuine and less instrumental. Realizing that he/she has been betrayed, used and then ditched, the child falls into despair. Psychotic confusion can be traced back to an obscure revelation of this kind, which shows the child that the dice have been loaded all along and everything he/she held to be certain and reliable was but an illusion. The aggressive component will be the more telling when what rankles most is having failed to bring the "winner"—the real object of his desire—to his/her knees.

In all cases, however, whether the patient flails about in confusion, withdraws into depression, or falls prey to destructive rage, or finally, whether he swings from one to another of these three moods, one thing he will never do is loosen his hold. His stake in the game does not allow for any backing out. The learning context in which he has grown up, built around his parents' stalemated game, does not allow him even to imagine the possibility of calling it quits or admitting defeat. Psychotic symptomatology will thus be the one weapon allowing him to prevail where "normal" behavior has failed. No longer will he be doomed to defeat; at long last he can outwit the "winner" and show the feeble, submissive "loser" what he— their son—is capable of accomplishing.

STAGE SIX: SYMPTOM-BASED STRATEGIES

When psychosis explodes, the family may immediately start implementing moves aimed at producing change. In some cases it is safe to say that such interventions are limited to the family circle, and we cannot rule out the possibility of the dramatic psychotic protest effectively bringing about a transformation, whereupon it gradually peters out and disappears. This may explain why psychotic episodes in adolescents and young people occasionally seem to recede and leave no traces. More frequently, however, such transformations elicited by the family will be mediated by the intervention of a third party on the outside. It will then assume the form of a request for specialized help, and in a certain number of cases this, too, will usher in a positive development, since when an outsider joins the family game the rules change.

In other cases, unfortunately, the patient's psychotic behavior will go on sliding inexorably into chronicity and the family will thus have reached the sixth stage in our model of the psychosis-inducing process. Each family member will organize an individual strategy around the child's symptom. This, in turn, has the pragmatic effect of enhancing the symptom. Behavior strategies such as these might be expected on the part of the "losing" parent, who stands to gain by those features of the child's symptomatology directly aimed at the other spouse, i.e., the "winner."

A typical example of this is the cantankerous, introverted husband of a lively extrovert, irresistibly attracted to social life: A psychotic son whose plight keeps this lady firmly at home and out of temptation's way will suit this husband perfectly. Thus, every time the patient seems about to shed the symptom, we will see the father throwing a formidable, albeit covert, obstacle in the youngster's path. This conduct will be even more confusing for the patient, since the father will simultaneously show infinite solicitude and patience for his child's condition. By his tolerance for the child's pathology the father is in actual fact helping to keep it alive.

All this is not new, and has long been known. One of the parents (the father, in our example) will signal by his conduct that he is far less enthusiastic about therapy than the other, and will more or less openly sabotage it, as though in some strange way he *needed* the child's symptom. However, if the psychotic process under way in the family has not yet reached the sixth stage, the other parent will come on as a staunch advocate of therapy. In our example we would expect the mother to be only too glad to rid herself of the burden the child's symptoms have placed on her and eagerly latch on to any help that promises her her freedom. If the point at which chronicity sets in has been reached, however, not only the "loser" but also the "winner" will stubbornly and surreptitiously oppose any change in the "status quo."

The winner, by this time, will have worked out a strategy based on the premise that the symptom is here to stay, and his/her conduct will be aimed at keeping it alive. The "winner's" determination is not usually directly a move in the couple's stalemate game; generally speaking, he/she is simply using the symptom to keep an important ally on his/her side in the marital battle. As we illustrated in Chapter IV on the effects of our invariant series of prescriptions, a "winning" mother may in fact be extremely reluctant to agree to therapy if she feels this will be tantamount to exchanging what is "known" for what is "unknown." What is "known" might be the solidarity she is getting from her daughter, her special confidante, or her own mother (who in the past has always preferred one of her siblings). The mother's anxiety about the patient, in which she has successfully enlisted her ally, will be the bond that ties them together.

What is "unknown," and risky, is not only whether the patient stands to "get well" but also the possibility of the couple's stalemate game suffering even the slightest change after so many years of stereotyped immobility: It is the stalemate game, rather than the patient, that has become chronic! Once this stage has been reached, not only one parent, but often both, will to all practical purposes steadfastly resist the therapist's endeavors.

BEYOND THE TRIAD: THE PSYCHOTIC'S SIBLINGS

We have described our six-stage schema as though a family game always involved only three players, to wit, the parental couple and the patient-to-be. Only brief mention has until now been made of other possible characters in the cast. If there is more than one child, the game takes on fantastic complexity. Let us look more closely at a particular situation we have been able to observe in greater detail.

Selvini Palazzoli's article (1985b) on the prestigious referring sibling described a four-player game in which, in a spouses' stalemate situation, the son bent on reforming his parents' rapport was not the patient but her brother. This later had become enmeshed in an inextricable web of seductive maneuvering and calls for help coming from both his parents. So adroitly had they entangled him in their marital rapport that they were no longer able to do without him, and he himself was hardly able to imagine any future other than this highly gratifying role of "moderator" in his parents' affairs. Into this triad, which, we should stress, is no longer the spouses' stalemate, enters the patient.

A case in point was that of a young man we will call Ciro, who had for years been suffering from alternating bouts of anorexia and bulimia. He had given up first his studies and then his job, and had broken off all social ties. His brother Carlo, five years older, had been his mother's choice of a husband-by-proxy since his infancy. She was intensely disgruntled with her real-life husband, who instead of coming home after work would spend his evenings in the bars. Later in life, however, Carlo became the apple of his father's eye: A simple man, this father was exceedingly proud of having seen his son all the way through college and into a first-rate job.

The parental couple had been locked for years in a perfect stalemate situation. The wife's "active" provoking consisted of devoting an inordinate amount of time and energy to caring for her old parents, thereby neglecting her children and most of all her husband. Her husband's "passive" provoking took the form of retreating to the bars in order to escape the invasion of his home by a horde of in-laws.

Carlo waged a valiant battle, meting out blows even-handedly in both directions: In his role as a stand-in for his father, he would punch his cousins when they outstayed their welcome at the family home. Then he would regularly back up his mother when she started airing her grievances against her absentee husband. His allegiance to his mother was the more conspicuous, however. His parents had an additional storey built onto their house, so that Carlo would have an apartment of his own after his forthcoming marriage.

The family might have carried on in this state of equilibrium forever had it not been for the younger son, Ciro. Ciro was decidedly superfluous. Ever since his infancy he must have sensed that the only way for him not to be utterly invisible in the eyes of his parents — constantly trained as they were on their own game and how best to use Carlo to further their respective ends — was to imitate his prestigious brother as closely as possible, so that some of all the glory and attention would rub off on him. Having reached adolescence, Ciro saw another tempting opportunity open to him: Since his brother had taken up his mother's defense and was openly encouraging her insufferable whining against their father, Ciro would spring to his father's defense. Ciro felt his father was more than justified in rushing off to the bars if his wife made life unbearable for him at home by allowing the place to be overrun by nosy relatives. He therefore began exhibiting intense jealousy for his cousins and then went on to include his old grandmother in this conduct. Further, he started on an anorectic-bulimic protest.

This cut his mother down to size a bit but, to his great dismay, his father showed no appreciation whatsoever for the efforts Ciro was making on his behalf. Far from acting grateful, his father went to great lengths to provide Carlo with even greater financial independence by having him and his young wife over for meals every day, all the while insisting that Ciro contribute to the household expenses, on the grounds that the boy wasted so much food by vomiting! What was more, Ciro's symptoms, aimed at tying his mother to him more strongly and prying her away from all those relatives (and especially from Carlo), only thrust her more firmly into his big brother's arms. She took Carlo into her confidence and told him all about her anxiety over Ciro's "illness."

Carlo, apparently doing all he could for his brother, initiated a deceitful maneuver all his own: Helping Ciro was tantamount to confirming his own preeminent position in the family hierarchy once and for all by acting as his brother's savior and healer. So this is an aspect on which we, as therapists, must concentrate when working with the family of a prestigious son or daughter—not the original stalemate situation, by this time usually rooted too far back in family history, but the current overlordship of the "healthy" son, who clings like a parasite to his self-image of success and stoops to offer his poor brother a helping hand, thereby aggravating the latter's pathology. When this aspect of the family game is brought out into full view, the pathetic weakness of this ostensible "family pride and joy" stands revealed, and the idol is seen to have feet of clay. Having been precociously pressed into assuming the role of "go-between" to the couple, Carlo now finds it very difficult to step down from this throne of infantile omnipotence: He will have serious trouble achieving any degree of autonomy outside the family.

Our experience has taught us that in the case of a family with chronic psychotic offspring, the first-order problems most readily owned up to are those concerning the sibling rapport, such as a greater degree of esteem or preference bestowed on one or the other of the children by one or both parents. As for interactive entanglements entailing members of the extended families, these too are quite frequent; however, at this stage of our research we do not yet know how to fit them into our general model.

CHAPTER X

The Anorectic Process in the Family

A SYNDROME PECULIAR TO THE AFFLUENT SOCIETY

THE ONLY PSYCHIATRIC SYNDROME which in the course of our research into its functioning gave rise to a complex epidemiological hypothesis was anorexia nervosa. Mara Selvini Palazzoli started studying anorexia nervosa in 1950 (Selvini Palazzoli, 1978). Her working hypothesis, basically, was the following: *The anorectic symptom emerges only if a considerable number of factors converge.* These may be roughly classed under two headings: (a) those pertaining to the Western cultural model, and (b) those deriving from the special way in which a given family's interactions organize and evolve.

Very briefly, here is the essence of what Mara Selvini Palazzoli had to say in an article originally written for the *Transcultural Psychiatric Research Review* (1985a): Anorexia nervosa is defined as a syndrome peculiar to the affluent society, this being the sociocultural context in which anorectic behavior can materialize. The first intimation leading to this hypothesis was triggered by the startling fact that medical literature does not report any cases of anorexia nervosa ever having occurred in third world countries, where food is a scarce and contended commodity. On the other hand, in Japan, where a Western lifestyle and widespread affluence are recent phenomena, the number of such cases is increasing exponentially. An abundant supply of food, lavishly and insistently proffered, develops into a strongly conditioning social cofactor.

Paradoxically, however, the affluent society prescribes an inverse relationship between food intake and the acceptable body image. Fashion demands that people, especially *women*, be thin. This peremptory edict is diffused by the mass media, so influential in Western culture as to convey it to literally millions of people in all walks of life. Young girls the world over see themselves as being too fat and go on drastic reducing diets.

This double-sided sociocultural factor (the slimness fad coexisting with a plentiful supply of food) then joins with two no less significant circumstances in influencing sociofamilial subculture in an affluent society. The *first* of these is a notable shift in the position the child holds in the family, from a relatively peripheral one to one of paramount importance. Social prestige accrues to being a good parent, and a bad parent is severely disapproved of, so that proper parenting has become socially discriminating. The *second* factor is the ever-lengthening period of the offspring's life spent dependent on the parents, due to longer periods of higher education and difficulty in finding a job. At the same time, the parents continue for a longer period to feel responsible for their offspring.

In sum, as far as its sociocultural context is concerned, anorectic behavior, which is a (covert) hunger strike, will only appear if (a) there is an abundant and easily available supply of food, (b) it is fashionable—*almost mandatory for women*—to be thin, (c) the well-being of the offspring is a prime concern of the parents, and (d) the children depend on their parents during an increasing part of their lives and responsibility is assigned at an ever later stage.

Having said this, we will now describe our model of the process whereby anorectic behavior develops in a family.

FROM THE PARENTS' GAME TO THE DAUGHTER'S ANORECTIC SYMPTOMS: A SIX-STAGE PROCESS

In describing the course of the anorectic process within a family, we selected as our arbitrary point of departure the game played by the parental couple. This consisted basically of each parent's constantly provoking the other and failing to get an appropriate response. For example, a wife will start nagging her husband about something, whereupon he will either dodge the issue by remaining silent or else blow his top the moment she begins airing her grievances; in both cases, he successfully blocks all possibility of interaction. These two reactions, differing but producing an identical result, stem from the tactical choice the husband makes in the couple's game. We find that the most frequently recurring tactic is that of the silent, forbearing husband, powerless in the clutches of a meddling, harping, know-it-all wife. The tactic we find much less frequently is that of the domineering overlord. However, a close look at the transactional game will show that, even in families with a husband of this second stamp, the wife, ostensibly a victim or referred to as such, is likely to be a very provoking victim indeed. Not only does she go on endlessly about her martyrdom, but she also knows all too well how to make the most of her inferior position in order to get back at her husband in countless crafty little ways. Her husband, however blustery he may seem, has to put up with these subtle acts of revenge—such as, for example, his wife's fulfilling her inarguable duty towards her old parents, devoting so much time and energy to them as to keep her husband fuming with impotent rage.

At this point we must pause and set the record straight on a very important matter: A stalemate situation of the type described above can also be found in families that do *not* have an anorectic member. However, it assumes specific forms and effects within a given set of rules variously described by a number of authors (Haley, 1959; Jackson, 1965, Minuchin, Rosman, & Baker, 1978; Selvini Palazzoli, 1978). We shall recall just the best known of these rules here very briefly:

- The rules of the family game grant every member the right to reject anything he or she is offered, be it something concrete or simply a definition of the relationship.
- Nobody has the right to assume a leadership stance: Each will tend to justify his/her behavior as obeying the requirements of others or general principles (that which is best, most convenient, or most suitable for someone else in the family). Individual requirements are always proclaimed to be subordinate to those of others. Refusal to shoulder any of the blame—thus placing it all implicitly on someone else—is characteristic of this type of interaction.

The couple's mutual relationship almost invariably features a wife resentful of her husband. In line with the system's rules, her endless grievances never relate to a personal claim of her own but appeal to his duty as a father on behalf of the children, etc. For his part, the husband dodges his wife's invective and recrimination by setting up his own definition of those same duties, which contradicts hers: He may, for instance, manage to get his workload increased in order to spend even less time at home, and will suffer her incessant griping in stoic silence. This is his way of conveying that *he* is going about his main duty, namely to provide financial security for his family, with unswerving diligence, all the time doing his best, although sorely tried, to keep peace in the family by refusing to rise to her taunts. It also allows him to show *her* up as failing to fulfill her duty as a loving, well-balanced mother. The children's various requirements will, of course, be depicted in a totally different light by each parent, each staunchly rejecting the other's interpretation.

Once we had managed to discern a general pattern for the game played by the parental couple, we went on to work out *a six-stage model* for charting the family's interactional course as it eventually leads to anorectic behavior.

Stage 1: In which the parental couple is seen playing the game described above. The stalemate will almost invariably enmesh members of the extended family as well.

Stage 2: In which the anorectic-to-be at a very early age starts getting involved in her parents' game. As to the manner in which she gets involved during childhood and preadolescence, we were able to identify two separate types, described here under the headings A and B:

Type A: The daughter due to become an anorectic is totally in the fealty of her mother, who often confides to her the suffering she endures at the hands of her husband and, in some cases, of her in-laws as well. The daughter tends to espouse her mother's relational viewpoint. She feels pity for her, although she does not really hold her in high regard. She is the only one in the family who will volunteer to help her mother with the housework. Given this context, the girl soon acquires the notion that she is a morally superior soul and has a deservedly preferential rapport with her mother, empowering her to keep her behavior above reproach at all times.

Type B: The future anorectic has always been her father's favorite, quite overtly so. He feels she takes after him, and he greatly appreciates her many good qualities. She, too, admires her father and considers him far superior to her mother. She can see no excuse for the way her mother rants at him.

In this initial stage, future anorectics of both types do not actively take sides against one of their parents: They steer an even course between the two.

Stage 3: Adolescence brings on a series of decisive events in the life of a future anorectic, abruptly changing the way she sees her father or else tying her to him all the more closely.

Type A: Mom's "special little love" discovers, either with dramatic suddenness or through gradually becoming aware, that her mother's real love has shifted somewhere else, usually to a sibling with whom the mother engages in constant emotional bickering or, more rarely, to some new object of affection. Feeling forsaken, she turns hopefully to her father: this stage is marked by highly intense, albeit subtle and disguised, seductive maneuvering on the part of both father and daughter. The daughter starts to see her father in a new light, attributing to him a fellow feeling of loneliness and abandonment and coming to appreciate his intrinsic qualities. She welcomes and reciprocates the hints and promises of a special affinity he holds out to her (what a perfect wife *she* would be for him!). At this stage, when her parents interact, the daughter covertly sides with her father: in her heart of hearts she longs to see him react firmly and sternly to some of her mother's behavior, which up to that time she had not noticed as being so provoking. For his part, the father takes every opportunity to signal to his daughter how trying and frustrating his wife is—even as regards their intimate relationship—and how he puts up with all this torment solely for the sake of peace in the family (mutual instigation against the mother).

Type B: As the future anorectic reaches adolescence, the seductive bond between father and daughter occasionally assumes embarrassing proportions. The (mutual) instigation heightens in intensity.

In both types, due to this "father bias," the future anorectic feels very much bound to him—they are both "victims" of this insufferable woman.

Stage 4: This is a period of intense relational distress, during which the "diet ploy" comes onto the scene.

Type A: Forsaken by her mother and egged on by her father, the future anorectic feels a compelling urge to distinguish herself from her mother. She loathes the idea of resembling her in any way. She takes the unprecedented step of acting on her own behalf and sheds her mother's behavioral tenets in favor of those currently in vogue with her age group, in an as yet hazy attempt to achieve autonomy.

Type B: The diet is seen right from the start as a challenge to the mother. It is immediately flaunted in defiance. We have hypothesized that precocious amenorrhea frequently occurs in these cases. The decision to resort to dieting is often sparked off by some specific behavior on the part of the mother that is especially disturbing to the father or the daughter herself.

No matter how the lowered intake of food gets under way, it rapidly develops into silent protest and rejection of the mother. Future anorectics of both types tend to view their decision as ushering in a change. *Against the girl's expectations, however, the reduced food intake sets off an interactional spiral in the triad—mother/father/daughter—that actually reinforces the parents' game and, consequently, the daughter's involvement therein.* We now have the mother poking her nose into her daughter's dietary habits in her usual meddling fashion, the father feebly attempting to shut up his wife (and failing, as usual), and the girl getting angrier and angrier all the while, with her urge to rebel leading her to eat less and less.

The drift towards a radical hunger strike is furthered by her father's attitude: She sees him as irresolute, utterly incapable of following her shining example and joining in the fray. To be sure, he deplores his wife's outrageous behavior, but he does nothing whatsoever to grasp at the sceptre his daughter silently holds out to him. He passes up the opportunity of rallying to her side and joining in the exciting adventure that could ally them in the (covertly promised) special relationship he had so often hinted at before. She senses that she has been left in the lurch and that her father prefers not to endanger his relationship with his wife any further.

Stage 5: This is marked by the father's volte-face. The daughter feels let down by her father and her attitude towards him is now resentful, occasionally despairing and spitefully contemptuous. She reduces her food intake to absurd extremes. This is the only way she has of getting her mother to knuckle under and of showing that faint-hearted deserter of a father what lengths his daughter can go to. . . .

Stage 6: In which the family game proceeds according to what we have termed "symptom-based strategies." The anorectic has tasted of the extraordinary power the symptom confers upon her, in that it allows her to recapture the illusory privileged status she enjoyed during childhood and preadolescence. She often ties her mother to her by a pseudo-symbiotic bond barely masking hostility and control. Eventually, each member of the family will think up self-serving strategies based firmly on the notion that the symptom is here to stay: Should the anorectic attempt to shed the symptom, she would face strenuous, albeit camouflaged, resistance from somebody.

As can be inferred from this general pattern of things, the entire course of events described is thoroughly shot through with deceit: This we have termed *"imbroglio"* (see Chapter V). Imbroglio stands for a complex interactional process that apparently gets under way and develops around a particular strategy consisting in *holding up as "privileged" a transgenerational dyadic relationship (mother/daughter, father/daughter) which is actually nothing of the sort.* Such bogus privilege, in fact, is not genuinely grounded in affection, and is really a tactical weapon to be used *against* someone — usually the spouse. Tactics of this sort are generally pathogenic per se, in that they are transgenerational. They set up a precarious equilibrium which, when it comes crumbling down, ushers in a series of events that glaringly unmask the fiction of the presumed privileged rapport, with devastating effects.

CHAPTER XI

Some Remarks on the Psychotic Behavior of Small Children

THE CHILD AS A STRATEGIST

EACH TIME OUR CLINICAL CASEWORK compelled us to face the cruel quandary of infantile psychosis, we went through a period of intense theoretical and emotional upheaval. The little patients we were asked to help seemed so severely impaired in their development that we often wondered whether their condition had not deteriorated beyond all hope. Some organic deficiency, or an anomalous evolution during a very early phase, had seemingly wrought irreparable damage.

After a long, soul-searching debate on how to handle these cases, the team resolved to abide by the model presented elsewhere in this book (see Chapter IX), which was increasingly being used in dealing with the psychotic crisis in families with adolescent patients. We decided to test whether its range of applicability could extend to cases of infantile psychosis.

With this in mind, we tested the model on a certain number of families. Our manifest intention was to compare our model with the specific situation the parents themselves were experiencing and reporting to us. There was clearly very little we could learn directly from the patient, usually a very small child whose verbal expression was either severely impaired or altogether absent in direct communication. Moreover, the patient would normally be an only child, or one whose siblings were in his own age group, so that we often had to do without the valuable help that a couple's "healthy" offspring can provide. Nonetheless, there was often striking correspondence between our theoretical assumptions and what the parents had to tell us. Such correlations were at times grudgingly admitted by the family and at times strongly denied, as though they constituted a menace.

This substantial approximation encouraged us to relinquish our doubts and proceed along this line of research.

The main problem lay in estimating to what degree such a very young patient's arrested development could be considered actively intentional, and how we should interpret it as the opening gambit the child makes when he enters into the parental couple's game. Although it was relatively natural to ascribe intentionality to the provocative conduct preceding the onset of a psychotic symptom in an adolescent, we found it difficult to assign deliberate awareness to a subject whose pathological career had commenced at such a very early stage. Our cultural stereotypes tended to make us consider the little patient as a passive victim, whose stunted evolution was the product of having been deprived of the opportunity and stimuli necessary for him to develop.

The first few sessions with such a family would hint at the fact that highly complex relational games, spanning several generations, were under way. The patient's parents, usually deeply involved in these intergenerational games, were hampered by frustrating constrictions. *This probably accounted for their having failed to give their own child adequate affective priority: Their emotional roots in their own family history were too deep. In other words, family history was still so powerful an influence on their lives as to constitute, more often than not, the very core of the spouses' stalemate.* The obvious conclusion, then, was that the child had been sadly used as a pawn in his parents' dueling, and the latter had been unpardonably blind to his need to "belong" and to grow. Severely deprived, the child had ostensibly become the unwitting victim of a game he had had no hand in starting.

We realized, however, that adopting such a premise would not take us a single step beyond what existing models had to offer, which had shown very little potential either for eliciting information or for contributing to therapeutics. The truth is that if the psychotic infant is assumed to be irremediably handicapped, no change in the ongoing family game will fill in the formidable gaps in his evolution, and a more sensible choice would be the kind of "psychic retutoring" provided by in-depth individual therapy.

It is pointless to tackle the spouses' stalemate, which frees the parents from the intrusive meddling of their own families, unless one is willing to see the child as a human being *at present* actively playing his trump card by being a patient. If such reasoning obtains, the patient will be seen as making moves suited to his elementary powers of reckoning (his self-knowledge, at this early stage, must be considered very rudimentary). Only by leading from the assumption that the patient was actively refusing to learn, to grow, and to adapt were we able to explore new paths and verify the therapeutic results ensuing from such a premise. If the child is perceived to be covertly reacting against a frustrating relational situation by refusing to avail himself of his potential for growth, then—and only then—can these perturbing relations be modified and the child reconciled with those whose duty it is to raise him. Only in this way can one hope to enlist the child's cooperation.

It was essential, therefore, to take a bold conceptual plunge and train ourselves to view such a very young child as an active strategist.

INFANTILE PSYCHOSIS AS AN ATTACK ON THE MOTHER

The literature on relational topics hypothesizes the psychotic symptom as a covert attack the child makes on its parents. Our clinical records, however, indicate that both parents do not react the same way to such an attack. In almost all cases, the mother appears far more stricken and anguished than the father. It will almost always be the mother who requests therapy. The father's attitude, though this obviously varies with personal characteristics and the specific family situation, will generally tend to be one of resignation. A father often chalks the symptom up to some organic impairment and thereby justifies his reluctance to consider psychological therapy. If one judges by its effects, the patient's attack will be especially hard on the mother. This is clearly a feature of the specific family game but also derives from a societal definition of motherhood, which tends to assign responsibility for a child's defective upbringing mainly to the person most closely involved.

Whenever we reconstructed the process of transformation such a mother had gone through, we were quite astonished: She had generally been a very active person, competitive in her profession, definitely the stronger personality in the couple. Her pregnancy had usually been unwanted and she now felt unable to extricate herself from the dismal pressure the child's illness was exerting on her life. For the child's sake she had relinquished her career, reneged on her principles, and pandered to the whims of her all-powerful victim as she never would have done for anyone else, least of all her husband. The child, using his pathological clout, blackmailed such a mother and extorted from her all that her husband had always failed to obtain.

It is a well-known (and unfortunate) fact that, in our line of work, the only phenomena we are truly able to observe are those we previously hypothesize. Discoveries are very rare indeed! Once our eyes were better trained to look out for them, we began finding analogies linking the patient's extortive use of the symptom to some profound (albeit tacit and repressed) grievance of his father's.

We found amazing correlations. Was the husband silently reproaching his wife for being too cool and standoffish towards him? The child would be constantly kissing and pawing his mother, who was so terrified of upsetting him that she would hide her exasperation and submit to being slobbered over for hours on end. Did the father loathe his in-laws and deeply resent their interfering in family matters? The child would do his best to make life unbearable for his grandparents by enacting symptomatic acts of retaliation, such as stomping all over Grandma's flowers or tormenting Grandpa's rabbits. Mother would frantically hasten to repair the damage, but she was forced to put up with her family's obvious disapproval and with watching them leave in a huff.

Now, let us try to imagine the husband's feelings when he assists at what amounts to a protracted vendetta. He watches the woman who has been such a disappointment to him, who after all these years is still holding out on him, being cruelly put to the rack by their child's illness. How can he help seeing this as her just deserts? Might he not perhaps be resigned so easily to his child's pathology because, on the level of simple reckoning (not knowingly) he stands to benefit by it? Led astray by his warped consciousness, might such a father not actually be fostering his child's pathology and relishing the idea of his wife's atoning for all the frustrations he has suffered? This hypothesis, i.e., that the father might be instigating the child against the mother, needed to be proven (for a discussion of the concept of instigation, see Chapter VI).

One of the authors clearly recalls her emotion when she first heard the father of a psychotic baby girl admit to himself and to the therapist, at the same moment, that this hypothesis was correct. In a personal meeting with the therapist (such individual encounters can be useful for getting to the bottom of problems in the spouses' stalemate), this father blurted out a full confession: He said that when he watched their daughter persecuting her mother by her provoking behavior "it was like balm on my wounds, to see my wife, always so cold and haughty, lose control and wait hand and foot on Chiara, like a slave. It's a feeling I've always been ashamed of, and I've never admitted to it before. I must say, though, that when my wife would ask me to get tough with Chiara, I just couldn't do it. I felt that the two of us, the child and I, had been through such hell because of this woman that I'd just let things ride. I couldn't scold her . . . this was my way of being extra loving in order to make up for her mother's cold, undemonstrative behavior."

FROM THE DYAD TO THE TRIAD: TWO PHASES OF A PROCESS

Some of our queries were gradually finding an answer, but new ones kept cropping up. The precocious onset of symptoms in infantile psychosis raises the problem of understanding *why* so small a child "wants" to punish his mother. It is not easy to accept the idea that the child deliberately takes the side of the "loser" in the couple relationship—i.e., the father—(as had been hypothesized for the psychotic crisis during adolescence), to the extent of bringing the parent he sees as the "winner" down on his/her knees, on the "loser's" behalf. A small child's powers of perception and discrimination are too underdeveloped for him to have even an intuitive, inaccurate notion of the complex tangle of relationships we have come to call the spouses' stalemate.

We therefore assumed that the process in infantile psychosis (autistic disorder, or pervasive developmental disorder, according to *DSM-III-R*), from the patient's subjective point of view, leads from a dyadic stage to a later triadic one. The child will at first only be reacting to a frustrating experience coming from his mother. He obviously ignores her reasons for being circumstantially unable to fulfill her biological duty to nurture. He is also quite unaware that, should he rebel, he would find a potential ally in his father. The child merely feels that something is vexing him. He reacts to this, and the feedback unclenched by this first reaction is what brings on the psychotic process.

Clelia, the mother of a six-year-old psychotic boy called Andrea, provided us with very enlightening information on this issue. While she was pregnant, Clelia went through a period of suicidal depression. Her father died, after a long illness during which she had nursed him devotedly. He left most of his fortune, including the house in which Clelia and her family had been living for 10 years, to his firstborn son, so that Clelia and her family (the parents and two children, eight and five years old) were suddenly homeless. Her father's "betrayal" shocked Clelia deeply, and she sank into prolonged apathy. She was also full of resentment towards her husband, who, instead of rallying to her side, mocked her for having sacrificed herself for her father (thereby probably getting back at her for having had to put up, for so long, with the scraps of attention left over after she had ministered to the old man).

When Andrea was born, his mother was in an appalling condition. She wasn't strong enough to take care of him. She made three suicide attempts, each of which landed her in the hospital. Through all this, little Andrea lay at home, virtually unattended, for the first months of his life. He was a very quiet baby and caused no trouble whatsoever. Then his mother finally got a grip on herself, snapped out of her apathy, and decided she was going not only to take proper care of her child but also to start working on a job about which she was very enthusiastic.

At once, Andrea, six months old, started being a problem. He would cry for hours, and then vomit. What had happened to him? Probably the lack of proper stimuli endured during the period when he was abandoned, plus the sudden appearance of an overanxious and very much present mother, eager to make up for her inadequate conduct of the past, had registered with Andrea: Like the crafty little "strategist" he was, Andrea began making his presence felt by a series of "disturbing moves," promptly magnified by his mother's overanxious attitude. However, the inevitable escalation involving an increasingly anxious mother and an increasingly obstreperous child would probably eventually have petered out had the mother, under reactive pressure from the child, learned to respond consistently to the child's tantrums by either repressing or appeasing them. Sooner or later, after much floundering and a good deal of misery, their relationship would have reached an adaptive equilibrium satisfying the needs of both. Instead, as Clelia told us, she was not consistent: "At times I'd heed him; at other times I'd simply ignore him altogether."

If we consider only the mother–child dyad, there is no way we can account for the psychotic trajectory. The clinical data gathered in the course of our research indicate, at this point, that the third player's polarity is now fundamental to an understanding of why the relationship takes a psychotic turn.

Let us go back to what Andrea's mother told us:

> At that time, I could cope all right during the day, but when my husband was around I'd feel terrible. He'd start giving me dirty looks because the house-work hadn't been done properly, and then he'd carp at me for letting Andrea fret in his crib instead of dropping anything I was doing and rushing to pick him up! The reason he was always criticizing me was because he wanted me to give up my job. So, there I was, doing my best to keep everything under control at the same time, because I like to think I'm able to cope with things . . . but I'd get so terribly nervous and jumpy, and he'd say this was what was making the child so restless and why he wasn't growing properly. Every time Andrea cried while my husband was home, I'd panic. I felt that Andrea's wailing, and later his constant vomiting, were like an accusing finger pointed at me, because I knew I'd neglected him in the past and still wasn't really giving him very much of my time.

As for Andrea's father, he admitted that he was seeing his wife in a different light since she was raising the child. He hadn't paid too much attention to their other children, but now he suddenly began noticing how careless and messy she was. He was bitterly disappointed at having failed in his own profession, his hopes of a successful career having vanished into thin air. Crestfallen, he had taken refuge in his own home, expecting to find a loving wife eager to heal his wounds — especially now that his father-in-law had died and the family had a house to themselves at last. Instead, Clelia, intensely put out by her father's ungrateful disloyalty, was full of invective against her husband for not looking after the family's interests and for not making enough money. She rubbed it in, greatly humiliating him, by finding herself a good job in order to contribute to the family's upkeep. Her manner towards him was cold and disaffected. She was disgusted with him for being so weak and ineffectual and for having failed so miserably in his profession.

In short, his wife had thrown a wet blanket over his fond expectations of solace at home, and Andrea's father was now balefully alive to his wife's failings and ready to pounce on her shortcomings as a mother. He would never pass up an opportunity to make acrimonious remarks on how cold and impatient Clelia was towards Andrea (instead of voicing any complaints of his own). The truth was that he did not dare claim any tokens of affection from his wife, for fear of a rebuff. Quite understandably, the mother–child rapport deteriorated badly in such an ambience. The more intractable Andrea became, the more his mother would be exposed to her husband's reprimands, and the more she would long to escape the frustrating chore of caring for this child who was the living proof of her inadequacy.

As for Andrea, he reacted to these signs of impatience on the part of his "bad" mother: He claimed his rights by moving to protect himself. His mother, too, was trying to protect herself by escaping from this child, whose behavior laid her open to her husband's cruel attacks. The father, in turn, was carping at his wife so insistently in order to even the score between them: If *he* was a failure in his profession, *she* was a failure as a mother. This, for him, took the sting out of the sharp criticism implicit in his wife's contempt. Thus, the psychotic spiral had started on its tragic course.

THE FATHER–CHILD COALITION
STABILIZES THE PROCESS

The patient-to-be, as we have seen, does not at first perceive the importance of his father in the family structure, nor does he react to his father's behavior. At a later stage, this situation changes radically. The father begins to play a leading role in the pathological process, which he fosters by his overly permissive indulgence. Chiara's father, in our first example, openly stated that he wanted to compensate his daughter for her mother's hardness of heart. A father will very often rationalize his indulgence towards his psychotic child this way, both to himself and to the therapist. His warped awareness does not allow him to perceive (or, at any rate, to admit) that his conduct is seriously undermining his wife's efforts to educate the child.

So the covert alliance we hypothesized in connection with adolescent psychosis is at work here also: We have a husband deeply disappointed by his wife and powerless to make his influence felt with her, and a child reacting against his/her mother's negligence and remoteness. In Chiara's eyes, her father was the "good" figure: prodigal of gifts, lenient about breaking the rules, indulgent when it came to shirking one's duties. The father's favorable image was enhanced by the fact that the mother, who felt she alone was carrying the whole burden of the child's education, was overanxious and extremely irritating by her insistence on discipline. So, Chiara was all for her father. However, her share in the father–daughter rapport was anything but a genuine one: The child probably dimly perceived the patronizing contempt that went with his permissive attitude.

The patient's father is always an untrustworthy ally. The child, who is the living proof of his mother's existential failure, is not the real object of the father's affection. The father sees his child solely as the product of his wife's mismanagement, and the child is "that poor thing" everyone has given up on.[1]

Highly interesting effects were observed when, in the wake of therapy, the father's indulgent and permissive attitude (and, with it, the disregard) were modified. Andrea began feeding himself at the table, and a month later had started speaking of himself in the first person. Chiara increased her attention span and corrected the psychomotor instability that had hitherto impeded her learning. Within months she managed the extraordinary exploit of learning to write in block letters. This achievement provided all the incentive her father needed to face up to, and eventually overcome, the serious marital conflict.

When the patient is no longer required to function as a vehicle for the claims one spouse makes against the other, therapy may be said to have attained its goal.

The spouses' stalemate, then, is at the heart of the problem, and merely exhortative attempts to modify the father's attitude will not suffice to check the patient's undesirable behavior. To be effective, such attempts need to be associated to a different relational self-image of the parental couple, which is something the child will be quick to perceive.

---

[1]We have purposely limited the considerations in this paragraph to the triad, in order to avoid complicating the picture. In clinical work, however, one must always begin by extending the field of scrutiny beyond the boundaries of the nuclear family. Our experience has taught us that the most "malignant" cases are those in which members of the young wife's family of origin more or less openly side with her husband. At times we discovered that the husband had adroitly seduced his in-laws; more often, however, this unnatural and confusing partisanship was rooted in some unsolved problem besetting the young wife and her own mother. In such cases, the maternal grandmother may unwittingly be instigating the child against its mother, or may have done so in past. Relational tangles of this covert and contorted nature require much more study.

CHAPTER XII

Adolescent Psychosis
and the Couple's Stalemate

WHY COALITIONS AGAINST THE
MOTHER ARE MORE FREQUENT

HAVING OUTLINED OUR DIACHRONIC models for the principal types of pathology that make up our caseload, we will now add a few remarks on the subject.

One aspect of our clinical work that puzzled us for quite some time was why the preponderance of the patient–father coalitions against the mother should be so substantial *in cases of psychoses arising during adolescence or young adulthood.* It is easy to see why such a coalition should predominate in the anorectic process, where the symptom, as we have seen, comes onto the scene once a daughter begins viewing her parents as an overbearing mother and a henpecked father. Anorectic fasting will then follow coherently from this perception and be directed against the mother, traditionally the purveyor of food. In infantile psychoses we encounter a similar perception of polarized roles (father = apparent victim; mother = apparent victimizer) and here, too, the refusal to learn, an essential feature of the psychotic block in infancy, obeys the tenets of our culture by attacking the one whose duty it is to nurture the offspring—essentially, the mother.

But why does this same scheme of things hold true when psychosis erupts during adolescence? Here, too, the tendency will be for the child to side with a father seen to be kowtowing to a domineering wife, yet it is difficult to attribute this to any essential difference in parental roles where an adolescent is concerned—except, of course, in the case of anorexia, which will *always* single out the nurturing mother as the favored target. So, some other factor must be at work here.

It is in keeping with our society's accepted gender roles for the father to play the active provoker. This conforms to the stereotype of the strong, domineering, self-reliant male, a figure to whom a host of special privileges still accrues. So, although the father is the one who plays the role of active provoker in the couple's game, this does not gainsay what we have previously asserted about the way a child is roped into the parents' game and about the presumed ally's volte-face: The child will indeed exhibit unusual and undesirable behavior, yet this will very rarely be psychotic.

Even when the mother first pits the youngster against his father, portraying her husband as a violent, heartless ogre, and then fails to back up the child when he rebels against this dastardly father, such a betrayal will be unambiguous and not take the child altogether by surprise. True, his mother has led him to believe, for years now, that all she really craves is to be free from the tyrant's clutches; true, the child hopes against hope that his mother will jump at the chance he offers her, sever her ties with her husband and rally to the side of her faithful knight-errant. But if his mother, when the time comes, lacks the courage to take this step, and reneges on her promises, what is to be done? The betrayal smarts terribly, of course, but it is quite in line with a well-established, time-honored conditioning, which takes the edge off it and makes it reasonable, if disappointing.

The truth is that in our current social pattern, the wife is still expected to play the weaker role in the couple's rapport—psychologically, but especially economically and socially. So even if a mother has been complaining for years about how bossy her husband is, it is no surprise that she will not be able to make a decisive move and tear herself free. When the mother does her volte-face, the youngster's revolt escalates into flagrant antisocial behavior (theft, drugs), because he senses that his mother is not coming to his aid and that he is desperately alone. This will make him all the more determined to press charges in his mother's name and see to it that his father pays dearly. His mother's defection, however, will not be so world-shattering as to bring on a psychotic upheaval.

Our families with seriously disturbed patients are more likely, then, to be up against a two-fold factor of confusion. On the one hand, the father is a *passive* provoker, which contradicts the normally accepted gender role. He seduces the child and sets him up against the mother. Secondly, when the moment of truth comes, the father will not "dare" to back up the child's rebellion against his mother. On the contrary, he will often take his wife's part and turn on the youngster, showing his disapproval. When this occurs, the adolescent's dismay and confusion are compounded by the fact that, in our type of culture, it is usually the father who wields sufficient sociocultural clout to put decisive pressure on his wife. He will often be a man of considerable prestige in the outside world, respected and even revered: How can anyone imagine such a man acting like a doormat for a wife who is so obviously his inferior? Hence, our casebooks register a large majority of fathers who *fail* to conform to the stereotype of the strong, domineering male, and whose chosen strategy, in the spouses' stalemate, is an almost absurdly spineless and passive stance.

THE COMPLEX ROOTS OF THE SYMPTOM

The reader will have noticed how in the foregoing, as well as in Chapter X on the anorectic process, we refer to cultural factors. These are posited as coexisting with the specifically intrafamilial factors that have hitherto been our sole concern. The new sphere, as yet virtually unexplored, was laid open to our research by the introducing into our "complex thinking" of the game metaphor. The game metaphor, in fact, enabled us to link sociocultural and individual determinants, where in the past we had seen them only as contrasting and mutually canceling each other out.

At present we see the psychotic symptom as grounded in three causative levels: (a) sociocultural, (b) familial, and (c) individual. The sociocultural level determines the special way psychotic malaise will manifest itself during a certain period of history (viz. hysteria in the sex-phobic bourgeoisie during the 19th century). The second level, that of family relations will, as long as the family remains the individual's biological and affective matrix, be the breeding ground for certain relational patterns that may usher in psychic disorder. The individual level is related to personal traits and circumstances that may cause one member of a family rather than another to find himself in an untenable position.

As family therapists, our specific field of interest has always been the second of these three levels, the one at which the "games" we are examining get underway. Moreover, the familial level is also, to our mind, the most profitable point from which to start when attempting to trace the origins of a mental outbreak and draft an intervention, even when this latter may ultimately be some sort of individual therapy. However, this preferential focus on family relationship does not make us blind to the social backdrop against which the symptom arises.

The glaring example of drug addiction is most enlightening on this point: Drug addiction, like anorexia, will be conditioned both by the youngster's family organization and by a cultural environment in which drugs are at the same time readily come by and taboo. There will be no addicts where there are no drugs, or where the use of drugs is acceptable, as among opium growers. These latter may well be physically wrecked by the constant use of the drug, but no social disapproval or ostracism penalizes those who use them.

As to what takes place on the individual level, we had resolutely put aside this whole sphere while we were training our minds to work systemically. Individual factors have now started to surface anew in our reasoning. However, we are still searching for an approach to the study of the individual that is consistent with our basic premises; therefore, we are not yet able to blend into our theorizing the data assembled by others who work within a contextual framework that differs from ours, such as intrapsychic dynamics, both conscious and nonconscious, or genetic factors that forebode mental disorders.

To these three interrelated levels, in which the symptom is rooted, one must also always add the causal factor of chance, happenstance or the accident, all of which can upset the fate of an individual and the history of a family.

CHAPTER XIII

When the Decision to have a Child is a Move One Spouse Makes in the Couple's Game

HUMILIATING AND RETALIATING

THE DOTING PARENT, whose all-absorbing interest in life seems to center on a son or daughter, is a recurring figure in everyone's experience. It is also very common for this fond parent to be particularly proud and appreciative of precisely those traits in the offspring that are lacking in the other parent, as though this dissimilarity were evidence of a parthenogenetic conception. The fact that these phenomena are so widespread and apparently trivial caused us, in the past, to overlook their importance and sidetracked us from probing into the issue with a view to reconstruing the underlying game. We will now invite criticism by outlining the nature of this game, even though our findings are far from conclusive. We present them in the hope that others will feel encouraged to test our working hypotheses in their own clinical work.

There is a danger that these cases of parental enthrallment, which present an extremely banal surface pattern, may lead one to overlook the underlying existential game. This we did on two occasions; only when we were dealing with our third case did we become aware of the ongoing game at an early enough stage to provoke some in-session reactions. These immediately confirmed our hunch.

Let us look more closely at the matter. We are examining here the particular situation in which one spouse, at a given moment in his/her evolving relationship with the other, senses that he has been humiliated beyond all endurance. "Humiliation," we think, is a word that covers the great diversity of reactions called forth by an equally wide range of mortifying behavior. In two of the three cases we encountered, the unbearably humiliated spouse was the wife, and the interactional patterns looked to us as follows:

In case A, the husband (a wealthy man) exercised so absolute and meticulous a control over his wife (who came from a poor family) as to class her explicitly as one of his possessions and deny her even token reciprocal control over him. In case B, the husband (a bookish university don) sent quite distinct behavioral signals to his wife (who had not gone beyond grade school) that her proper role was that of a faithful handmaiden perfectly content to wait on the great man — in worshipful silence, so as not to interrupt his august train of thought.

In case C, the humiliated party was the husband and the interactional pattern assumed the following shape: The wife, a low-brow, rather vulgar woman, came from a somewhat superior family, and several of her relatives were successful in their professions. Her husband, on the other hand, was of very humble peasant stock and had lost his parents at an early age. Despite these handicaps, he had succeeded, with the help of an uncle who was a priest, in going on to land a university degree and an important public office. The wife chided her husband incessantly for being an incompetent bigot and despised him for not earning a higher salary. She had taken full charge of running the household and raising the three daughters and never once considered his wishes or asked his opinion on anything.

Regardless of how the situation arises, the humiliating condition is intolerable for the one who realizes he has sunk into it, especially because the victim also feels that he/she has a number of good reasons for harboring a low opinion of the victimizer. Above all, the victim feels utterly powerless even to make the spouse understand his discomfort and possibly work out some way of jointly changing the situation, let alone to openly rebel or act on the slim chance of in some way getting even. The spouse trapped in such a position desperately needs a strategy that may, at least in part, extricate him from his predicament but does not oblige him to stick his neck out by making his intentions manifest.

The insistently proclaimed wish to have a child, then, is an ideal strategic move. Warped consciousness probably makes the parent feel that it is a genuine desire. If he/she is able to persuade the partner, the child will be born, and from that moment on, the "generating" parent, i.e., the one whose idea the child originally was, will have an unimpeachable strategic stronghold resting on love and unassailable parental duty — *a duty, moreover, that the other parent is compelled to share.*

THE TACTICS EMPLOYED BY THE "GENERATING" PARENT

A global strategy of this kind comprises a series of moves in a time sequence and adjusted, as the game proceeds, to the child's special nature (sex, personal traits) and to the events, favorable or unfavorable, that mark his growth and development. The tactics a "generating" parent brings into play during infancy all more or less resemble each other. By invoking the sacrosanct needs of the child, the "generating" parent will easily succeed in (a) denying his spouse certain prerogatives (something he would never have dared do in his own name), and (b) extorting certain concessions from the spouse (which he would never have dared claim for himself), in a perfectly unaggressive way that will not upset the long-defined equilibrium of their relationship. If anything, should the need arise, the "generating" spouse will resort to veiled, guilt-inducing remarks on the duties of a *true parent*. During his son/daughter's childhood and adolescence, the "generator's" tactics will become ever more complex. They will center specifically on pedagogical methods and will vary according to the youngster's natural characteristics.

In his rapport with the son/daughter, the "generating" spouse will steadfastly assume a stance exactly opposite to that of the other parent. He will be easygoing if the other is strict, thorough going if the other is absentminded, generous with his time if the other is cursory, and so on. Moreover, he will eagerly discover and foster those qualities in the youngster that he feels are lacking in his partner, thereby virtually assigning to his own son/daughter the future role of a triumphant antithesis.

Here is a profile of case C that illustrates what we are referring to: This father, whose wife has humiliated him ever since they first married, has suffered a further tragic blow with the loss of the couple's third daughter. Secretly, he blames his wife's negligence for the girl's death. He is the one to passionately advocate another pregnancy, with the idea of filling the void left by his favorite daughter.

When a fourth girl is born, he develops an intensely tender feeling for the baby. He ministers to her needs during the first long, sleepless nights, never fails to put her in her crib and tell her a bedtime story. As the girl grows older, he fashions her into a sort of anti-wife. He praises her discriminating taste (his wife is vulgar), her passion for learning (his wife is uncultured), her disregard for money and liberality (his wife is greedy and stingy), her fastidious attention to detail (his wife is lackadaisical), and so on. By so doing, he weaves a tangled web around the girl, who comes to believe that she is truly privileged; at the same time he sets her up implicitly against her mother by taking over the latter's proper role.

This is not all, however. If the youngster, as he/she grows older, shows any special feature or accomplishment (physical beauty, outstanding scholastic achievement, a knack for athletics or an artistic temperament), the "generating" parent, beneath his legitimate parental pride, will taint the child's prowess with a very subtle, irritating competitive coloring by comparing him/her with the spouse, almost as though the child were his vindication personified.

Case B illustrates this very clearly. This humiliated mother never passed up a chance to contrast her husband, old and ailing, with her son's dashing athletic vitality, the old man's plodding diligence with the boy's quick-wittedness, the father's tiresome erudition with the boy's creative flair for drawing. We believe it must have been this irritating competitive coloring, *additionally enhanced by the underdog spouse's absolute failure to react,* that at long last antagonized the youngster and led him to renounce his qualities and achievements and move over to the other spouse's camp, in the hope of setting up a less designing rapport there.

HOW THE OTHER SPOUSE AND
THE SON/DAUGHTER REACT

How does the "nongenerating" parent react to his partner's strategic maneuvering? In line with the rules that govern the couple's stalemate game, he will on no account let his partner notice (this would be tantamount to an admission) that he feels at all frustrated, left out, or jealous. He will stick scrupulously to formally prescribed parental behavior while stealthily building up, in his heart of hearts, a mounting feeling of hostility towards his child. Furthermore, and this is the dark core of the matter into which we must as yet probe in greater detail, he will never stop communicating to the youngster in a number of ways his lack of esteem for his spouse, whose blameworthy conduct he tolerates solely for the sake of keeping the peace in the family.

The "generating" parent's behavior by itself would not suffice to propel the youngster towards self-destructive decisions: The chameleonic behavior of the "nongenerating" parent is what compounds the problem and deludes the child into believing that he can, at last, win over this latter parent, who has been the object of his desire all along. Only a hope of this kind, fostered in some subtle way by the parent himself, can induce a youngster to make certain decisive moves under the illusion that he will be understood and accepted when, in rebelling, he renounces those very qualities and achievements that so manifestly gratified the "generating" parent.

Witness the first rebellion enacted by Federico (the child in case B). At the age of 17, Federico resolves to sabotage his physical beauty, so highly valued by his mother, by developing overwhelming anxiety concerning his nose (he would refer to it sarcastically as being "as hideous as Mom's!") that finally lands him under the plastic surgeon's knife. His fond hopes go unfulfilled. Punishing the manipulative parent and depriving her of the instrument she used in competing with her husband—who, for his part, failed to react—is not enough to allow the youngster a deeply desired rapport with this sought-after father of his. Instead, he feels the full brunt of his father's contempt.

It is as though the father were seeing all the many years of repressed resentment, of jealousy, of painful concessions made to his wife in the name of her total devotion to the child, suddenly receiving proper justification. As though, at long last, he could exclaim, "Well, there you are, this is what you get for all that devotion, that ridiculous glorification! I could have told you it would end this way!" The parent does not utter these sentiments aloud, he keeps them well to himself, but they show through increasingly in his facial expression and long, meaningful silences.

As to the youngster, he finds himself absolutely alone. He was the one who decided to ditch the "generating" parent, but his move has been misunderstood by the parent he was out to win over. The latter neither joins him in his endeavor nor acknowledges his overtures. This child has been raised in a symmetric learning context that does not allow for retreat; therefore, he will not be sidetracked from his chosen design, i.e., to punish the "generating" parent, and will carry on with it alone. How does the "generating" parent react to all this? He or she can only follow the strategic course upon which she originally set out. For better or for worse, he/she will stay bound to the child he/she so fervently wanted and keep on using the child to extricate him/herself from the spouse's clutches.

THE SCHEMA OF A CASE
AND ITS EVOLUTION

To give a clearer picture, we will schematically report on the course of case A, which led to the son's schizophrenic psychosis. This illustrates how flexible such a manipulatory motive can be and how it can take advantage of all the factual events that punctuate the child's growth and development.

Here we have a wife exasperated by a controlling husband who treats her as one of his possessions. She longs desperately to bear a child. Massimo is born. As an infant, he is sickly and asthmatic. His mother is morbidly devoted to him, and her single-minded dedication deprives her husband of his share of attention. She wheedles him into sending her and the child away on lengthy stays at renowned climatic resorts, in order to cure Massimo of his asthma. The father complies with the pediatrician's orders.

In preadolescence and adolescence, Massimo grows up to be a fine, strapping youngster. He is clever and good at sports. His school record is brilliant and he is a crack tennis player. His mother encourages him to play tournaments and hires a pro to coach him. She is ecstatic over his first victories and positively basks in her son's reflected glory. All this time, the father acts as though he were too much absorbed in his work to take any notice of his son's doings.

At the age of 16, during his first year of upper high school, Massimo starts falling behind seriously in his schoolwork. He also stops playing tennis. He claims he feels dejected and ill. His mother hovers over him constantly and does her best to stimulate and encourage him. During a particularly severe bout of anxiety, Massimo is taken to a private psychiatric clinic—money is no object with his father, where his son's health is concerned.

At 19, Massimo is a chronic psychiatric case. He is under heavy medication, obese, and lives the life of a recluse at home with his mother, whom he torments with the most absurd demands. If she so much as leaves his side, he walks out of their apartment and assaults any neighbor he runs into on the staircase. This compels his mother to spend every hour of the day and night at his side, entirely given over to caring for him. The upshot, of course, is that she has managed to condemn her husband to a virtually nonexistent married life.

The reader will easily see that this outline leaves a number of questions unanswered. The most important of these *concern the process of reciprocal relationship that grows up between the "nongenerating" parent and the child.* This, to our view, is as covert as it is decisive for the flaring up of the tragedy. Careful study of a great many more cases is needed, along with a powerful dose of humility and patience, if we are to get to the roots of these and similar queries.

PART FOUR

Testing the
Therapeutic Methods

CHAPTER XIV

Conducting the Session and the Therapeutic Process

THE INVESTIGATIONS OF
M. VIARO AND P. LEONARDI

W E FIND IT RATHER DIFFICULT, at this writing, to discuss the methodology of conducting the session and choosing therapeutic strategies. Our manner of conducting the session is at present in a phase of very rapid evolution. It is therefore not easy to theorize about, or systematically frame, what is still being tested experimentally. We will merely indicate the general lines along which our research is developing and enumerate the many doubts and queries we are trying to solve.

The technique for conducting the session implemented during previous stages in our clinical work has been accurately analyzed by M. Viaro and P. Leonardi (1983). A good many of their observations concerning method are still relevant today. The authors refer to a *basic technique* of session strategy applied during the phase of "paradoxical" procedure. This technique was also the subject of an article: "Hypothesizing, Circularity, Neutrality: Three Guidelines for the Conduct of the Session" (Selvini Palazzoli et al., 1980b). Much has changed since that time; what has not are the fundamental rules governing a therapeutic setting, which Viaro summarizes as follows:

By therapeutic setting, we refer to the spatio-temporal environment in which the interview takes place and to communicative exchanges between family and therapist. Some of these are constant or codified (Selvini Palazzoli et al., 1978) and can be briefly described as follows.

The first contact between the family and the therapist is made by telephone; the therapist asks a number of standard questions and fixes the date of the first appointment. Save for rare exceptions, he asks the entire nuclear family to attend the first session.

In all sessions observed by us, the therapist is consulted in his capacity of

family therapist, regardless of any other professional (psychiatric, psychological, etc.) qualifications he may have. The family turns to him for the specific
purpose of family therapy, following advice received from other sources. The
therapist, having fixed the original appointment, explains that the sole aim
of the first session is to establish whether family therapy is indicated. The
therapeutic contract is concluded at the end of the first—and more rarely
the second—session, provided the therapist agrees to treat this particular
family. A maximum of ten sessions is stipulated with an interval of one
month between each session. The contract also stipulates the voluntary
acceptance by everyone of several definitions: the therapist and the family
agree, at least overtly, that the problem is a family problem, whatever meaning is attached to the term; that the therapist is an expert in family therapy;
that the aim of their relationship is the solution of a problem and a change of
attitude.

The room in which the sessions were held was equipped with identical
chairs, greater in number than that of the participants. The family members
enter the room first, taking any chair they wish, and wait for the therapist.
The therapist arrives and takes one of the chairs left empty. The room is
linked, by means of a one-way mirror and an acoustical device, to an adjacent
room in which one or more therapists act as supervisors. A session can be
interrupted at any moment at the behest of the supervisors to enable the
team to discuss and decide the appropriate action in the absence of the
family. (Viaro & Leonardi, 1983, pp. 29–30)

The team sets aside approximately three hours for each session. There
is a presession discussion of roughly half an hour, during which the information on the telephone chart (in the case of a first session) or the synthetic report the acting therapist has drawn up after the foregoing session is
examined. The session itself will be split into three or four parts by intervals during which the team gets together to talk about the information that
has been obtained and decide on a future course of action. Our team is
made up at present of the four authors of this book. We have learned that
full-time attendance of three people behind the mirror is unrealistic, as it
does not allow everyone sufficient opportunity to creatively contribute, by
their observations, to the proceedings. Therefore, one acting therapist and
two supervisors usually work together.

The conditions Viaro describes have remained unchanged also with
regard to the rules of directive session management, i.e., only the therapist
controls certain aspects of the conversational exchange. Here are these
rules, as Viaro defines them:

The interview is essentially a conversational game, but an asymmetrical one,
inasmuch as certain moves are open to the therapist alone, and are thus his
sole prerogative. By and large, they grant him the exclusive right to direct the
conversation. More precisely:
    1. The therapist has the exclusive right to decide what topic may be
discussed, that is, to choose the succession of conversational topics, their
articulation into subtopics, and the moment when a particular topic must be
dropped and what other must be substituted.

2. The therapist has the exclusive right to decide who may speak at any given moment, that is, to decide the succession (allocation) of turns in conversation. The therapist indicates a member of the family and the next interlocutor often in an unequivocal way, much more so than would a participant in an "informal" conversation.

3. The therapist has the exclusive right to cut anyone short and even to interrupt those whose turn it is to speak. This rule gives the therapist the exclusive right to censure the behavior of others and to establish what anyone may or may not say. It is important to stress that the term "censure" does not have a negative connotation: by cutting someone short and censuring him, the therapist simply labels a certain form of behavior as "not useful" to the inquiry at that particular moment. Since the therapist does not communicate his or her own hypotheses, he or she alone is able to decide what is relevant to their verification.

4. The therapist has the exclusive right to stop a conversation. Only the therapist can decide when to break off or how long to continue. The interview has no set duration.

5. The therapist has the exclusive right to put questions, to sum up, and to make organizational glosses. Such glosses render the organization of the conversation manifest — by stressing the hierarchical relationship between topics and subtopics, by explaining that an argument must be considered closed, etc. Such glosses, accordingly, are not comments by the therapist on the content of what has been said, but references to the organizational structure of the conversation. It must be stressed that, with few exceptions, the therapist does no more than that during the interview: nothing but asking questions, summing up and organizing what has been said. The family, of course, tries to impose another set of rules on the therapist. This question will be treated below. (Viaro & Leonardi, 1983, pp. 30–31)

It is quite clear, then, that these rules concerning directivity assign a pivotal position in the session to the therapist and veto all conversation among the family members that by-passes the therapist's control.

All these "rights," however, must not lead the reader to imagine the atmosphere in the session to be akin to that of a court of law. The therapist's active steering and the directive manner in which he or she conducts the session are never inflexible or authoritarian. He almost always succeeds in properly controlling the therapeutic relationship (keeping the upper hand and maintaining an asymmetrical therapist/family situation) with a friendly, relaxed atmosphere. The therapist's style will be that most congenial to him: He will definitely not try to adopt any ready-made jargon or mannerisms culled from "the perfect therapist's handbook," yet he will at all times keep in mind the rules basic to a qualified setting and to efficient therapeutic strategy.

In a later article, Viaro and Leonardi (1986) aptly describe the techniques implemented during the so-called "prescriptive" phase in our clinical work, i.e., when therapy was based on the experimental use of the "invariant" prescription. This prescriptive phase was a transition period linking the "paradoxical" period to our present-day modality.

Our technique today centers primarily around our endeavor to draw up a model for psychotic processes, and our therapeutic strategies focus mainly on this modeling. During our first years of work with the invariant prescription, a paradoxical "mentality" still prevailed, but paradoxical interventions were implemented during the interview and not, as before, at the end, during the conclusions (which would be predetermined by the pattern the invariant prescription assumed). Such midsession interventions, which Viaro calls "openings," gradually gave way to our first deliberate attempts at making the family game explicit by unmasking it.

A GENERAL GUIDE FOR
DRAWING UP HYPOTHESES

During the "paradoxical" stage, as well as during the stage of prescriptive therapy, we were without efficient road signs to guide our hypothesizing about the specific family game. The general model of the psychotic process in the family that we have now been able to outline has provided this long-lacking guide, a plausible general roadmap to help us find our bearings in the labyrinth of psychosis.

During the paradoxical period, our concern was the pragmatic intervention rather than an increase in knowledge; our main purpose was not so much to know as to conjure up a disconcerting intervention. Our inquiry into family relationships was designed mainly to ferret out, as covertly as we could, any information that could help us by bearing out or adding weight to our paradoxical intervention. To this purpose, we concentrated on discovering what advantages parents and siblings stood to gain by their relative's predicament.[1] To this end, the session was conducted in a way that strongly emphasized ascertaining the symptom's pragmatic effects.[2] Inquiry was well grounded in the here and now, since the ostensible advantages accruing to family members were also necessarily to be observed in the present, the symptom being active in the present. Any curiosity or concern about the historic and evolutional process of a subject or his/her family was relegated to the background.

Once the functionalist premise was abandoned (i.e., the focusing on advantages accruing to "healthy" family members), the pattern of conducting the first interview with a family underwent a radical change. The

[1]*Example*: patient acts as watchdog over the mother, which suits a jealous husband, or patient's plight is the occasion for reunification of estranged couple, etc.

[2]We need only mention the procedure of rating everyone according to how upset he/she is by the patient's problem, and the attention given to immediate reactions to the symptom elicited by such questions as: "What does Dad do when Mom yells at Elvira because she refuses to speak?" "What has changed in the way your life is organized since Elvira fell ill?" "What would happen between Mom and Dad, according to you, Riccardo, if your sister Elvira suddenly decided to get married and go off to Australia?"

general model of the psychotic process became the principal guide for our work. At present, we follow a preeminently cognitive line in our hypothesizing. The aspects more intimately related to theorizing about "what, in psychotherapy, brings about change?" now constitute our main field of rethinking. During the paradoxical period we were inclined to have very strong opinions about the unimportance of insight, the limits of verbal communication and the superior "therapeutic value" of experimentally "doing" something before (or without) thoroughly understanding what was going on in the family. Today, we are pondering these difficult questions again and subjecting our experiments to more flexible, less dogmatic principles. In Chapter XVIII we go into this all-important matter in detail.

CONDUCTING THE SESSION:
THE EMOTIONAL AMBIENCE

As we have seen, one principle to which we have remained loyal throughout the years is that according to which the first session does not take place until we possess the information on a carefully planned telephone chart. This furnishes a description of the symptom and an outline of its history, together with essential data concerning the nuclear and extended families. During the presession, the team studies the contents of the telephone chart very carefully and spots any omissions or incompleteness of the essential information. One of the main tasks during the first session is to fill in these missing parts without actually resorting to a formal interrogation. It is of the utmost importance to avoid any bureaucratically importunate prying into affairs (which are generally organizational, such as someone's work schedule or what year Grandma died) during the opening encounter. We keep such questions in abeyance and introduce them casually in the course of therapeutic conversation, in order to properly fill in the gaps in our information.

Lately we have been assigning increasing importance to the chronology of events leading to the onset, evolution, and possible later flaring-up of the symptom.[3] If this type of information is missing on the telephone chart—and this is highly possible when we are dealing with long, drawn-out illnesses with unstable symptomatology—the matter is tackled directly during the first part of the first session. We believe it advisable to speak directly to the patient, and certainly in his presence, about how the problem has varied with time. This will call forth immediate connections with other important events in the family's history and open the way for relational hypothesizing.

If, on the other hand, the telephone chart lacks information pertaining

[3]See the later section in this chapter: "The symptom's chronological history provides a clue for unraveling the family game."

to a description of the *present* state of the symptoms, we believe that it is counterproductive to start off in the first session with a transaction such as, "What has Pierino been up to lately?"[4] We will choose instead to "do without" such missing information for the time being, and fill it in casually later, without resorting to an outright inquisition.[5] True, we shall be obliged to look into the missing items at a later stage in our work, but there will be less risk then of brutally focalizing everyone's attention on the patient.

Our style entails transforming the session into a highly emotional experience. To this end, the therapist (and the team) directively heads the conversation towards topics the family would much prefer to avoid. Were we to allow the family members to take over the situation, they would simply reproduce once again, in the context of the therapeutic consultation, the interactional patterns that are their customary trademark: obstinate silences, trivializations, recriminations, accusations, etc. In our view, inferring the specific family game in the session does not necessarily involve leaving the initiative to family members; it is far more rewarding to observe how they respond to the therapist's initiatives.

In previous articles on the subject we have perhaps failed to make sufficiently clear that our choice of beginning therapy only when we hold a properly completed telephone chart is linked to a particular purpose: We want to be able to conduct these first sessions in a manner conducive to arousing, as early as possible, a highly intense emotional atmosphere. Only if we hold valuable and abundant information do we have any real possibility of rapidly getting to the heart of the matter. Without this information there is considerable danger that the therapist's "provocations" will be too unspecific and off the mark. The telephone chart supplies a baseline of pertinent information and enables the therapist to avoid getting bogged down for too long in fact-finding, which may well serve the therapist's purpose but will prove bureaucratic and tedious for the family.

FROM PICKING UP THE TRACES
TO MAKING
EXPLICIT INTERVENTIONS

The telephone chart provides the first traces along which the team pursues its inquiry. These are not bits of information we can immediately fit into our general model of the psychotic process: A trace, in this special sense, is a difference or peculiarity we notice when examining the family's

---

[4]Indeed, a transaction of this type would strongly contradict what Viaro and Leonardi have called "the individual competence presupposition," to which we shall refer in Chapter XVIII.

[5]It will be clear, by now, why the telephone chart must be designed with a view to eliciting a description of the symptom and all its manifestations.

chart, which reveals how it is in some way *different* from what one would normally expect of a family with its cultural and social background. Traces are "oddities," unexpected items. Here are some examples of the questions we ask ourselves after studying these basic data: "Why is it that this woman aged 30 (which means she attended school well after the Italian law was passed rendering secondary school obligatory) never got beyond fifth grade?" "Why were these children raised by their grandmother, even though their mother has never worked?" "Why were these children, who lived in a big town, sent away to boarding school for so many years?" "Why does this woman insist on keeping her modest, nongratifying job instead of playing the lady of leisure, a role her husband's high social position allows her to hold?"

Once we have ferreted out a rationale for these oddities, which often point to crucial aspects of intrafamily relationships, we decide whether to tackle one or more of the following general issues:

1. How each parent's relationship to each of the children has developed over time: Here we use the well-known circular method that addresses questions preferably to a third party, i.e., a more-or-less neutral observer of the dyadic relationship we are examining. For example, we will say: "Mrs. C. (grandmother), can you describe for us how Elvira's relationship to her mother has evolved over time? What was Elvira like when she was a small child? And when she reached adolescence?"
2. Individual reactions to important life events, such as death, retirement, divorce, or serious illness in the family.
3. How each member's relationship to his/her extended family has changed over the years: What we are trying to get at here are indications of one or more relatives' interfering in the couple's rapport and in the raising of the offspring.
4. How strongly each of the parents is still tied to his/her family of origin and what position this parent held in the family hierarchy in the past, as well as the present implications of having played such a role. For example, Dr. P. was the privileged son in his family. His parents encouraged him to go through medical school and then appointed him tutor to his handicapped siblings. Dr. M. was sent off to boarding school and virtually forgotten there by his family; he reacted by becoming a brilliant student and then a highly successful professional. Mrs. V., though married and the mother of five, never really accepted her maternal role because her father had assigned her a managerial one in the family business.
5. Problems hinging on the parental couple's marital rapport.
6. The symptom's pragmatic effects: One needs to find out who, in the family, is most deeply affected by the symptom. There are

clues to this in the telephone chart—the most affected is normally the one who comes out most strongly and actively in favor of therapy. But there are other issues which require looking into; for instance, which parent is most effectively "nailed to the cross" by the child's psychotic behavior?[6]

These are the six general areas one can explore in search of useful information when formulating a hypothesis. During the first interview, however, the therapist will not dwell on them in a plodding, systematic fashion (point 1, point 2, and so on). He or she already possesses some information (from the telephone chart, from initial in-session behavior, from a close look at the traces) and will move swiftly and smoothly to uncover useful information for testing the general model in the specific case.

This first phase of simple inquiry will take only a few minutes if the special nature of the family game comes into view at first glance and fits neatly into the general categorization of our model. As a rule, this phase will in any case not extend beyond the first part of the second session. Its duration will depend on how complex the situation is, on the family's reticence, and on the therapist's personal style.

The following phase, during which information is scrutinized in greater detail, starts with the therapist's enacting an intervention. Using the data at his disposal, he will put before the family a more-or-less comprehensive interpretation of the psychotic symptom. Such in-session interventions are what Viaro and Leonardi have termed "openings." As these authors put it, "the therapist introduces his own expert point of view *as soon as he can* in the interview, that is, as soon as he has observed some 'signals' corresponding to one of the hypotheses in his repertoire . . . " (1986).

We give here an example of such an "opening," from the transcript of a first session with the family of a chronic anorectic girl. All live-in members of the family had been summoned, i.e., the parents, two daughters, the maternal grandmother. The first part of the session was given over to inquiring about everyone's reaction to the fact that the maternal Grandma had come to live with them a few years earlier, after her husband's death. After roughly 20 minutes of this, Grandma was dismissed and the session proceeded with only the nuclear family.

---

[6]See the case of the Galli family (Chapter VI, p. 107). Inquiring into the symptom's pragmatic effects was already a prime concern during our "paradoxical" phase. There is an important difference, however, between then and now—at that time we were seeking out only the propitious influence of the symptom, whereas today we consider it a move in a game and probe into its covert intentionality and actual effects.

THERAPIST   Now, I want to introduce the subject of today's conversation. As you know, we see very many families like yours, so we know from experience that anorexia is always a form of protest . . . a sort of undeclared hunger strike . . . against somebody . . . that somebody is the mother . . . who is seen as a very trying personality, who makes life at home impossible for her husband. This protest, at least in its first stages, is not enacted in the child's own name but *for Dad's sake*, in Dad's defense. . . . What I would like to know now is . . . what does Mom do to make life impossible for her husband — so much so that he spends as much time away from home as he possibly can?

Other possible "openings" can be paraphrased in a like manner, e.g., "Caterina, if you've decided to clench your teeth to such an extent that you've lost a tremendous amount of weight in just a few months, you really must have been hopping mad at somebody. Which of your parents was it that let you down?" (This is an "opening" on imbroglio and volte-face). Or, "If Giorgio so vehemently resents his mother and wants so badly to get back at her, this can't be due only to his own resentment. He must have noticed an equally resentful look on Dad's face or on Grandma's" (an "opening" on instigation).

Other interventions, if based on more detailed and specific information, will obviously be a great deal more subtle, but all will develop fundamentally along these lines. The more straightforward "openings" are simple enunciations worded as questions, such as, "Paolo, how long did it take you to find out that not only your mother, but your father, too, has a soft spot for Ernesto?" More complex and finely honed interventions may even be made in the very potent form of a blunt statement.

In the transactions that follow such interventions the therapist switches back and forth between statements and questions. Should she consider it necessary, she will work on two concepts central to the general model, namely (1) serious problems in the parental couple's marital rapport (the stalemate) and how they evolved over time, and (2) the way in which the patient has become involved in the stalemate, and the phases this involvement, which is at the root of his predicament, has passed through.

All in all, the therapist's task consists essentially of revealing to the family the true causes of the "illness," as though she were voicing a diagnosis. As to the way families react to such "openings," Viaro and Leonardi stress the prevalence, during the last period of prescriptive therapy, of a reaction of surprise, followed by disavowal, i.e., an attempt to reject the therapist's point of view. Our recent experiences extend to a wider range of reactions: anger, enthusiastic agreement, belittling, outright negation, silence, partial approval, etc. Whatever they may be, these reactions always shed considerable light on each single member's strategies and elicit new, crucial information: Anger, for instance, will often prompt someone to tell us out of spite something he would never have revealed otherwise. This information shows us what direction to take in our therapeutic venture.

We hope that what has been said has made it quite clear that our team, when face to face with the family, will not go about gathering information via a reassuring, matter-of-fact, routine procedure. Quite to the contrary — therapy is conducted with great energy and emphasis and unsettling statements are "dropped" on the participants like so many bombshells, making everyone feel decidedly ill at ease. We do, however, avoid engaging the family in a tug-of-war or an outright battle of the wills: Viaro and Leonardi have pointed out how the therapist keeps to a minimum any deliberate clashes with the family and prefers to rely on diversionary tactics, such as introducing another subject apparently quite unrelated to the foregoing one. The therapist may turn the spotlight on an important issue hitherto neglected. Very often the information that emerges from this inquiry, viewed together with the family's objections and resistance to the therapist's earlier "opening," provides new significant data. In fact, the participants' reactions to the opening, and perhaps some further digressive questioning, will enable the therapist to decide whether to change tack altogether or "re-present" the initial hypothesis in a more accurate and convincing way, conceivably arousing less resistance.

THE SYMPTOM'S CHRONOLOGICAL
HISTORY PROVIDES A CLUE FOR
UNRAVELING THE FAMILY GAME

One of the deservedly famous dicta of the first, great pioneers in family therapy is Murray Bowen's "Let the calendar speak." The calendar has much to tell us, and we cannot afford to ignore it. Bowen's advice is more pertinent than ever to our present way of working. In order to reconstrue a family's interactive process, we must map the time sequences and focus on them as closely as possible. This, as everybody knows, can be tough going with families of the type we see.

All time sequences relative to the symptom, such as the date of its onset, later periods of abatement and stability, together with any dramatic flare-up, are of paramount interest to us. Our time-honored, standard hypothesis — that symptomatic behavior is an interactive response to the behavior of others — guides our efforts as we set out to investigate and piece together events in the patient's life immediately preceding any of the above-mentioned symptomatic phases.

Our model is of great help here: Suppose, for example, that we are starting therapy with a family whose daughter has been anorectic for several months. In line with our model, we will assume the symptom has exploded in the wake of some specific conduct of the mother's (that has aroused the girl's fury or caused her acute distress) and that it has been strongly enhanced by an inadequate behavioral response to mother's behavior by the girl's father. Although we will obviously take into account the family's special characteristics and life events, our inquiry will head in this direction.

In the case of Giuditta, a proud 15-year-old redhead, we learned almost at once that her "hunger strike" had begun immediately after the family moved to its new home. Why? What we discovered was almost unbelievable. Her mother, who had always kept very close ties to her own parents (who detested her husband and blamed him among other things for not keeping their daughter in the style to which she was accustomed), had accepted their offer of a new, larger apartment. She had never said a word about this to anyone in the family, and certainly not to her husband, so that he came to learn of the change of address the day they were to move. His reaction to this "surprise" was a sulky, demoralized moodiness that lasted a few weeks and then subsided. Giuditta judged this reaction to be grossly inadequate and ushered in one of her own, as an object lesson to her father. This was a case where scouting about for news concerning the onset of the symptom proved extremely helpful and brought to light a veritable tangle of conflicts spanning all of three generations.

More often, the events that foreshadow the symptom (in that they bring on the future anorectic's suffering and the ensuing symptomatic behavior) are far less obvious. Take, for example, Vilma, once Mom's special favorite, who grudgingly admitted she had suffered terribly when her mother, on countless occasions, had allowed a maternal aunt to compare Vilma to her own daughter, a girl Vilma's age whose superior talent, poise and charm the aunt would praise for hours on end. Vilma's mother never once stood up for her daughter. All this time, her father, who openly professed to despise his wife's relatives, never even noticed that his daughter was being so deeply humiliated. It must be said that it is extremely difficult in a case like this to get the patient to speak out and come clean. She will often be too ashamed to bring up the subject, fearing that it will be considered trivial or self-important. This has taught us the importance of presenting our hypothesis to the family members in a straightforward manner and encouraging them to speak by citing undramatic examples of similar cases. The idea is to let them know we are *not* looking for spectacular facts but merely for distress caused by perfectly commonplace circumstances.

In chronic cases with years of symptomatic history behind them, inquiring about how and when the behavior manifested itself will elicit a long report of ups and downs, so that we find it more profitable to concentrate on the period immediately preceding the latest flaring-up or relapse, and specifically the worsening that has led to their turning to us. Very dramatic connections often surface and shed much light on the situation. We recall the case of Dea, a lovely girl of 22, who was in the throes of her second "bipolar disorder" with manic behavior when the family contacted us. Dea's family of four had, in fact, approached our center four years earlier, during the girl's first crisis, which was far less acute than the second. At the time of our first attempt at therapy, we worked with the whole family during the first two sessions and noticed that Dea, involved in the parental couple's stalemate, was siding with her father who, quite unconsciously, had enthralled her and instigated her against a wife too overpowering for him to handle alone. After the two exploratory sessions, we dismissed the two daughters and intended to see only the parents from then on. However, in those days we were inclined to be much less explicit, and when we bid Dea good-bye we told her only a small part of the many things we had learned. We failed to tell her that her father had unconsciously been using her in order to take his wife down a peg. All we said was that she, Dea, was naïve in believing she was really closer to her father's heart than her mother was.

Unfortunately, this intervention was cut short: Therapy was discontinued. The father, who showed up with his wife for their third session, refused to accept the secrecy prescription: He felt he could not tell his elderly mother that Dea, her favorite grandchild, was ailing. Announcing the prescribed secrecy was tantamount to revealing the reason why they were seeking therapy. Besides, he added, Dea was fine now, so that he preferred to wait and see. He called some time later to let us know that Dea had found a job and was very happy in her work.

The family's second call for help came four years later, essentially in the form of a dramatic account of Dea's second crisis. This had been in full swing for several months before their call, but the family had wanted to wait, in the hope that medication would take care of the problem. The crisis had meanwhile blossomed out into gross manic conduct. In a very short time, Dea had managed to squander huge sums of money on clothes, furs and jewelry. The trouble was further compounded by a delirious notion that her mother wanted to poison her: Dea refused to eat anything at home.

During the second session, with the whole nuclear family attending, the therapist centered her inquiry mainly on events leading up to this second outbreak. A very significant fact came to light when the mother spoke up: The family, who had been living in rather cramped quarters, had been offered the chance to buy a small apartment adjoining theirs. Quite a large sum of money was needed for this, and Dea's father suggested buying the extra space on a mortgage; with Dea's salary as guarantee. Dea's mother was very emphatic about how strongly the girl had reacted to this suggestion: She had not only flatly refused but it upset her terribly, although she never mentioned the matter again. Dea's mother was quite positive that this incident had brought on the girl's relapse. Dea simply had not been herself ever since. A few days later, the girl took all her savings out of the bank and in a couple of weeks spent all her money, 14 million lire, on worthless, frivolous things. From then on, for almost a year, she had failed to recover, despite psychiatric treatment.

When the mother volunteered this information, the father looked absolutely thunderstruck. He said it was the first time anyone had ever linked Dea's crisis to his suggestion about the mortgage. The therapist, meanwhile, felt that something akin to an exploding mine had opened a rift through which she could see into the "dark pit." This new opening led into territory she would have to explore with great tact and very sympathetically. Why did it happen to be the father who had the idea of a mortgage guaranteed by Dea's salary? Did he realize that this would mean signing away the future of a 22-year-old woman? What did Dea's love life look like at the time? Was she going out with a boy? Who was it who had most yearned to move into that extra living space, Mom or Dad? And why did Mom, who had linked her husband's proposal to Dea's predicament, fail to mention this to her husband, so that he was now hearing about it for the first time here in this session? And so on we went, picking up one clue after another, with one answer leading to the next question in a painstaking journey back through the maze.

Professional secrecy prevents us from supplying some details, but what we have reported should be sufficient to show our colleagues what we mean when we speak of using our model as a stencil and matching it to a specific set of variables, to see how it fits the case. The general model we have devised is merely a compass to guide us through the subtle, idiosyncratic complexity of each separate family. And yet, the model is invaluable. By pointing to a hypothesis, it will often give us the stamina and confidence to carry on in the face of unbelievably stubborn reticence.

We are reminded of our desperate attempt to save Albina. The daughter of working-class parents, this chronic anorectic was carried to our center on a stretcher in a terminal condition. What impressed the team particularly on the telephone chart was an outline of the symptom's history. It had begun very violently, when Albina was 14, and had then settled into a less acute form. Her body weight had stabilized somewhere in the region of 36 kilos (about 79 pounds)—since she was 1.50 meters tall (4'11"), this was compatible with a normal life. However, during the months prior to the session she experienced a disastrous loss of weight which was not arrested by a stay in hospital.

Albina arrived at our center weighing 25 kilos (55 pounds). She was unable to stand and her voice could barely be heard. Her two parents, who came with her, were pathetic zombies, utterly impassive and expressionless. It turned out that Albina herself had asked to come here and her parents, reluctantly, had condescended to please her. After we had read the telephone chart, the therapist immediately focused on the events preceding the sharp drop in weight. She at once came up against such a formidable wall of reticence that she decided to skip any beating about the bush and told them frankly what she was looking for: "After years of experience with girls like you, Albina, I now know for sure that if a girl decides to clench her teeth and not swallow anything, this happens because she has suffered very deeply and is very, very angry. This suffering has been inflicted on her in her own home, and it is her own family she is angry at. . . . Something has happened that is 'the last straw,' something she simply can't stomach."

It would take a film to convey the thunderstruck silence that followed this statement and, immediately afterwards, the furtive glances and hurried, mumbled escapes into trivial digressions. The therapist was not to be sidetracked and urged Albina to recount the events that had preceded her breakdown. It turned out that an uncle on her father's side had been killed in a road accident. Her father had suffered a severe blow and mourned his brother deeply. The dead man's wife and two daughters had been left almost destitute. Albina's father was full of praise for the elder of these cousins, who left school after her father's death and found a modest, very tiring job.

What did all this have to do with Albina's decision to go on a hunger strike? The therapist worked tirelessly along first one track and then another, like a mouse in a labyrinth. What were the father's ties to his sister-in-law? Could there be jealous feelings between Albina and her cousin? Might Albina's father have more regard for his niece than for his daughter? At last the mother, who had been sitting motionless with her eyes riveted to the floor, spoke up: "There's something you ought to know, doctor. Albina has kept alive all these years because of the restaurant. She won't eat a thing at home, but in the evening my husband would give her money for a meal at a nearby trattoria. She would eat everything they served her there, and thus managed to feed herself. Well, shortly after her uncle died Albina went to her father one evening as usual, to ask him for money for her meal out. He gave it to her, but he said: 'How can you possibly want to go off to a restaurant when your uncle has been killed!' From that day on Albina has stopped eating at the restaurant or anywhere else, and that explains the state she's in."

Once again, a mine had blasted a crack in the wall of silence, affording the therapist a passage into the "dark pit." She jumped at the chance and stumbled on a long history of tribulations and errors. Albina's father, who had lost both his parents at an early age, was raised by his older sister, who had been a mother to him. He was already greying at the temples when he got a fellow office worker his own age pregnant and married her "out of decency." He took her to live with him in his sister–mother's house, whereupon a bitter, nonstop duel between the two women got underway, which saw Albina's father always siding with "his" family. His deep sorrow over his brother's death was a token of this allegiance, as was his wish to use the money Albina was so inconsiderately spending by eating out to help his nieces, who were facing such grim prospects. So, this was "the last straw" Albina had not been able to bear—and, here again, chronicling the symptom's evolution provided the indispensable clue for unraveling the family game.

THE PROBLEM OF RETICENCE

"Reticence" means avoiding saying all one knows, or feels; in short, it means keeping something concealed.

During our "paradoxical" stage, the therapist was deliberately reticent while effecting the circular inquiry preceding the intervention, intent as he was on not letting his expert point of view show through (Viaro & Leonardi, 1986). At the moment of the closing paradoxical intervention the therapist would actually resort to outright deception: He pretended to abandon his reticence and voiced what seemed a diagnostic opinion, when in actual fact he was not saying what he really thought. In other words, he did not actually believe the patient was sacrificing himself for others but was using this functionalist interpretation in a strategically provoking manner. We were able to verify that the paradoxical therapist's duplicity can be dangerous, especially in the case of lengthy therapies: The clients, albeit confusedly, will smell a rat and become suspicious and distrustful of the whole idea of therapy: "What's he up to this time, I wonder," they'll ask themselves, always on the lookout for hidden intentions in the therapist's every word and deed. The relationship will become gravely warped and founder in a farrago of reciprocal hoodwinking, with ominous consequences. The phenomenon is analogous (yet with more severe implications) to that engendered in a number of families who, when *Paradox and Counterparadox* was first published, turned up for their sessions having read our book (Selvini Palazzoli & Prata, 1980).

At present, our research technique rejects all concealment and duplicity: We inform the family at length about anything we have understood, even when all we have to go on are some intuitive notions stemming from the "guesswork" we do by comparing their case to that of similar families.

Right at the start of the first session, the therapist will announce his plan: "The first thing I want to do is explain how we work. We will try to find out what has gone amiss in the relationships between people in your family, as we are convinced that the patient's personal predicament is directly linked to his rapport with his family, and especially to the marital problems of his parents. All this I cannot do without your help." With this statement, the therapist tackles head-on the fundamental problem of the family's reticence or duplicity. If any member of a family finds it difficult, or even impossible, to speak out, the reasons for this must be sought on at least three contextual levels, to wit: (1) one or more members of the family may not be sufficiently motivated for therapy; (2) the ongoing family game is of a covert nature — reticence is almost never aimed directly at the therapist, and if family members don't speak up, it is because this is incompatible with the rules of their particular game,[7] which require everyone to keep his cards face down, hidden from the other players; (3) individual members may be resorting to vital self-defensive measures by negating reality, or by self-deception. Reticence, then, is often due to real, factual confusion or to an incapacity to significantly link real events, behaviors, and relationships to one another.

The therapist abandons his own reticence in order to:

1. Encourage the family to collaborate, by offering them an open, empathic rapport.
2. Clear the decks of some of the more conspicuous aspects of reticence: By attempting to grasp intuitively some of the key points of the family's game and render them explicit, the therapist takes upon himself the responsibility of being the first to turn up his cards. When this happens, many of those present will feel free either to bear out the therapist's statements or to react to them with objections they otherwise would never have dared to voice.
3. Induce more realistic personal attitudes, by pointing out the need individual members have felt to defend themselves and justifying such defensive attitudes on the basis of their personal life script.

CHOOSING THE RIGHT TIME
FOR INTERVENING:
HOW MUCH TO SAY AND WHEN TO SAY IT

Choosing the appropriate time for presenting our most comprehensive and incisive "opening" is of the utmost importance, as is the choice of how to word its contents. There was a time when we were inclined, especially when we felt the family was poorly motivated, to put before them a hypothesis based on our six-stage model in a very early phase of therapy, even during the first session. In such cases, our diagnosis of the symptom's etiology would inevitably be rather unspecific, since we had little definite information to go on, aside from the data on the telephone chart and a few opening transactions. This meant that we risked making highly dramatic statements and then being forced to back down and substantially disavow our interpretation when the family's evidence to the contrary proved convincing. So, what we had hoped to gain in emotional intensity by making the family more amenable to producing information would cost us our

---

[7]Lack of proper motivation of one or more members and a covert game are usually closely linked, as will be seen in Chapter XVIII.

credibility when we were obliged to bow to the evidence and reconsider our previous statement.

Still another factor argues against a strategy based on making interventions too early in the process: They will deprive some of the participants of the opportunity to express all they consider relevant, so that they will not feel they have had their say *before* the team comes up with an expert diagnosis.

However, we have also learned that procrastinating as a strategy often simply means a waste of time, in that it permits the family's closure and reticence to crystallize. If the atmosphere in the session is allowed to stagnate and grow cold and listless, we will fail to call forth the strong emotional response we feel is vital if we hope to fascinate and engage the family. Only if these efforts are successful can we elicit reactions that will enlighten us and allow the family to experience something out of the ordinary and therefore potentially therapeutic.

It is difficult to strike a proper balance in choosing the right moment for an intervention without forfeiting the necessary emotional tension. It is mainly a matter of discarding ready-made strategies in favor of an adjustable, well-aimed effort to get team and family on the same wavelength. Above all, the team members need to gauge as accurately as they can just how far they can "bet" on their own experience and models when making the family game, or at any rate some crucial aspects of it, explicit. One also needs to carefully evaluate the proper moment for this "opening," which implies realizing in time when an inquiry is no longer yielding significant information.

WE STOP CONTESTING THE FAMILY

During these last few years, our research has often risked becoming confined by a self-imposed, rigid manner of conducting the session. This was due to our eagerness to verify the aptness of our model of the psychotic process at all costs. Our ambition to find confirmation of our six-stage model would sometimes make us resort to a certain amount of verbal impetuosity. We would lock horns with the family in order to prove to the patient (and to ourselves) how "true" our models were. The danger of such an attitude is that it will curb the family's objections "a priori," leading us to view them negatively as attempts at sabotage or as outright lies. Instead, immediate reactions to our "revelations," as well as later reactions to therapy as a whole, should always be considered the experimental terrain on which our general hypotheses can be made more specific and be more finely tuned.

In due time, we found that it was a mistake to have thought of our model as a dogma, a "truth" that required confirmation in each single case. What it is, actually, is a general, loose schema to be fitted over a case in order to observe recognizable patterns. Not only that: We hope eventually to be able to proceed in our research towards specifying the various sub-types of psychotic processes. This goal has led us, in the case of anorexia, to pinpoint the distinction between types A and B, as we have reported in Chapter X. This was a major breakthrough in the direction of identifying more specifically the various possible subtypes of anorectic process that can affect a family.

The general model of psychosis in the family should, therefore, be viewed as an initial theoretical schema that needs to be tested and refined by matching it to the separate realities of anorexia, infantile psychosis, schizophrenia, etc. For example, the first stage of our model, involving the couple stalemate, was given a somewhat stereotyped interpretation in our first article on the subject (Selvini Palazzoli, 1986), as though all couples were alike. Today we see very clearly that there are many types of couple stalemates, and also that one and the same stalemate can vary over time.

Our objective today is to find the link that exists between the specific type of stalemate with which we are dealing and the other five stages in our model, in just the same way as there is a link between the type of stalemate and the type of symptom the patient develops. A researcher must avoid the temptation to impose his personal prejudices on the family if he is to acquire the flexibility that will bring with it therapeutically significant results (it is the therapist who adapts to the family, not the other way round), as well as a relevant gain in knowledge (i.e., progress in refining the system of "road signs" that guide our hypothesizing).

So our strategy, at present, entails renouncing the *confrontational attitude* we often assumed in the past. The antagonistic spirit that characterized the paradoxical phase was caused by our strategy of "hiding out" (reticence) until we were ready to drop our bombshell and startle the family into changing. Lately we have realized that we were slaves to this spirit of confrontation when we insisted on carrying out a verification of our general model of psychotic games, and today we are concentrating all our efforts on acquiring an open cognitive and therapeutic spirit, based on genuine collaboration.

THE THERAPEUTIC PROCESS

We will now draw a general outline of the therapeutic process. Therapy begins with the crisis we provoke by revealing the game (during the first two or three sessions), proceeds at the prescriptive level, and at the end, allows the therapist to revert to the game with more significant elements in hand concerning (1) factual data about the couple's stalemate, obtained from observing the way the parents have (or have not) carried out our prescriptions and, in a later session, from the therapist's getting the parents to "open up" and reveal their secret moves; and (2) factual data on the way the child has become involved in the parents' game — this derives from the way the therapist has felt he has been triangulated into the couple's stalemate, a feeling that allows him to understand what happens to the patient.

A hazard one needs to avoid is that of no longer being able (once one has moved from the revealing to the prescribing phase) to revert to unmasking the game with more telling arguments than before. We have occasionally found ourselves back at the point where we needed to render the game explicit with nothing more effective to offer than a lame little lecture that substantially repeated what we had said in the first session. When one is forced to do this, it means that the parental couple has used the prescription to send the therapist on a wild-goose chase of some kind, such as, for example: (1) an almost ritualistic, uncritical use of the prescription (we ourselves tended in the past to overestimate the direct therapeutic effects of the invariant set of prescriptions), or (2) an equally uncritical belief that the alliance he sets up with the parental couple will overcome the patient's pathological power.

So, it is very important for the therapist to keep his sights trained on unmasking the game. Bringing the game to light is a process that passes through intermittent moments of insight and requires monitoring the collaboration between team and parents. The moment when the prescription is issued will, therefore, be the occasion for testing whether there have been changes in the game (for example, for verifying the couple's capacity to cooperate) and whether the stalemate has been broken and new forms of rapport can be induced. It is also a running test for gathering information on the game itself.

The therapeutic process, then, starts with the interventions aimed at unmasking the game and then tackles the family's reactions to this revelation, whereupon it uses the prescription to obtain concrete evidence of change.

FROM THE INVARIANT PRESCRIPTION
TO SPECIFIC PRESCRIPTIONS

In 1986, we introduced a very important modification into our therapeutic methodology: We gradually started to abandon the use of the invariant set of prescriptions. This can be easily explained: Six years of clinical work with the systematic use of the invariant set of prescriptions, thanks to the information it enabled us to obtain and classify, had made it possible for us to devise a general model of psychotic processes in the family.

At a later stage, this model, which guided our hypotheses about a family's ongoing game, was matched to the specific set of variables we found for that family. This way of working is proving so useful at present in reconstruing a specific family's game that it actually allows us, if we consider it useful, to implement "ad hoc" prescriptions that can be as specific as the game itself. We therefore believe we are on our way to gradually foregoing the invariant set of prescriptions altogether. In certain therapies, especially those with families of anorectics in an early stage, clarifying the problem and making it explicit during the first few sessions and then dismissing the patient is at times sufficient to bring about the symptom's arrest.

We still use the prescription occasionally today, but we no longer do so according to the standard ritual procedure we held to during the six years in which we treated and tested prescriptively. For instance, as we shall see in the next chapter, dismissing the patient and his siblings is no longer the cryptic move it used to be. If, at the end of the consultation sessions, we decide to enter into a therapeutic alliance with the parental couple, we will use the secrecy prescription as a sort of acid test for the appropriateness of this decision; at the same time, the secrecy prescription will act as an effective therapeutic move.

As for the prescription involving "disappearances," we implement it only with a small number of the cases we see at present. When we do prescribe disappearances, we do not always follow the invariant routine but adapt the task assigned to the parents to the special situation and link it explicitly to our hypothesis about the ongoing game. Also, when an "ad hoc" prescription is issued simultaneously to both parents, the text of the prescription will resemble the one we used in the days of "invariant" prescribing, in that it will foster a physiological "underpropping" of the parental couple. Even the decision to summon only the mother of an autistic child, leaving his passive and sabotaging father at home, is a move aimed at the couple: It should help convince the wife that her husband has no choice but to act like a dead weight for as long as she keeps on flaunting her stultifying hyper-efficiency.[8]

We have reported on this evolution in our methods because we hope — quite unreasonably, but most fervently — that some kindly disposed celestial spirit will now suggest to us a new strategy, affording further knowledge.

---

[8]In the case of an only parent, or when the parental couple is undependable or divorced, the prescription will be adjusted case by case and will quite definitely require a much more difficult and complex procedure.

CHAPTER XV

How to Dismiss the Patient from Further Sessions

THE PATIENT'S "INVOLVEMENT" IS REVEALED AND DISCOURAGED

A T THE END OF THE second or third session, when with everyone's help we feel we have succeeded in making clear various key phases of the process of family interaction leading to a child's psychotic behavior, we enact a crucial intervention, with a twofold purpose: (1) to reveal and discourage the patient's interference in his parents' problems, and (2) to create a therapeutic alliance with the parents.

As explained in the first part of this book, when families seek help for a child or an adolescent, we find it more effective to enlist the collaboration of only the parents. For this reason we dismiss the patient and any siblings as soon as possible. In the past, this dismissal was done in a cryptic fashion. Nowadays, before we dismiss the patient, we make an important move: We clearly reveal his active part in the dysfunctional game of the family and center our remarks on the fact that he is siding with one of the parents.

Years of experience with so-called paradoxical interventions have taught us that we must restore to the patient the dignity of carrying out voluntary, comprehensible actions. We never consider the patient's behavior compulsory, uncontrollable, or incomprehensible. We always assume individual competence, which implies the existence of a behavior obeying to precise motivations and intents.

As described in the first chapter, some of our paradoxical interventions caused things to change when we succeeded in pinpointing key links in the family game. The patient would then be the one most affected when the exalting of his symptom as a "sacrifice" for the good of the family was properly reinterpreted by a sarcastic provocation. However, the danger of being too generic and vague, and therefore ineffective (due to our lack of a guiding model), was disturbingly high.

What is our present purpose? It is to clarify in detail how and to what extent the patient *has become involved in his parents' relational problems as a couple*; how *he (she) has thought up his own idiosyncratic interpretation* of these problems, and how, in line with this interpretation, *he (she) has sided with the parent he considers the underdog*, identifying with him/her; also, how *he (she) subsequently gets drawn into playing an active part in the game*, both in order to champion the underdog and to induce him to join forces and challenge the parent (considered) to be abusing his/her power; finally, how *such active involvement turns into a total failure*—useless to the couple's relationship and disastrous for the child himself.

When, using all necessary tact, the therapist gives the patient an "explanation" of this kind, some surprising, often very moving reactions can ensue. Take the conclusion of the third session with Miriam's family. Miriam is 21, an only child whose chronic anorexia is complicated by delusional ideas and exhausting, obsessive rituals. At the start of the session, the father (a typical yes-man who kowtows to a domineering wife) has described to the therapist how worn out his poor wife was from constantly having to cater to Miriam's every whim. Having received this information, the therapist, following our model, works gently and at length to bring into the open a possible understanding between Miriam and her ostensibly feeble father. Nothing emerges. Everyone, including the girl herself, insists that Miriam is totally on the side of her mother.

Towards the end of the session, having decided to start dismissing Miriam anyway, the therapist addresses her affectionately and says: "Look, Miriam, from what your father told me when we started talking today, it seems that after so many years of hard work you really have finally persuaded your mother to submit to you. Now, tell me, do you think your father, at this point, is also beginning to make some progress in this direction? I mean, is he learning the lesson you are trying to teach him, does he sometimes assert himself with your mother the way you do? Have you managed to get your father to change a bit?"

"Doctor," comes Miriam's immediate, unexpected reply, "I wouldn't exactly say that Dad's changed, but Mom has begun to ask his advice. When there's a problem, she'll say, 'Let's wait till tonight and ask Dad'—and she never used to do that before!" After this, it was easy for the therapist to show Miriam what poor results she had achieved after wasting seven long years of her life!

During the first sessions we try mainly to show up how one parent has unwittingly been "using" the child in the long-standing battle with the other. At the moment of dismissal, however, it is essential to make quite clear how the child has become actively involved in the game by behaving in a "stupid" fashion. Our choice of the word "stupid" is not casual. It stems from observing a widespread phenomenon peculiar to our culture. Many people do not seem to mind being labeled nasty or even crazy nowadays — in fact, these traits may at times even appear quite desirable when they are construed as meaning "tough" or "bizarre." No one, however, accepts being referred to as "stupid" without getting very angry, even though only a part of his behavior is being thus criticized.

Now, what we are out to obtain is precisely such an angry reaction, which is what can trigger change. Nevertheless, for therapy to be effective, the team must have grasped in detail the specific reasons behind the patient's connivance with one of the parents. A generic provocation would only be offensive, not helpful. At times we considered it suitable to stress how naïve the patient was in imagining herself to be the most important person in the life of a parent who, in real fact, was completely absorbed in the problems of the marital rapport. Sometimes we have pointed out very emphatically the patient's fond illusion that she can alter her parents' relationship by tormenting the one she considers the "winner," not realizing that her behavior has failed to make the parent she considers submissive any more courageous and enterprising than he was!

However, we are quite often unable to understand the true essence of the patient's collusion in the game, and therefore have to give her a rather vague "talking-to" before we dismiss her. Still, until we acquire greater skill, we feel that such a prelude to dismissal is nonetheless indispensable if we are to establish our therapeutic alliance. We shall now try to explain this.

THE RISK OF INDICTING THE PARENTS

Using our model — and, above all, clinging to our basic conviction that it is mandatory to break down the barrier around the couple's stalemate — entails a risk, in the first sessions, of heaping too much blame on the parents. To counteract this, we make quite clear from the start that, in order to help, one must first understand. Our tone of voice and choice of words tend to make our involvement dramatic and emotional, rather than incriminating. This, however, is not enough. Especially in the case of a patient who exercises strong pathological power over his parents, it is very dangerous not to hold the patient himself responsible for having "butted in" on the game. In fact, if the first sessions were to point out only the misdeeds of the parents, the patient, who already feels aggressive towards them, will very likely use this evidence to increase his attacks and strengthen the dictatorship he is already practicing. Another less obvious but equally insidious danger is that of indicting the parents so heavily as to plunge the patient into sterile hopelessness and despair: "With such disastrous parents," he will be inclined to feel, "whatever can I hope to do with my life?" This would bring on a provocative and guilt-arousing passivity, which may perhaps engender a call for help, but for the sole purpose of proving that "nothing is of any use."

The risk of kindling provocative explosions in the patient was a very close one during the second session with the family of Marcello, a 15-year-old encopretic exhibiting serious manic behavior. This behavior worsened in the period between the family's first and second session: In addition to his encopresis, Marcello managed to have two accidents on his scooter and had smoked pot at home in front of a horrified maid. The team pondered the possibility of Marcello's behavior being his reaction to our inquiry into his parents' conflict. We decided to dismiss the boy at the end of that session and agreed that the manner of his dismissal should underline the active, voluntary aspects of his symptomatic behavior (soiling his underwear and bath towels with his feces instead. of using toilet paper and sanitary napkins) as a "stupid" attempt to punish his mother in the name of a father he considers weak, thereby forfeiting his own social identity—a pretty high price to pay!

In the second part of the session, therapy began with a question addressed to the patient: "Marcello, why is it you are so determined to punish your parents for what you see as their shortcomings? You seem to have lost sight of yourself completely. *You* are the one who's all messed up. I could understand such behavior if you were three years old—punishing your mother by giving her piles of things full of shit to wash every night because she's ashamed to let the maid see them—but the fact is, you are the one who's really being punished. And now there's this business of the hash, too, and the pranks at school, and showing off on your scooter—all this just to punish your father for his inertia! This is ruining you, you're like a little baby who thinks there are only two people in the world, Mom and Dad. One really wouldn't think you were all that stupid, to look at you."

Marcello turned red and mumbled something in his own defense in answer to the therapist's pressing question: "What about the girls? Don't girls have noses? How can you possibly ask a girl to ride on the back of your scooter when you smell of shit the way you do? Oh, you'll never find a girl friend, and if you don't snap out of this soon, your love life will be an unholy mess. You, of all people! You who think you can show Dad how to bring Mom to her knees! Marcello, you're really dumb!"

This intervention may help the reader understand our twofold purpose: The first concerns the patient. An intervention of this kind is used by the therapist in order to give the patient back his psychic integrity while showing him proper respect. He is defined as stupid by what he *does*, not by what he *is*. The therapist speaks in a frank, intense, confidential tone, but with the authority and severity one usually shows towards an adolescent for whom, despite everything, one still has respect. The family issues touched upon are specific and serious, and the closing remark about his chances of becoming a man who can shoot off on his scooter with the girls, free from the snares of his childish world, holds out a strong invitation.

The second, indirect purpose concerns the parents. Declaring that the patient is behaving like a fool and a nosy-parker not only aims to give the patient back his sense of responsibility, but is also a fundamental move to counterbalance the parents' feelings. It is not at all fair for the parents to feel they are the only ones on trial. In order for them to be properly motivated to self-criticism, they must feel that the therapist understands their plight. They also need to be certain enough of the therapist's competence and neutrality to accept such a painful reconstruction of their past history. For this, even dismissing the patient in the way referred to above does not seem to suffice; the therapist must also manage to mirror back to the family nucleus a "reparatory" image of the parents, an image that shows them as two people who have indeed made mistakes, but not knowingly and who, moreover, have been through an excruciating ordeal.

In the case of the encopretic adolescent, the first part of the second session concentrating on this second objective saw some very touching moments. The father's loneliness in his family of origin emerged, together with his present crying need for affection within his new family unit. Sent away to boarding school at a far too early age, this man had suffered terribly. He had courted and married a woman with less schooling than his own, and less well off. In this way he intended to make sure he would have her all to himself, as a devoted homemaker. His spouse, however, escaped from her assigned role as a housewife by getting an office job, thus slipping out of her possessive husband's clutches. He made life unbearable for her with his constant vigilance and humiliated her by flaunting his superior education. So the mother, too, was reframed by us as standing in need of self-defense, in order that the offspring should see how the couple's stalemate was a trap into which each spouse, by trying to safeguard himself or herself, had caused both himself and his partner to fall.

CONTRAINDICATIONS FOR
DISMISSING THE PATIENT

A good rule is judged on the merits of its exceptions. With some families the team may decide to break a rule—once the third session has been held—and *not* dismiss the patient. Let's see why this is done.

As we all know, work in the first sessions centers mainly on investigating such issues as the all-important evaluation of everyone's willingness and motivation with regard to therapy. We can cite the case of the family of a widowed mother and her two children (see Chapter V, p. 86). The patient, Lia, aged 25, suffered from chronic anorexia. During the first sessions, despite certain aspects inherent to the syndrome, we noticed that the patient possessed resources that might eventually allow her to become independent from her family and achieve economic and social stability. The girl also seemed genuinely desirous of getting out of her wretched condition. We concluded that she would be made to feel too much of a "baby" if we dismissed her and her brother and continued therapy with only her mother. We therefore decided to invite her to an individual meeting. During this, the therapist concentrated on firmly proving to Lia that her behavior was nothing more than childish fury at not having been chosen as her mother's special confidante in place of her aunt, and that her stupid determination to make her mother pay for this by stubbornly staying cloistered away at home in order to get back at her was making life miserable for everyone. Our intervention caused an immediate change in Lia.

When an intervention of this kind fails to produce an effect, one may proceed with a lengthier, individual course of therapy (as indicated in Selvini Palazzoli & Viaro, 1988). Such a departure from our rule is not uncommon in cases of chronic patients over 20 who show the necessary requisites. In other words, the more adult the patient is and the more personal and social resources he possesses, the more his exclusion from therapy will make him feel he is being considered a child. Individual treatment is actually mandatory in cases where the parents do not seem at all motivated to therapy. There has been only one case, up to now, where after a few family sessions we offered individual therapy to a very young patient: She was an exceptionally gifted bulimic anorectic whose parents were not married, did not live together and exhibited rather unusual behavior patterns. Neither of them seemed a reliable subject for therapeutic work, and we opted for individual therapy, which fortunately was successful.

HOSTILE AND REJECTING FAMILIES

Finally, we should like to stress another point we consider very important. Inducing a crisis in the patient must always be done *after* the parents have been made to face their responsibility.

In private family therapy centers, the problem rarely arises—parents who request family therapy are not rejecting their child and are prepared, at least partially, to admit they have made some mistakes. In different situations, particularly in a public institution where family therapy is not directly requested, parents are often hostile and even rejecting towards the psychotic child (although anorexia nervosa is always an exception, in that even among the less privileged it will tend to induce strong guilt feelings in the parents).

In such cases, the first step in the therapeutic process will be to show the parents how, unwittingly, certain difficulties in their marital rapport and with their respective families of origin have unfortunately harmed their child's development. Only if we manage to convey this can we approach the patient in the way we have described above. If we fail in this intent, an intervention based on dismissal, undertaken in the presence of impervious parents who do not see themselves as part of the problem but merely as victims of the patient's misdeeds, will have a disastrous twofold effect: It will strengthen the parents' rejection and fuel the child's rage.

CHAPTER XVI

Constructing Synchronic Models

INCORPORATING THE THERAPIST INTO
THE COUPLE'S STALEMATE

A DIACHRONIC MODEL IS A loosely constructed, general pattern that gradually becomes more detailed as we fit into it the chronological events of a family game's evolution. Over the years, such a model has greatly improved both our hypothesizing and our technique of conducting the session. Synchronic models, on the other hand, are instant, almost photographic projections centering on the immediate, ongoing phase of the family game and its development here and now. Such models were conceptualized at a later stage in our clinical work. Significantly, the need for such synchronic models arose when we came up against certain particularly perplexing situations in the course of therapy, in which an impending danger of failure made it imperative for us to understand what was going on without the slightest delay.

As is well-known, a gain in therapeutics carries with it a gain in knowledge. The essential feature of a synchronic model is that it must include the therapist. The notion of such a model originally evolved around the need to manage deadlocks encountered in the course of treatment. It was intended to provide the therapist with a clear picture of how the family's relationship with him was developing right there, during the session. With this understanding to guide him, the therapist would be able to infer the interactive phenomena responsible for the impasse and subsequently find a way to overcome the difficulty.

Some examples ought to help make the issue clear. Our first example was also the team's first venture into the construction of synchronic models. The upper-middle-class family it concerns has already been introduced to the reader in the section on "Imbroglio in schizophrenia" in Chapter V. The phase of therapy we are focusing on now is an advanced one, and the team has for some time been seeing only the parental couple. The couple has carried out the invariant set of prescriptions, and has been bravely battling, with uneven results, their son Filippo's pathological power. In what has up to now fortunately been the only case of its kind in our experience, Filippo's move in this battle was spectacular and frightening. His parents had made a desperate attempt to counter Filippo's hold over them by resolving to close down the family abode, a large villa, and move to their little country house: Filippo was to be settled in a service flat, on his own.

Filippo got wind of this and retaliated, while his parents were out, by starting a fire in the kitchen of the villa. The fire spread to other parts of the house, causing damage that ran into millions of lira. The exploit landed Filippo in the psychiatric ward of the local hospital for some time. He emerged a changed man. At this point he has been living on his own in the service flat and working fairly regularly in his father's business. He pays for all his expenses out of his salary and has found himself a nice girlfriend, who is extremely attached to him.

When the parents arrive for this crucial session, repairs on the villa are almost complete. It is late autumn, and the couple needs to come to a decision: Are they to go back to living at the villa or should they sell the place? It is important to note that the therapist had already expressed her opinion on the matter a few months earlier: If they were *really* determined to stop acting like solicitous nursemaids to Filippo and take up their role as co-therapists, the villa would have to be sold. Otherwise, once they moved back in, how could they possibly turn down their son's bid to go back to living with them?

News about Filippo isn't as good this session as it had been the last time the parents came. They report that he has started to play truant, is idling on the job, and has turned gloomy and taciturn. Here is an outline of the transactions that took place in the session, from which the reader will see how each parent followed a strictly repetitive pattern of conduct.

Father: Every time he mentions Filippo's name—and he does so very frequently—his whole face lights up and his intense, tender feelings toward his son become very obvious. He speaks with great warmth also of Filippo's girlfriend and of her family, who seem to be giving the boy the affectionate family atmosphere he so badly needs. This enthusiastic, approving attitude persists even when he refers to Filippo's fire-setting and to the huge amount of money required to refurbish the villa (not exactly subjects that normally inspire terms of endearment). We are quite intrigued by this attitude, especially in view of the fact that the father had formerly always treated his son patronizingly. How are we to account for this newfound love?

Mother: Every time her husband, who is sitting next to her, remarks on something the therapist is saying, she puts her hand on his thigh and squeezes it gently. She repeats this gesture eight times, with no noticeable effect on her husband, who neither refrains from voicing his opinion nor shows any sign of impatience at being silently censured.

The team members interrupt the proceedings in order to discuss what seems to be happening. They agree that an explanation for the therapeutic impasse must be sought in the peculiar repetitive behavior both parents are enacting. The bone of contention around which the couple's squabbling is centered right now is, what to do with the newly reconditioned villa. Our guess is that the wife doesn't want to go back to live there, although she is very careful not to come out and say so; instead, she backs her claim with the overruling prestige and authority of the therapist. Her husband is the one who wants to move back in, and he, too, is very careful not to come out and say so—he bases his claim on the unquestionable moral certainty of his (lately rekindled) love for his ailing son, to whom he wishes to restore a home and a family. The combined effect of these two strategies points to a stalemate game: The more enamored you are of the therapist (and agree with her that the house must be sold), the more enamored I am of Filippo (and determined to give him back a family and a home, even against his best interest). And, vice versa, the more enamored you are of Filippo (and wish to give him back a family and a home although this is not what is best for him), the more I will be enamored of the therapist (and endorse her opinion that we should sell the house, for Filippo's sake).

This juxtaposition of two strategic infatuations is a component that apparently often recurs in the couple stalemate. When a game of this sort is discovered in an advanced stage of therapy, as in this case, therapy is doomed to failure. Even if the team succeeds in seeing through the couple's maneuver and makes a concrete statement about the synchronic pattern of their game, the therapist will by this time be too deeply enmeshed in the game to be able to modify it. In the case we are examining, it was obvious that the team had failed to grasp and forestall in time the danger threatening the therapist. By advocating the idea of selling the villa and moving away from it as the most expedient way of getting Filippo detached and gradually nudging him towards independence, she had unwittingly taken sides with the wife. The latter was now using the therapist's authority as a weapon against her husband and he was using his son to counter it.

Once we had learned this bitter lesson we realized we needed synchronic models for the interactions made during sessions, in order to be able to use them *at a very early stage* of therapeutic treatment. It became clear to us that such patterns, which would have to include the therapist, would allow us (a) to gauge each family member's attitude towards therapy and the therapist, (b) to infer each player's position with regard to the game under way, and (c) to spot any dangerous strategies and nip them in the bud.

AN INTERVENTION TO SAFEGUARD
THE THERAPIST

Let us see if we can clarify, albeit very summarily, how we succeeded in heading the course of a therapy in the right direction precisely because we were able, in the second session, to identify and neutralize a major threat to the therapist.

This was a three-member family with a lower-class background. The couple's only child, Rina, age 18, had been diagnosed in her childhood as a case of "autistic disorder." The family came to us for help because Rina's care and upkeep were proving too onerous for her mother, who was getting only very perfunctory help at home from the local district psychiatric service.

First session: The behavior patterns are essentially the following: *Father* (Vico): Very suspicious, and on the defensive. He interprets everything the therapist says as criticism and retorts ill-naturedly. *Mother* (Gemma): Conveys to the therapist that she is mainly the victim of an inefficient psychiatric service. *Daughter* (Rina): Her attitude is catatonic—every minute or two, she spits on her hand, then wipes it dry on her skirt. She spends most of the session with her head on her father's knees. She responds incoherently to the therapist's questions.

The therapist directs her inquiry towards the present situation and the chronicle of events leading up to it. It turns out that Gemma had very strong ties to her own family in the past, especially to her mother. These ties tended to exclude Vico. The therapist expresses sympathy for all of them, including Vico and Rina.

Second session: The behavior patterns are now the following: *Father:* Still wary, but no longer hostile. *Mother:* Very excited, almost breathless. *Daughter:* She no longer acts catatonic, and no longer clings to her father. She resorts to her provocative stereotype of spitting and wiping only twice. During the second part of the session, she starts walking briskly up and down the room. She is attentive and answers the therapist's questions quite rationally.

During this second session, the therapist concentrates on Gemma's rapport with the practitioners (all of them women—a psychologist and several less qualified operators) who provide her with home care. A repetitive pattern is observed: Gemma tends to have very deep, meaningful relationships with these women, and this has a negative effect on Rina's condition.

When the therapist leaves the room for a moment, one of the supervisors notices the following: Gemma exclaims eagerly: "What a fantastic woman!" This produces no visible reaction from Vico, who sits silently looking at his feet, while Rina goes on pacing the floor. The supervisor calls for an immediate team discussion on what he has noticed, and the interac-

tion is diagrammed as follows: Gemma has already set in motion the strategy she habitually resorts to in the couple's stalemate game — she is falling in
love with the therapist and scorning Vico (and, unwittingly, Rina as well).
Vico and Rina have begun to like the therapist and might be willing to
enter into a rapport with her, but Vico is wary and Rina is tense, possibly
because they resent Gemma's growing enthusiasm for the therapist.

Once she has caught on to what is happening and sees the risk she has
run, the therapist feels relieved and perfectly at ease. She is now determined to set things right. She goes back to the family and enacts an
admirable intervention. She addresses Vico and Rina, and in a folksy, ban-
tering tone admits that she's already got herself into a bit of a mess, just the
way the women from the district service had: She feels Gemma is falling
for her, and she is falling for Gemma. If this were to happen, she says very
emphatically, it would lead to a real disaster, as Rina and her Dad would be
forced to dislike her intensely, which would send any possibility of collaboration down the drain, for why should anyone want to collaborate with a
detestable therapist?

Turning serious, the therapist zooms in on events in the past. She explains how all the kind, well-meaning people who have come to help them
at home have unwittingly wrought great harm on the family. By responding
to Gemma's loving overtures, they turned her husband against her — how
was he to compete for her attention with such wonderfully kind, selfless
women? So Vico would grow hostile towards the practitioners as well,
because he felt left out and unappreciated. And Rina? The practitioners'
home calls would always be a great disappointment and source of anger for
her. She would feel betrayed by the very people who professed to be there
on account of her but then spent the whole time chatting warmly with her
mother.

Everyone present reacted to this intervention first with surprise and
then by joining in a chorus of consent. Gemma gave an embarrassed little
giggle, but nodded. Vico looked for all the world like someone who has
come into his own at last. As for Rina, not only did she understand perfectly what the therapist was talking about, but she also complied readily and
lucidly with the therapist's request to list the names of her mother's many
"girlfriends." In winding up the session, the therapist put herself back into
the picture by confirming that she was in danger of falling into the same
trap in which her colleagues from the district service were floundering, and
entreated Vico to help her steer clear of it. The intervention was a huge
success. The therapist had managed to enlist the husband's collaboration
without forfeiting that of the wife. Treatment proceeded towards what was
eventually a favorable outcome for the whole family.

Synchronic models that "freeze" a picture of the game as it is developing
in the session are useful on two counts: In the first place, they enable us to
detect the trap the stalemated couple is setting for the therapist, which the

latter can avoid only if he gets wind of it immediately. In the second place, they tell us that there is not an infinite variety of such games. Apparently, each spouse will be safeguarding his/her survival by (covertly) opposing the other. The therapist, too, will be enticed into an incompatible relationship with them, since the more one of the two accepts him, the more the other will refuse to do so. The effects of this incompatibility will effectively annul any therapeutic gain. One must keep the risks inherent in the couple stalemate well in mind; they are definitely repetitive, even though they may emerge in a variety of behavioral patterns. This enables one to intervene promptly in order to forestall the danger and place the therapist out of harm's way.

Not only that—a skillful intervention, at an early stage of therapy, may in itself be successful in breaking up the stalemate. Such an intervention, in fact, proves that the therapist has seen through the strategy one of the spouses is implementing against the other via an instrumental use of the therapist himself! This can be quite a breathtaking revelation and may conjure up a lot of strong feelings, certainly much stronger than those aroused by a learned, abstract explanation that fails to involve the therapist in the first person.

The idea of constructing these synchronic models came to us once we had resolved to adopt a zig-zag manner of thinking as part of our striving for complexity (see Chapter XX). We realized that we needed to learn to think in a shuttle-like pattern and build a lattice that would apply the diachronic model to a family "out there" and the synchronic model to the therapeutic system in the "here and now" comprising the family and the therapist as actors, plus the team as the conceptualizing agent that meditates on what is going on *while* it is going on. We will revert to all this in detail in the last chapter of this book.

CHAPTER XVII

The Parental Couple's Self-Therapy

THE PARENTS BECOME CO-THERAPISTS: FROM PATHOGENIC TO THERAPEUTIC RESPONSIBILITY

OUR REMARKS IN Chapter XVI about how the therapist becomes triangulated into the couple's stalemate usher in a crucial theoretical and practical subject, namely, whether the pathogenic parental couple can be "cured." Our current clinical outlook encourages us to try and change this grievous stumbling block into a springboard, i.e., to have the pathogenic couple transform into one that can "cure" their child and, in the process, "cure" themselves by modifying their relational pattern. We elaborated this concept after going through a number of phases in our work in which we experimented with several other solutions to the problem of adversely blaming the parents.

It is a well-known fact that prescribing psychotherapy for the whole family, in the case of a disturbed child or adolescent, will inevitably entail finding fault with the child's parents. Braulio Montalvo and Jay Haley, in a famous article published in 1973, stressed the difficulty, as well as the necessity, of not making the parents feel they were being indicted. The team that authored *Paradox and Counterparadox*, in its first experimental ventures into family therapy (from 1972 to 1977), tried to solve this ticklish problem in a number of ways, since 90% of our caseload at the time consisted—as indeed it does today—of families of severely disturbed children and adolescents.

THE PHASE OF POSITIVE CONNOTATION

The best-known of these attempted solutions was undoubtedly the tactic we called positive connotation, which implied not only abstaining from criticizing anyone in the family but also pointedly playing up everyone's commendable behavior, obviously including that of the child's mother and father. This tactic paved the way for the so-called paradoxical prescribing of the symptomatic behavior itself.

As we think back on it today, we note that the idea of positive connotation, originally designed as a means of guarding the therapist against both counterproductive clashes with the family and dropouts (see Chapter I), was a strategically flimsy device: Outright praise did not really camouflage an implicit indictment. We need only consider the "logical structure" of our paradoxes, which essentially consisted of reframing the situation by viewing the patient's symptom as sacrificial, designed to prevent the serious problems in his parents' marital rapport from coming to a head (i.e., not exactly connoting the latter's behavior as positive!).

What has failed to change, in these 20 years of research in family therapy, is our firm conviction that there is a link between a dysfunctioning family and the patient's symptom. Our current social structure still features the nuclear family as its fundamental unit, and the relational etiology of so-called mental illness must be sought for mainly by identifying a link between the specific type of disturbance that besets the couple's rapport and the child's symptomatic behavior. Such a basic hypothesis makes it altogether impossible not to involve the parents and assign responsibility to them: The problem is not whether this is to be done, but how.

THE PHASE IN WHICH PARENTS WERE IDENTIFIED AS PATIENTS

In the late seventies, before Mara Selvini Palazzoli's split with her former associates, the team experimented with a method that diverged from positive connotation with several families of anorectic patients. This method consisted of labeling the parents as patients in cases where four or five sessions with the whole nuclear family were not only failing to produce any noticeable results but were also bringing to the forefront a long-standing marital conflict, extremely distressing for everyone. In such cases the therapist would end one of these plenary sessions by dismissing the offspring "who had already done so much to help their parents" and promising to take over for them and do his best to free these parents from the painful situation in which they had unwittingly come to find themselves.

Now, what would you expect to find, after making such a statement, when the parents came for their next session? What you *do* find is a couple passively sitting there and signaling in every possible verbal and nonverbal way that the team's generous efforts are doomed to failure. These parents are telling us that they know all too well that their marital relationship is hopeless and nothing can be done about it. This type of attitude eventually led us to understand that we were facing a relentless logic here: These parents sensed that if their child were to shed his symptom and their conflict were to remain unchanged, the causal link between the couple's conflict and the symptom would stand disproved, so they preferred to act the part of the hopeless couple, past helping, and put the onus of "curing" their child back onto the therapist, who was getting paid to do this. The fact that we encountered such a phenomenon frequently, even in cases where the patient had actually shed the symptom, was a source of much perplexity for the team: had we really done our job properly?[1]

THE PHASE OF THE
INVARIANT PRESCRIPTIONS:
A BALANCING ACT BETWEEN
BLAMING THE PARENTS
AND RAISING THEIR SELF-ESTEEM

Our work with the invariant set of prescriptions enabled us to draw up a repertoire of strategies we could use to *counteract the indictment of the parents that our basic hypothesis about the onset of psychosis inevitably entailed.*[2] Parents are not first accused and then excluded, as in other therapeutic procedures, nor are they left stunned into apathy by the harshness of the accusations brought against them. Instead, they feel properly appreciated and can be enlisted in collaborating actively in a process designed to bring about change. In this sense, then, appointing the parents as co-therapists is an eventful move.

The two aspects, i.e., blaming the couple and raising their self-esteem, must be carefully weighed against one another for the duration of therapy.

In the first sessions, before the offspring are dismissed, the therapist will center his efforts on pointing out some prominent features of the family game, such as (1) the way the parents have obviously been "inveigled" (manipulated) into a game played by their family of origin, which has warped their personality. This is done in order to show understanding and sympathy for their plight and helps assuage their resentment both towards their offspring and towards each other. (2) The way some member(s) of the extended family has been instigating either one of the spouses or one of the offspring, producing rifts in the couple's rapport, or else has incited the patient against one of his parents. (3) The active role played by the patient

---

[1] A typical example of this can be found in "A Systemic Course in Family Therapy" (Selvini, 1988): see especially the seventh session (pp. 323–359).

[2] There are, of course, other approaches to the problem (such as a psycho-educational one with families of schizophrenics) that quite definitely do not imply any blaming whatsoever. Anderson, Hogarty, and Reiss (1980), for instance, acquit the parents on the reassuring grounds that schizophrenia is a biological disturbance and the parents' task, therefore, is merely to take good care of the patient and avoid any stressful factors that may bring on a relapse.

himself, who "stupidly" decides to interfere in his parents' affairs, with harmful consequences for them and for himself.

At a later moment, the countervailing aspects of blame and commendation will also be made apparent by the fact that only the parents will be summoned to family therapy sessions. This will in fact be interpreted not only as bestowing top priority on the couple's identity as such, but also as a move to point out who the "real" patients are. In this phase the therapist lays great stress on the value of the parents as co-therapists and on their alliance with him in fighting the patient's pathological power. He thus clearly conveys to them that carrying out the prescriptions and keeping a firm stance towards the child's prevaricating are essential if they wish to save him. At the same time the therapist will move swiftly and incisively to attack the parents when he discovers they are persevering in their stock pathogenic games, as in the case we describe in the following section.

THE COUPLE'S CO-THERAPY
FUNCTIONS AS SELF-THERAPY

An adage as old as the world itself has it that the crew of a ship, however much they may quarrel among themselves, will be quick to join forces if the ship is in danger of sinking. However, our casebooks on families with schizophrenic and psychotic offspring defy even this old truism. In the severe cases we see, and especially if chronicity has set in, the parents are hardly ever motivated to the same degree or equally desirous to extricate themselves from the tragic predicament that has befallen them. In the case of an anorectic patient, it is the rule for the mother to wish to carry on with the therapy at all costs, since *she* is the one who feels she has been hit the hardest by her daughter's symptoms. However, in cases of psychotic behavior, and especially in schizophrenia, we will face a couple stalemate in which each parent will take a different, usually opposite stance towards therapy. One of the most demanding tasks a family therapist then needs to undertake will be to bring all his skill and tactical acumen to bear on the situation in order to persuade both parties to collaborate and thereby break up the stalemate.

Here is a case in point, with a very moving outcome. Sergio, age 26, affected by paranoid schizophrenia, was the only son of fairly well-to-do parents. He had been repeatedly hospitalized and for a long time now had been considered a chronic case. His long career as a mental patient, in and out of expensive private institutions, and the long procession of psychiatrists, psychologists and psychotherapists who had been called in one after the other to counsel the parents, had not prevented the latter from becoming utterly enslaved by their son, who by now had got thoroughly out of hand and impossibly demanding.

It became clear at once, during the first two sessions, which Sergio also attended, that the boy was siding with his father and that 90% of his bullying was aimed at his mother. The latter, given her husband's pitying, indulgent attitude towards this poor, sick creature, not only felt quite powerless to rebel but also was covertly keeping up an escalation with her son by signaling "the more you mortify me, the more forbearing and meek I will be and the more eager to fulfill my duty by you."

The parents had reached this sorry stalemate as a result of a long, complicated history with roots in their own families, as is so often the case. Giulio, the husband, was the son of a widow who had reigned supreme over her own shop. He had married Wanda, a pretty, hardworking girl from a working-class background. Wanda had suffered unspeakably from the humiliations her mother-in-law inflicted on her during the first years of their marriage, which her husband did not dare to challenge. Then, patiently and tirelessly, Wanda succeeded in winning over this formidable woman, whom at last she nursed through her fatal illness.

After her mother-in-law's death, Wanda took over the shop: She found herself instated there as queen and her new status totally eclipsed that of her husband, who meanwhile had taken to drink. Sergio, as a child, had perceived his mother to be the victim and had sided with her. He now became violently jealous and resentful of all this infatuation with her role as shopkeeper, and went over to his father's side.

As therapy continued with only the parents, we noticed that the more enthusiasm Wanda showed for therapy, and the more willing she became to collaborate and take the initiative, the more Giulio withdrew and became sullen. It was clear that the fact that we had unmasked the ongoing game in those first sessions had utterly failed to budge the stalemate situation.

In her anxiety to get out of this fix (and under pressure from her team, who kept insisting that she, too, was becoming infatuated with Wanda), the therapist did something that was very hard for her to do: She criticized Wanda relentlessly and browbeat her to the extent of making her quite depressed. She did not hesitate to point out all the pieces of behavior that showed Wanda to be lapsing into her old bad habit of humiliating her husband. All the while she was upbraiding Wanda, the therapist was pleading with Giulio to help her and prevent her from falling prey to Wanda's charms like the customers at her shop. Giulio, she insisted, was the one whose help she desperately needed in order to get Sergio to behave.

Very slowly and cautiously, Giulio began to come out of his shell and take action. He made all the decisions about when and where the couple was to "disappear." The crucial test, however, came when the couple set out to battle Sergio's pathological power. Giulio no longer held aloof. He and Wanda were constantly in the firing-line, and they fought and suffered together. There was much suffering, too, since Sergio, as his part of the game, went to extremes to discourage them from persisting. Still, by the end of their tremendous ordeal, which had a successful outcome, Giulio and Wanda had turned into a "real" couple, and so they remained, from that time on. Parents who struggle and suffer together so bravely in order to rescue their child not only succeed in teaming up as his co-therapists but also in radically modifying their own relationship.

CHAPTER XVIII

Therapy and Change

THE THERAPIST POSITED
BETWEEN HIS TWO ROLES
AS "HUNTER" AND "BREEDER"

UNDERSTANDING "what makes for change" is clearly one of the primary objectives of research. To this area of inquiry the various teams who worked with Mara Selvini Palazzoli devoted painstakingly careful consideration. The need to properly understand how change occurs often led them to implement some very radical modifications in methodology. In this connection we need only briefly mention the decision to abandon the classical psychoanalytic approach and the resulting shift to communications theory as a new framework for our investigation. They soon discovered this theory to be specious and pretentious, and to contribute little or nothing to a theory of change. Teaching someone to communicate adequately is an inconsequential pursuit when one is facing the vast complexity of psychotic phenomena, of which impaired communication is but one of many manifestations.

At a later stage, our quest for a reliable theory of change proceeded within the framework of systemic-holistic doctrine and paradoxical methods. Although not altogether explicitly, the new focus was instrumental in effectively severing all remaining ties with the time-honored concept of psychotherapy as a significant personal relationship conducive to cognitive and emotional growth. Having definitely decided that education and psychotherapy are two very different things, we began to cast the therapist in the provocative role of catalyst of change (Selvini, 1988, p. 89).

In the "interventist"-paradoxical approach, change is viewed as being engendered by an upheaval, a sort of severe jolt to the family's *Weltanschauung*. This is a concept of discontinuous change—change comes about by jumps (Watzlawick et al., 1967). This strongly contradicts the notion of change coming about in the steady, gradual flow associated with personal evolution, heightened awareness, progress in learning, and so on. Using a metaphor, we might say that the paradoxical therapist acts like a "hunter" and that his intervention is somewhat like a harpoon (Selvini, 1988, p. 233).

In a literal sense, paradoxical therapies essentially involve inducing crisis. The notion of the therapist as a cross between pilot and experienced traveling companion along the road to healing and recovery (which, in our metaphor, would assign to the therapist the role of "breeder") is totally foreign to this concept. Indeed, if we look back at the average number of sessions we would hold with each family during our paradoxical phase, we see that they were very few — usually three or four.[1]

We have for many years now been increasingly dissatisfied with strict adherence to this radical position and the "all or nothing" logic it implies. We find it interferes with a more accurate control of how the therapeutic process evolves over time. In an initial attempt to ameliorate this drawback, we decided to fuse paradoxical interventions with prescriptive ones. Today we feel that this mixed approach also tended to rely too much on the therapist's "power" and on that of the messages he conveyed. It was equally over-optimistic with regard to the family's self-healing capacity.

Our current line of research proceeds towards a new synthesis that places the therapist in a twofold role as both "hunter" and "breeder." During the first sessions, with the whole nuclear family on hand, crisis-inducing dynamics will undoubtedly prevail (and the therapist will be "hunting"). At a later stage, when the parents are appointed co-therapists and the first prescriptions are handed them, a middle-term therapeutic alliance will be drawn up (and the therapist will be "breeding"). Everyone's response both to the alliance and to the prescriptions will in turn yield pertinent factual information for when we revert to the "hunting" phase and track down the couple's stalemate and the ongoing family game.[2] The crisis-induction that takes place in this second "hunting" phase must, however, leave the ongoing therapeutic alliance unimpaired!

Basically, the therapeutic process hinges on the team members' skill in preventing their interactions with the family from breaking off at too early a stage in the proceedings. Such an untimely split may of course come about in the form of a drop-out, but it may also be the result of the too

[1]This figure was reported by the team that authored *Paradox and Counterparadox*. It was borne out by a number of practitioners who later followed paradoxical precepts. The same average was reported both for the experience at the District Psychiatric Center of Corsico by M. Selvini and the private professional practice of S. Cirillo and A. M. Sorrentino.

[2]We hope we will not insult our reader's intelligence by stressing once more that we use this venatorial jargon solely in a metaphorical sense, and that no one should be alarmed into believing that we think of our families as "fair game" and go after them with inhumane weapons.

hasty dismissal that is typical of paradoxical therapies. The team must also be ready to diagnose, at a very early stage, any possible danger of getting personally involved in the process that is keeping the dysfunctional game alive, so that the serious risk of stubbornly plodding on down the wrong track can be avoided. We will deal with this problem in greater detail at a later point in the discussion, and merely wish to point out here how our current idea of therapeutic change takes it to be a highly complex process, which gets under way *both* through discontinuous transitions (crisis induction) *and* through gradual evolution (the therapeutic alliance with the parents and the feedback of the effect of the parents' change on the patient).

CHANGE AND THE META-GAME

Here again, the game metaphor stands us in good stead in illustrating our work, in which we view psychotic processes as phenomena "out there." Therapy is a game, and we ourselves are players. There is a fundamental premise behind viewing the therapist's moves and the changes our therapies elicit in terms of a game: Any move in a functional relational game cannot *but* belong to one of two distinct categories. It is either a move in the game that is under way or one that ushers in a new, different game, inviting the players to adopt it (a meta-game move).[3] Significant moves by the therapist must obviously always be made on the meta-game level.

THE INDIVIDUAL COMPETENCE PRESUPPOSITION

The ground rule when making therapeutic moves on the meta-game level is for the therapist to adopt a basic attitude that sharply contrasts with one of the family's fundamental beliefs, namely that the child they have labeled as the patient suffers from an illness. The therapist stays firmly within what Viaro and Leonardi (1986) have termed the competence presupposition, an expression they use to explain the therapist's refusal to consider the symptom as a manifestation of illness. The therapist leads from the assumption that all behavior can be understood (in its interactive aspects), providing there is enough knowledge of the context in which it arises. When confronted with behavior that appears incomprehensible, there is only one procedure we can follow that is compatible with this basic assumption, namely, intensifying our inquiry into the context. Thus, should the patient refuse to speak, the therapist will refer to this as a freely

---

[3]This clear-cut distinction applies in the case of functional games: in psychotic games many of the moves will be hard to classify and will seem to be partaking of both categories, i.e., the meta-game and the in-game.

self-imposed decision of the patient's which he (the therapist) has every intention of respecting. Or, should the patient be delirious, the therapist can either cut him short by saying that session time is far too short for idle digressing or, if he can make any sense at all out of what the patient is saying, point out the logic underlying the apparently meaningless flow of words. Over and above the specific exchanges during the session, the therapist will at all times take pains to signal that he considers the patient's conduct intentional and comprehensible.

REQUESTING FAMILY THERAPY: A MOVE IN THE GAME

Again, according to this basic rule, the first level on which therapeutic meta-games are planned comprises the first fundamental decisions the team must make after studying the data on the telephone chart. Specifically, these are: "Are we, or are we not, to undertake therapy with this particular family?" and "Who should be summoned to the sessions?" In order to answer these queries we need a rough outline of how the therapeutic game with this particular family may be modeled. This allows us to decide whether our moves in response to any ingrained dysfunctional patterns we detect in their history are to be "meta-game" or "in-game" moves.

For example, is the therapist's game to involve introducing something entirely new, to implement a transformation of the ongoing family game? Or will it simply merge into the game already under way and contribute a merely formal or quantitative variation on the same repetitive theme? Hence the need to make assumptions about the family game at an early stage and to gauge immediately the possible retroactive effects our questioning may generate in the family.

In our holistic-systemic era, we entertained a naïve notion about the "family that requests therapy," as though the family were a "person," a single, undifferentiated entity. Today we know that "requesting therapy" often comes about on the initiative of one particular family member who persuades the others to follow suit. This member will be pursuing some strategy of his own, and we must be quick to get to the bottom of it. Requesting therapy may, for instance, be a move designed to reinforce someone's leadership position or to place other members of the family under a cloud by emphasizing their negligence or other blameworthy conduct towards the patient. In other cases, the request may be the end result of much haggling by the parental couple; exhausted by the patient's constant harassment and by their own dispute, they may have decided they need an umpire. Or again, the couple have conceivably reached an agreement about keeping another of their children, who is about to detach himself from them, tied down at home by entrusting his "sick" brother or sister to his care.

We cannot review all the possible interactive configurations that may prompt a request for therapy: We merely wish to point out how hypothesizing and investigating along the lines indicated above allow one to draw up a first rough synchronical model of the family game based on how the request for therapy is made. A study of our past records showed up a few typical "trouble spots" that must be explored. One of the most emblematic of these was the subject of an article of Mara Selvini Palazzoli on the prestigious sibling as referring person (1985b). In a family of the type discussed in that article, a child's psychosis is constantly fueled by his covert and confused rage at a sibling ostensibly desirous to help him in every possible way who, in actual fact but quite unwittingly, "uses" him to maintain and reinforce his own position of prestige in the family, even to the extent of outranking one of the parents in the family hierarchy. The patient, however, will be willing to die rather than hand this formidable sibling an umpteenth trump card by letting him get credit for having "healed" his sick brother/sister. This explains why going ahead with family therapy would be an irreparable error here.

THERAPEUTIC GAME-PLAYING AND
THE COUPLE'S STALEMATE

More frequently, a move on the meta-game level, in one of the various phases that characterize the psychotic process in a family, will tilt at the couple's stalemate, thus decisively affecting the evolution of a dysfunctional game. In that case, if the move to request therapy has been made by one spouse *against* the other, therapy is very likely to head up a blind alley. A typical situation will also at times see the stalemated couple assigning roles of "responsibility" and "irresponsibility" to each spouse: The "responsible" spouse will then be the one for whom requesting therapy is a part of his habitual strategy based on hounding and blaming the other, held to be "irresponsible" because of a tendency to be weak, listless, selfish, ineffectual, lacking in family feeling, superficial or whatever else.

Carrying on with therapy in a case such as this, without first having grasped the particular game of which the request for therapy is simply another move, portends certain failure. The therapist is bound to get ensnared in the couple's game as an implicit ally and accomplice of the "responsible" spouse, whereupon the "irresponsible" one will be equally bound to do everything possible to sabotage therapy (usually by wielding his accustomed ultimate weapon, passive resistance).

THE INVARIANT SET OF PRESCRIPTIONS

The second level on which meta-game moves are enacted is that of the prescriptions. Even prior to the first consulting sessions, the team must make ready to carefully register the effects of the "therapy game" both on the couple stalemate and on the family game as a whole. Right from the time we first invented and started to systematically apply the invariant set of prescriptions, we began to ask ourselves how exactly the changes we witnessed so frequently were coming about.

As is always the case when one lacks, or fails to apply, the proper "code" for deciphering a cryptogram, we got lost in tangles of complication, in countless compounding elements. We shared the fate of Kepler, who used up almost a thousand folios in calculating the orbit of Mars, working with the Ptolemaic code of "celestial spheres," before he at last followed his own bold intuition and switched to a code in which orbits are ellipses rather than circles, whereupon he got down all the necessary calculations on just a few folios. So we, too, spent years pursuing our query, whereas when we now look back on the invariant prescription and see it in terms of a game, we easily find sufficiently straightforward and convincing answers.

At the end of the first stage of treatment, consisting of two sessions, the therapist will not only have sounded out each parent's motivation and willingness with regard to therapy but also have worked to enlist and reinforce the parents. This means the parents will have accepted a complementary, subordinate position in the family-team relationship. The team will use this upper hand as a lever: Implementing the secrecy compact is tantamount to making a move (in the meta-game) that invites the couple to start sharing in a new game to play with each other but also, by teaming up, against all the others. (*With each other*: by agreeing to remain on an equal, non-competitive footing; by agreeing to act as sworn accomplices, which will qualify them strongly as a couple and set them apart from all the others. *Together against all the others*: by accepting to be labeled, within the therapeutic metasystem, as allies of the therapist, which splits them off from all the other family members, both of the first and the third generation.)

In this fashion, the therapist's preeminence, which the parents acknowledge, becomes the matrix of their own autonomy with respect to all the others, in that it bars the others from directly participating in the therapeutic system while at the same time elicits information about the others for the system, via the reports the parents write in their notebooks and hand in to the therapist. When the therapist gets to the second part of the invariant set of prescriptions, namely the "evening outings" (once the couple has proved it has accepted and duly started to play the game implicit in the compact and in "keeping the secret"), the therapist does not switch to a new game; rather, he carries on with the one that has begun and makes an (in-game) move by raising the ante. He prescribes a further move, which, since it pertains to the in-game level, no longer touches on their rapport with him or even on their rapport with each other, both of which have by now been clearly defined by the (meta-game) move enacted in the previous session. He now emphasizes the relationship that exists between the couple, on the one hand, and everyone else, on the other.

By staking a claim to a time and space of their own, in their own name and without forewarning anyone or explaining anything, the couple marks its autonomy with regard to family members of both the first and the third generation. Logically, as is true of any prescription, this one cannot causally determine change in the game merely by being issued (or even formally complied with). What the prescription does is provide an occasion for experiencing the possibility of change. It is an invitation to start playing a different game, and it will always be unforeseeable to a large extent whether the novel experience the prescription provides will or will not spark off a transformation in their relationship. For example, will those cozy tête-à-tête dinners at a restaurant, during the evening "disappearances," restore to them a sense of shared enjoyment, or will they just be one more in a long series of terrible disappointments, an empty ritual for spouses who have nothing more to say to one another?

The invariant prescription invites the couple to play a relational game vastly different from that which has been going on in the family with a psychotic child. One need only think of its "disentangling" effect on the children, who will tend to give up intruding in their parents' marital problems, or of the crucial move (made on the meta-game level) consisting of dismissing first the grandparents and then the offspring during the two initial consulting sessions. A long-term course of family therapy, on the other hand, with both generations attending the sessions, would inevitably sanction and enhance precisely the unwholesome entanglement we consider decisive for the onset of psychotic processes in the family.

It will now be easy to understand why so many parents panic and grow tense at the very idea of these prescriptions, an attitude that puzzled us for years. We kept asking ourselves why their reaction should be so out of all proportion. Why did these parents, who were faced with the tragedy of a severely disabled and intractable child, balk so stubbornly at the idea of carrying out such petty, trivial assignments? The fact is that they sensed all too well the danger of the prescriptions unleashing a hurricane over the delicate equilibrium of their rapport, with consequences they do not even dare to imagine.

REVEALING COVERT GAMES

In the foregoing we examined two levels of therapeutic strategy: (1) the therapist avoids getting entangled in the family game and thereby fails to further its dysfunctional, repetitive pattern, and (2) using the prescriptions, the therapist extends a very emphatic invitation to the family to start playing a different game.

We have often observed that these two levels of strategic action do not in themselves suffice to produce effective change; they do not guarantee an adequately specific therapeutic intervention. We feel it is essential for us to succeed in reaching a *third* meta-game level of therapeutic strategy, on which we may tackle the issue of unmasking the game. Our theory here obeys the fundamental hypothesis that the main characteristic of psychotic games is that they are covert. The most extreme manifestation of this concerns the parental couple's marital rapport. The two players may appear to be a model couple, or they may be at each other's throats day and night: Whatever they seem to be, one thing such spouses will consistently refuse to do is lay themselves bare to each other (or even to themselves, for that matter) and explicitly reveal the true reasons for their distress. Each of them is only out to save himself or herself, and each is convinced that the only way to do this is by resorting to devious tactics. Both have long ago lost any hope of being able to confide in the other, to vent some secret anguish and meet with the other's understanding or sympathy.

Until we are proven wrong, we shall go on thinking that our most potent instrument for change is a family meeting at which the cards are turned up, causing a general upheaval and a salutary demolishing of negations and of other camouflaging of reality.

We have therefore set ourselves the twofold task of, on the one hand, refining increasingly detailed models for the various types of process that lead to psychosis and, on the other, constantly checking the real therapeutic usefulness this modeling procedure offers for first "guessing at" and then unraveling the tangled skeins of a psychotic game.

Our move to unravel the game may appear to be overly direct, an explicit provocation; still, we feel that only hypotheses "that are more or less congruent with something that is occurring in the family" give such an intervention therapeutic cogency (Speed, 1984, p. 515).

In the past we were guilty of some loose thinking about *surprise*. We erroneously considered provocation and surprise as being our key therapeutic instruments. The truth is that an intervention will fly straight to the target and be properly effectual, while at the same time upsetting the members of a family cognitively and emotionally, *only* if it lays bare something that someone was trying to conceal both from himself (warped awareness) and from the others. In these circumstances, surprise and provocation are the only adequate strategic possibilities—no others will do the trick. The family's startled reactions will signal very clearly that we are probably on the right track. However, such a reaction should definitely not be aroused merely as an end in itself.

As we stated earlier, in this current phase of our investigations we are shifting away from our former confrontive attitude towards the family. During the paradoxical phase, and for the greater part of the prescriptive one, we tended to view the family from behind a screen of technical and professional aloofness. Paradoxes and prescriptions were devices that helped us keep our emotional distance. They were ascetic, dispassionate moves in an intellectual game. We never felt close to the family members, never really let them know what we were thinking and doing. We felt close only to our fellow team members and thought of ourselves as aligned together on one side of the playing field in order to play against the family members on the other side, albeit for their own good. At present, we concentrate on drawing up a wide range of models typifying psychotic processes and feel this allows us to approach the family in a far less arrogant, far more collaborative spirit. Such a change in tactics has had some significant effects: The therapist's revelations now tend to have less recriminative overtones, and the message will sound something like this: "A very unfortunate thing has happened to you; it could have happened to anyone in the same circumstances, including me." A collaborative atmosphere will enhance the family's willingness to listen, which in turn allows the therapist to listen not only with the head but also with the heart. It also lets the therapist feel free to ask the family members for help in understanding their dilemma.

When family members see the therapist as someone who has joined them in seeking a solution to their problem, and has abandoned all reticence in doing so, the all-round emotional atmosphere will undergo a momentous change for the better.

CHAPTER XIX

The Stalemate Behind the Iron-Clad Door

BEYOND THE OPEN CONFLICT

THE STALEMATE IN THE spouse relationship, as we came to call it, is a long-standing deadlock we find in the relational pattern of parents seeking our help for the problem of a severely disturbed son or daughter. The phenomenon is very much the hub of our current clinical research and entails a painstaking progression through quicksand territory that we now know is unavoidable. However rigorously we pursue our goal and follow the guidelines indicated by our model, however much we refine our inquiry technique and accumulate therapeutic experience, we will eventually always find ourselves up against this double-locked door, and once again it will be brought home to us that we absolutely must know what is behind it. For there, we are sure, lies the heart of the matter, the clue we cannot do without if we wish to be architects of change. If we fail to ferret out this heavily guarded secret, our work will never achieve its scope. Since we have too little knowledge as yet of the phenomenon, the quest for greater insight is our top priority at present. Here is a summary of our preliminary findings.

The first step in tackling the problem is to distinguish between the *stalemate situation* and the *conflict situation*. Stalemate is covert, whereas conflict is manifest, open and above-board—it is what it looks like. On the other hand, the couple's open conflict may be masking genuine distress and at the same time providing a suitable vent for tension. When we dealt with the parents of schizophrenics in the past, we all too often ended our inquiry once we hit upon the manifest conflictual pattern in the couple's relationship. Feeling that this supplied all the information we needed, we failed to realize that the open conflict was a coverup for something lurking underneath it, something that left the chute into relapse wide open, a gaping menace. Now, if *we* are unable to get at this hidden threat, how is the parental couple to do so, ensnared as they are, over so many years, in a hopelessly, confused tangle of what is "manifest" and what is "covert?"[1]

We will now relate, as clearly as possible, how we gradually gained a better picture of this tangled phenomenon.

At the heart of a couple's stalemate lies an overpowering fear (of betrayal, perhaps) one spouse feels with regard to the other. This is never shown or even acknowledged (for reasons we do not understand—possibly so as not to "show one's hand" and thus offer the other an advantage, or simply because this fear is so great that it cannot be confessed even to oneself). So, the spouse who lives in fear will mask this terror behind some pseudo-problem, conjured up much like a smoke screen. On this pseudo-problem he or she will harp far too much, keeping the "opposite player" under a steady barrage of heckling. The "opposite player," however, senses his partner's terror and joins the conspiracy of silence, all the while latching onto the pseudo-problem and using it to buttress his own stronghold. Thus, he/she will act as though accepting the pseudo-problem at face value and will eagerly contribute to keep the fire going (couple in a conflict situation). At the same time, he will use the pseudo-conflict to actively fuel his partner's secret terror: this behavior is due to the fact that he/she, too, harbors some special fear of his own, not so much related to the sexual-erotic sphere, perhaps, as to the degree of esteem and admiration he possesses in his spouse's eyes. This is why his spouse's fear partially reassures him.[2] The fact that the couple's respective fears are parallel and complementary to one another might account for the stalemate's stable equilibrium.

Parents of disturbed children may of course also fail to resort to an open conflict to mask the stalemate. Quite to the contrary, they may make a point of appearing to agree about everything, which only makes the therapeutic task of opening the stalemate door more arduous.

A couple that came to us for the problem of a 15-year-old chronic encopretic boy, Marcello, who was also exhibiting manic behavior, was a case in point of the manifest conflict type (see the description of this case in Chapter XV). The open conflict surfaced during the first session: The husband's efforts to found a family on the devoted ministrations of a

---

[1]If the game the couple is playing is a "clean," "open" one, no matter how conflictual, and allows them to lay bare their weaknesses and "show their hand" by voicing fears and desires, we believe that the parents' game will not prove so unsettling and pathogenic for the offspring.

[2]We are, of course, unable to gauge the levels of cognition at which such interactional patterns are played out; however, in those cases where we were able to ferret them out and hold them up for the couple to view, we often had the impression that the ensuing reactions of emotional upheaval and astonishment were due not so much to the revelation *per se* as to the fact that we had been able to decipher the patterns.

house-proud wife were thwarted by the wife's stubborn resolve, right from the start and throughout their marriage, to stick to her office job. During their engagement she had promised she would give up her job when their first child was born, and her husband, ostensibly in retaliation for her breach of promise, persecuted her relentlessly with disparaging remarks on how badly she ran the household, how untidy everything was, how his shirts always had buttons missing, and so on—all of which could be set down to the fact that she wasn't spending enough time and effort on her domestic duties.

In this case, as so often, it was the patient's symptomatic behavior that made us see that the true problem lay elsewhere. Even though the son, during the first and second sessions, hauled his mother over the coals on the subject of her domestic failings, acting as his father's mouthpiece and treating her as one would a *slovenly servant*, the boy's pathological behavior *was far too severe to have been triggered by such minor grievances*. Why was he smearing his feces on the bathroom tiles and fresh towels every single day, thus subjecting his mother to the humiliating task of having to clean up the mess? This was certainly not the way anyone would handle a slip-shod servant!

In our session with the whole family, we were struck by the erotic passion mother and son brought to their arguing. It seemed very likely that the son was identifying with his father, not only in their open strife but also in sharing his father's deep, carefully concealed fear of his wife's infidelity, which was nagging at the roots of the husband's married life. Their son, using his unsavory routine, was acting as a self-appointed avenger.

In the fourth session, with the children no longer present, the therapist had her plan ready: She intended to knock respectfully at the stalemate door, and to have it opened. She began by addressing the husband empathically:

> I have been doing a lot of thinking about everything we discussed and in-quired into during our previous session, concerning the problem you both have. I have given it very careful consideration, and at this point I must say that I honestly believe that what we talked about last time was not the real issue. I am quite positive now that your problem centers on something else ... and I believe it's fear, very strong fear, so strong that you can't even confess it to yourself—fear that your wife might be unfaithful. . . . I don't know if it's fear that maybe something out there, at that office of hers . . . someone, perhaps, attracts her and satisfies her more than you can. . . . I'm not using the word "jealousy," mind you—that would be much too trivial. . . . I'm referring to something deeper . . . something much more profound. . . . And, madam, I believe you feel this, too—you can sense this fear of your husband's, you perceive it, and you latch onto it for reassurance, because it's proof that he loves you . . . so, you do nothing to allay his fears, you even encourage them, instinctively, not only as regards what you do at the office. . . . And there's someone else who shares this fear, who has become infected with it and has put it into deeds . . . and that's Marcello. He's the one who

smears feces on your clean walls; it is as though he were calling you a filthy slut!

The effect of this grim statement by the therapist, and what happened in the wake of it, can only be seen in full by watching the videotape. There was a volley of telling facial expressions, first thunderstruck and then charged with emotion; there were reluctant avowals that gradually led to full confessions, until, at last, there came the outright confirmation that left no room for doubt. We provide the transcript here of the last moments of this memorable session, so that the reader may perceive the cogency of what was said and the passion that colors a situation such as this, in which we reach a climax in our clinical work.

Once the therapist had obtained confirmation of her hypothesis from the couple, she left the room for a short while, to hear her colleagues' impressions of what had happened. When she returned, with the intention of winding up the session and bidding the couple good-bye, she was unexpectedly handed the clinching bit of evidence on a silver platter: The wife, looking straight into her eyes, her face tense, suddenly exclaimed as follows:

WIFE   Doctor, you've got my husband really worried about what you said back there, about a possible threat . . . something outside our home . . .

THERAPIST   Well, you've always used your provocative power to let them feel "I can get aroused about things out there, whereas with you, here . . . "—that's quite a numbing message you're delivering there.

HUSBAND   There's often been lack of real give and take, on her part, in our sex relations. My advances were often rebuffed, and for long periods at a time, too. . .

THERAPIST   She wanted you to think there might be someone else, who . . .

WIFE   That's perfectly true, you know. I feel quite elated when he worries and gets suspicious! I'm afraid that's just the way I am . . . I can't help it!

THERAPIST   (to husband) You see? It's all done just to keep you on tenterhooks. Anyone who actually *does* things like that doesn't go around teasing about it, she lies low. . . . Well, good-bye, we'll be seeing each other four weeks from now.

This final episode proved beyond all doubt that the door to the couple's stalemate had swung open, to the extent that during the interval, when the couple went out for a cigarette, the husband was able to openly show his wife how terrified he was by expressing his urgent need to know what the therapist herself thought (about his wife's possible infidelity). His wife registered that need correctly and took the initiative in seeking the therapist's opinion, whereupon the therapist pounced on this and deflated the terrified husband's fears with reassuring good humor, making light of them by saying: "it's all just done to keep you on tenterhooks," i.e., it's a rough game, certainly, but that's all it is—a game.

TRUSTING THE THERAPIST HELPS
TO PRY OPEN THE STALEMATE DOOR

We have only lately learned to stand before that double-locked door with a determination equal to our respect. We know we must bring every skill at our disposal into play if we are to induce the parents to open a crack in the door, and we also know we can only undertake this after carefully fulfilling a series of prerequisites. One is to have forestalled, very early in the proceedings, the danger of having to deal with the antithetical stance many spouses assume towards therapy and the therapist, a stance which otherwise places the latter in an untenable position. Another is to make sure of having established our credentials in every possible way, by being sympathetic, honest, unassuming yet self-confident, so as to gain the confidence of both parties. It is our impression that, *if each partner really comes to trust the therapist, he/she will eventually also be able to trust the other partner as well.* Only then will a plethora of unbelievable things come to light, quite naturally, in the friendly, easygoing ambience created in our sessions. The therapist will be able to voice explicit hypotheses, and these important things can be owned up to, talked about.

We reached such a propitious stage in a case we can take as an example, where the therapeutic success was remarkable. This was Rina's family, which we have written about in detail in Chapter XVI. The absolute trust both parents afforded the therapist, and deservedly so, was rewarded by an incredible discovery. Taking their clue from the frequent "infatuations" Gemma, Rina's mother, had shown for the (female) psychologist and social workers looking after her daughter (a severe autistic from early childhood), the team drew up the following hypothesis: These "crushes" Gemma would develop for women were a threat Gemma was using to keep her husband constantly on the alert and in considerable alarm. In this particularly severe case, the nature of the couple's stalemate seemed even more badly warped than in the case previously described. Fear was not a paramount issue here; instead, there was a longing, but so intense, so overriding a longing as to encompass, by its very potency, the terror of despair—despair of its ever being fulfilled.

What Vico, Gemma's husband, so desperately longed for was to capture his wife's warm affection, the same warm affection he read into her every look and move when spying on her with *the women* around. Yet, during their seventh session, it was to a woman—namely the therapist, who on one occasion had asked him to guard her from his wife's infatuation, and had dared to propose a red-hot hypothesis (homosexual infidelity, though the therapist never used those words) — that Vico gently opened the door to the stalemate. In his lovely Tuscan accent, he said: "It's exactly as you describe it, doctor. Somehow, I'm always running scared . . . that's why I feel so relieved when I know Gemma is cloistered away at home with Rina. . . . Yes, it's just like you said: *When Gemma is with the women, there's too much of something . . .* "

After this, Gemma volunteered her own story. She said that her mother had always treated her disparagingly, holding up her elder sister's many good qualities for comparison. Yet, strangely enough, Gemma's mother was extremely jealous of all Gemma's girlfriends. She wouldn't allow them around, and would fly into a rage and abuse them verbally if they visited Gemma at home. This jealousy may well have been Gemma's only hint of the fact that her mother held warm feelings for her.

PART FIVE

Beyond the Systemic Model

CHAPTER XX

Learning to Adopt Multidimensional Thinking

The truth was that notions such as system, cybernetics and information, which had enabled me to go beyond my old way of thinking, carried with them an oversimplification of their own, the full implications of which I at first failed to notice. . . . One had to avoid becoming confined in notions that were liberating in the destructuring phase but would turn into veritable shackles in the restructuring phase that followed . . . one had to beware of the danger such momentary liberation entailed. I realized that the same impulse that had made me move towards such notions as system, cybernetics and information would inevitably also urge me to go beyond them. (Morin, 1977, p. 385, translated from the French by M. Selvini Palazzoli)

THE QUEST FOR AN EPISTEMOLOGICAL FRAMEWORK

THE MAIN PROBLEM OUR TEAM faces at present is that of moving beyond the systemic model in order to grow ever more proficient in multidimensional thinking. This is a formidable undertaking, the latest in a long series of ventures the several successive teams have attempted over these many years.

Back in 1972, when we resolved to throw over psychoanalytic thought for the systemic framework, we found we needed to use methodological devices (causing considerable uproar among the diehards in our field, who mistrusted the genuine nature of our effort to cast off causal reductionism) to help us tear our attention away from the causes of a phenomenon to look at its pragmatic effects. We were training ourselves to think (and sticking our necks out by writing) that a given person sitting in one of our sessions *wasn't* depressed but merely *appeared* to be. This line of speculation compelled us to zero in on the effects his "appearing to be depressed" was having on the other people present, instead of concentrating on figuring out *why* he was depressed. Such a turnabout, cynical though it may seem, was—for us, at any rate—an inescapable phase in training ourselves to observe pragmatic effects of behavior such as, in the above example, the influence of someone's sullen mood on everybody else.

Others may perhaps be able to drastically change their way of thinking without resorting to such artifices, and to switch without noticeable effort from pondering about the causes of behavior to taking stock of its pragmatic effects. For us it was very tough going. There were also some undesirable repercussions—notably, a certain emotional aloofness. However, the gain far outweighed these side-effects; in fact, it was remarkable. Shifting so radically from causes to pragmatic effects led us straight to the pragmatic concept of interactive exchange—in other words, to the idea that our morose friend in the example actually *expected* his behavior to affect the others.

Yet, only a few years later, we realized we had gone from the frying pan into the fire, that is, from psychoanalytic reductionism, which disjoins the individual from his interactions, to holistic reductionism, which disjoins the system (family) from its individual members. Indeed, so wary had we been in the past of explicitly focusing on the individual, his intentions and aims, that for lack of "real, live people" we found we needed to "personify" the system, endowing it with all the intentions and finalities of which we had so carefully dispossessed the individuals! The *system*, then, would be the one to request therapy, to resist change, and so on.

With the invention of the invariant set of prescriptions and its systematic implementation, our way of thinking underwent a momentous change, the extent and significance of which grew clear to us only gradually and when it had become a *fait accompli*. We were forced to acknowledge that the different individuals who made up a family would each react in a different manner to one and the same prescription. This prompted us to retrieve the dimension of the *subject*. Once we had recovered this dimension of reality, we found that we had together with it rediscovered another, very important dimension—that of *time*, and hence of *process, trajectory, history*.

This discovery actually frightened us a little at first. How could we have come to this? Was our little band of staunch standard-bearers of systemic thought *really* ready to forswear allegiance to a cherished model? What on earth was happening to us? Were we about to become a bunch of eclectics, bereft of any consistent conceptual underpinnings? We were obviously in dire need of an epistemological framework to buttress our new way of thinking and operating.

Edgar Morin was the epistemologist we had been looking for. We discovered this in a curious, roundabout manner, *a posteriori*, so to say. We will try to explain how this came about.

At the time when we were eagerly reading and rereading Bateson's essays, later to be published as *Steps to an Ecology of Mind*, our sights were set on a different goal. We were hoping that this entirely fresh point of view, which held out so much promise, would be of great help to us, and we made every effort to assimilate the teachings of this difficult writer, hoping we could transfuse his thought into our clinical work. Conversely, our encounter with Edgar Morin came about at quite a different time, and was in no way connected with our therapeutic efforts. We had for some time already conceived and implemented the method based on the invariant prescription, which had grown out of purely clinical considerations. The many cases we had treated by this method, however, were slowly but surely modifying and broadening our knowledge. Original observations were emerging, and a number of recurring phenomena had become foreseeable and could be grouped into set categories. Edgar Morin's *Méthode*, in other words, seemed to provide us with a definitive epistemological formulation of what we had in actual fact already experienced. Indeed, it appeared to "legitimize" what we had done and were doing, even though we had not been aware of any design behind our way of operating. Somehow, in endeavoring to meet our immediate need for greater clinical expertise and knowledge, we had begun to progress towards multidimensional thought patterns and were now using a dialectic fusion of concepts hitherto retained heterogeneous, all the while keeping these concepts perfectly distinct from one another. In some mysterious way, quite unawares, we were escaping from what we had so proudly referred to as our systemic rigor, having perhaps dimly perceived that we were in danger of becoming trapped in an ideology.

What follows is the account of how we "discovered" Morin and realized that we were already enacting the method he had expounded. To make our explanations more forceful, we divided them into brief paragraphs, each of which has as its heading a statement concerning the path to complexity posited by Edgar Morin (1982). We hope this will clearly show how our work, which at all times inseparably fuses clinical with cognitive elements, has shifted, or rather, intends to shift, in the direction of multidimensional thought patterns.

The principle of universality is valid but in itself insufficient. It must interact with the principle of intelligibility, which leads from what is local *and singular. The two are complementary and indivisible.* Our research had concentrated for years on attempting a general schema of the "psychotic" interactions in a family. It had centered on our daily effort to render intelligible what was taking place in the *local* situation of the *single* case. The expression "render intelligible" seems more appropriate than "understand"—even the single cases seemed to us so highly complex that in order to make them more easily intelligible we needed the help of artifices. This was the rationale that gave rise to the game metaphor and the invariant prescriptions: The first of these devices was essentially cognitive; the second primarily strategic. All in all, what we did was elaborate a strategy for

the growth of knowledge. The invariant prescription, which elicited con-
frontable reactions from the different family members, allowed us to use
these reactions as relational information we could then interconnect, inte-
grate, organize, group into categories, and even foresee. Finally, the information thus obtained enabled us to construct a diachronic schema of the
game under way in that particular family. However, when after years of
analyzing *local* situations we finally got to the point of drawing up our
general schema, we were forcefully reminded (if ever we had forgotten) that
such a general model would be instrumental in increasing the intelligibility
of each single case *only* if it could be fitted onto the specific, articulated
singularity and local aspects of that case. Such an operation would then
either *verify* (enhance) or *falsify* (Popper, 1934) our general schema. We
concluded from this that the intrinsic nature and limits of our intellect
made it necessary for us to pursue knowledge via a spiral pathway, keeping
up a steady dialectic interrelationship between what is general and what is
incidental and peculiar to the local situation.

The unforgoable need to bring history *and the* event *into all descriptions
and explanations.* Ilya Prigogine maintains that a complex system can be
understood only by referring it to its history and trajectory. This obtains
not only in physics and biology; indeed, it is even more clearly evident in
any type of *organizational* problem, where the interactive process must of
necessity be accurately reconstrued and properly dated step by step, tracing it back along its itinerary in time, whereby an arbitrary (although carefully considered) point of departure will of course be chosen. This sees to it
that one does not lose sight of the strongly dynamic nature of the process.
In our work we have always had to bear in mind that the analysis of an
interactive process must consider not only exchanges of behavior (or
moves) enacted by the members of a family, but also any chance events.
Should a housewife win the sweepstakes, this chance event might allow a
latent relational grievance to manifest itself in a spectacular manner. So,
events and pieces of behavior, before they are linked to one another, must
be accurately dated. This often implies dealing at length with the reticence, not to mention bouts of amnesia, with which the family is likely to
confront us. Yet, despite the unflagging attention we devote to a detailed
chronicle of how a given process has evolved in history (and this is evidence
of how indispensable multidimensional thinking is for our work), we have
always had to continue to favor the "here and now" dimension, basing our
cognitive operations squarely on it. Take, for example, the case in which a
particularly prestigious sibling of the patient is the one to request family
therapy—here the "here and now" dimension, and it alone, can provide a
key to the background situation we need to reconstrue and date the game
(keeping a firm foothold in the present so as not to get lost), by noticing
who made the request and how.

The need to link knowledge of single elements to knowledge of the whole of which they are a part. One needs to constantly bear in mind both the individual *and* the system of which he is a part. In other words, the individual cannot be considered disjoined from the family, nor the family disjoined from the individuals that constitute it. Given our former reverential fear of violating systemic doctrine, the task for us was mainly to rediscover the individual but view him as distinct — though not disjoined — from his family system. This was the reason why we did not revert, in our clinical experiments with families of psychotic children, to psychoanalysis. We had discarded the basic psychoanalytic premise, which assigns preeminence to *individual* endopsychic structure, in order to embrace the (perhaps equally arbitrary) notion that considers *relational* processes to be of overriding significance. What we feel is really important is to view relations (the family game) as presiding over the different individual endopsychic structures. These "regulative" relations will cause certain qualities to become conspicuous (qualities we may decide to label "psychotic") in place of others which will remain latent, blurred or hidden.

Our schema aims to lead from the family game, extend to the individual, and then revert back to the game. This is an approach based on the fact that a newborn child, with all its preexisting individual characteristics, will always be set into a preexisting family game, which it immediately affects and is affected by. Here, too, thinking in a multidimensional manner is important. Individuals must be retrieved as acting subjects and we must join them in the struggle to understand what feelings and intentions are animating them in a given interactive situation. Yet at the same time we need to keep a tight grip on the basic assumption that what is really essential is taking place within the framework of interreactions. This assumption holds the door open to a considerably more complex visualization of the actual development that is unfolding in the individual as well; this bears our Edgar Morin's statement that "the effects of actions are often 'perverse' with respect to the intentions from which they originated" and, as they evolve, "ends transform into means, means into ends, side issues become main objectives and main objectives turn into side issues" (1982, p. 197).

We have recognized such perverse effects time and again as the woeful histories of parents of psychotic children unfurled before us. We need only remember Wanda, the mother of a chronic schizophrenic son (see Chapter XVII). Wanda was the beautiful, highly intelligent daughter of a very poor family. A prosperous young shopkeeper, who owned and managed a big shop together with his imperious mother, chose her to be his bride. In her effort to get her domineering mother-in-law to accept her, Wanda devoted herself body and soul, for years, to the family enterprise. By the time the old lady died, Wanda had developed such skill in selling and in public relations that she immediately took over the role of queen dowager and soon became as sought-after and esteemed by her clients as her predecessor had been. At this point the course of developing events had swept Wanda way beyond her original goal (a poor, uneducated girl desirous of proving her mettle in difficult circumstances). Her husband now felt cheated and forsaken, and took to drink. Their only son, Enrico, resentful of his mother's triumphant career as a shopkeeper, crossed over into his father's camp. Highly gifted intellectually, he began by dispossessing his mother of his own brilliant scholastic achievement. How did Wanda reciprocate? How did she react to these bitter frustrations and to the concrete fact that her husband was not to be counted on for help, being usually too drunk to be useful? She tried to even the score by getting ever more wrapped up in her shop, thereby escalating the twisted rapport with both her son and her husband. Wanda's "means" (her devotion to the shop) had unwittingly turned perverse and become an "end." This example emphasizes the fact that we are quite unable to accurately determine, when we observe an ongoing family game, what the individual actor's original goals were when the game started.

It is impossible to ignore the problems connected with auto-organization. Here again, multidimensional thinking requires constant attention both to the individual, his needs, intentions and aims, and to the specific problems of organization.

If two people decide to live together, they must organize in some way. They will divide up between them everything that needs to be done, and since they are by definition two individual subjects, both biologically and due to the differing learning contexts in which they have grown up, the couple's self-organizing will involve a conflict of interests and much negotiating, as they are both physiologically egocentric. One must assume that individual family members will weigh the pros and cons of cooperating with one another. Problems of self-organization, however, will also arise as a consequence of some chance event leading to a crisis either in an individual member or in the way the organization itself is shaping up. Death, for instance, can be such an event. Mourning for one of the parents may of course cause a subjective problem situation, but it is also likely that death will disrupt the self-organizing process — we need to be on the lookout for signs of members of the younger generation starting a feud over which of them is to occupy the dead parent's position in the family hierarchy.[1]

---

[1] In one such case, a family with a schizophrenic son, we were able to reconstrue how conflict began after the father had been diagnosed as having a fatal illness. The diagnosis proved wrong, and this instance of a "death (mistakenly) foretold" had devastating consequences. This subject is also discussed in Chapter V in the section on "Imbroglio and the single-parent family."

TRAINING OURSELVES
TO THINK IN LOOPS

We owe it to our esteem for Edgar Morin to start out by saying that the heading of this section is not his but ours. Still, we believe it is an engaging proposal.

Traditional science elaborated a method based on the disjunction principle: An object to be examined was to be isolated both from its environmental context and from the observer, on the assumption that this would yield unadulterated "scientific" knowledge about it. Complex thinking, on the other hand, is the art of distinguishing without disjoining and then conveying what has thus been distinguished.

> For a very long time a lot of people believed — and many probably still do — that the social and humanistic sciences were handicapped in their development by their inability to free themselves to a sufficient extent from the manifest complexity of human phenomena in order to attain the dignity and unassailable prestige of natural science, which draws up simple laws, simple principles and establishes order through determinism. However, we see today that this type of simple, disjunctive explanation is in a state of crisis *precisely* in biology and physics, so that the ostensible non-scientific drawbacks of social science — namely, disorder, contradiction, plurality, complication and so forth — have now become a fundamental part of the present problem situation in scientific knowledge. (Morin in Bocchi and Ceruti, 1985 p. 49)

For our part, we consider it very likely that the social sciences (and especially research in the field of psychiatry) have lagged behind *precisely* on account of not having devised adequate strategies for increasing knowledge in their particular fields. They limited their efforts in this sense to taking over into their areas of inquiry the disjunctive methods of scientific simplification. These methods, faced with growing evidence for the complexity of the real universe, have finally been found lacking even in the realms of physical and biological science; they are even more lacking, of course, in social sciences, where steadily emerging evidence for the hypercomplexity of the universe of human relations has revealed the crippling inadequacy of present cognitive methods.

One can find instances of such theoretical floundering in the works of two family therapists quite dazzled by the aesthetic splendor of second-order cybernetics — neither of these books (Keeney, 1983; de Shazer, 1982) contains the slightest hint of the possibility of error, or rather, there is no word of warning to put a therapist on his guard against the possible irremediable errors he might commit. These authors consider an error on the part of the therapist as merely a stepping-stone on the trial-and-error path to knowledge, totally ignoring another fundamental aspect, namely the risk of causing a catastrophe in the process of treatment. Why such blindness? Possibly because these authors, entrapped in an ideological concept of the therapeutic system (i.e., family plus therapeutic team), have neglected to see the family and its members also as subjects "out there" and as potential agents of sinister, harmful patterns. These patterns, much like a "fata morgana," can mesmerize a therapist and dispossess him or her of proper therapeutic choice. Insufficient allowance for error appears to be a frequently recurring shortcoming of reductive thought, especially where such thought freezes into ideology.

So, here we have a first instance of why one needs to think in a to-and-fro pattern—that is to say, in *loops*. This very apt simile instantly suggests the unceasing to-and-fro movements of a rat exploring an unfamiliar maze, or the rhythmic motion of the weaver's weft continually going from one end of the warp to the other. Awareness of the "booby-traps" lurking in certain "historic" dysfunctional patterns of the family's organization leads the therapist to adopt very rigorous procedures, such as a meticulously accurate filling-in (both with regard to life events and relational information) of the clinical chart *prior to* the first meeting with the family (Di Blasio, Fischer, & Prata, 1986). Such a rough outline of the family's ongoing game will allow the therapist to detect any such booby-traps and steer clear of them.

Thinking in loops also tackles the problem of Aristotelian logic, which entirely permeates our daily life—we cannot escape from it. However, this does not mean that we need be confined by its limitations. In our "shuttling" we must simultaneously reach out beyond it and return to it, in a constant back and forth motion. In this fashion, linear causality (a retrospective, sequential instrument) will be confronted with complex causality (endocausality).[2]

The obligatory return to Aristotelian logic our zig-zag motion entails proves, to our mind, that a multidimensional way of thinking does not exclude *anything* from its scope. Even our simplifying devices may now be viewed as part of our strategy for moving closer to complex thought patterns. We need only keep in mind that when we use such artifices we do so in order to simplify, for practical purposes, not on the assumption that they will lead us to some quintessence of reality. Here, as Edgar Morin tells us, lies the danger of discarding as epiphenomena whatever does not fit into the simplifying schema, and deciding that only what can be simplified deserves to be labeled scientific.

---

[2]For a clarifying example of this in plain language, let us go back again to Wanda, whom we last talked about on p. 263. Wanda's decision to give herself over entirely to shopkeeping resulted in some brilliant, mundane games with the shop's clients; in time, these games became autonomous, no longer related to her original intention, and this in turn provocatively reinforced the family's in-game, exacerbating it.

The principle of distinguishing, but not disjoining, an object from its environment. Knowledge of any physical organization presupposes knowledge of how that organization interacts with the ecosystem. In our work of tracking the interactive game, knowledge of the ecosystem and hence of any subcultural, regional, or societal peculiarities is basic. Should we neglect to see this, such factors will mislead us into writing off some behavior as provocative or abnormal, when in actual fact it is ingrained in a particular cultural pattern, or vice versa, into considering quite normal some other behavior which stands in glaring contrast to its special sociocultural context.

Exigencies of credibility, too, should prompt the therapist to identify clearly the background against which a family game is being played out, as well as its particular language. With regard to this issue, it is known that research into the results of psychotherapy has pointed out the link between a successful outcome of therapy and the fact that therapist and patient shared a common cultural code.

The principle of relatedness between the observer (who conceptualizes) and the observed (what is conceptualized). The principle of introducing a device when observing or experimenting, thereby introducing the observer himself into a given physical observation or experiment. With regard to the problem of integrating the presence of an observer into the phenomena he observes, one would be hard put to find a team more enmeshed than ours in the process of its own research. Leading from a plan designed by clinicians for primarily clinical purposes, our research implied the use of purely clinical artifices, namely the invariant set of prescriptions. The prescription turned out to be not only a device for clinical observation and experiment but also an active "perturbing agent." And this was not all. In order to use the artifice to obtain an increase in knowledge, the team coupled it to a device designed to organize this information: the game metaphor. The combined use of these two instruments may be described as a *meta-strategy* for acquiring knowledge (complex knowledge). Furthermore, the team, being properly aware of the fact that within the framework of the therapeutic system (family plus team) it would itself inevitably be a part of the overall game each family was playing, used this awareness when formulating explanations. Any significant piece of behavior identified for a family member became a useful clue for first inferring and then reconstruing that particular family's game. Then, by charting and characterizing step by step (when possible) the various behavioral exchanges (moves) in the game, the team was able to group them into categories and place them in a schematic chronological order along the interactive trajectory (or process) that had eventually led to the onset of the symptom and to the possibility of its becoming chronic.

Is there any way to correct the conceptualizer's enmeshment in his own constructs? This is a crucial matter, a question we have over the years attempted to answer on several levels, all of them referred to "observing ourselves observing," i.e.:

1. By adhering to the implicit and explicit tenets of our successive *general* theoretical frames of references, from Bateson to Morin.
2. By constantly bearing in mind and confronting the tenets of our *local* theory concerning mental disorders, which in turn requires constantly referring back to the origins and roots of our basic hypothesis — reminding ourselves, in other words, of where it arose from and how it got there. Quite recently, having begun to hypothesize more explicitly and systematically about the individual and his strategies, we have started to ask ourselves what clinical theories of psychiatry (or what general psychological concepts) we might be using in this process, even if only in part.
3. By implementing the two-tiered level of observation guaranteed by direct supervision. Family and therapist make up a whole, within the framework of which direct involvement and participation are of the utmost importance. Supervisors, on the other hand, are in a position to observe this therapist-family unit in a very different emotional and cognitive state from that of the acting therapist. Using this methodological setup, the team paradigmatically implemented a synchronic process of self-observation (Selvini, 1988, pp. 90–92).
4. As for diachronic processes, the team was determined here, too, to "observe ourselves" as we proceeded, from within the time-span and the flow of technical and theoretical development. The instruments for this self-observation are our published works, the write-ups of our therapy sessions (that is, the reports the acting therapist draws up after each meeting with the family), and the videotapes, together with our examination of the immediate results of therapy and those we observe in our follow-ups.

We are under no illusion of being able to "cancel ourselves out of the picture." We will always be subjects. However, we are striving to become aware, at least in part, of the distortions and simplifications — the subjective elements, that is — we bring into our observation of phenomena.

There is another level, however, on which the therapist's knowledge is posited as akin to a collective mind that holds up for scrutiny the therapeutic system of which, together with the family, it is a component. In fact, although we have up to this point discussed the self-knowledge that posits us as "observers of ourselves" (also through the use of technical artifices), we now wish to consider a further notion, namely, that control of self-knowledge may be obtained also by an interaction that goes beyond us and involves the therapeutic system and the scientific community. This is an idea inspired by Edgar Morin's reflection (1986, p. 17) on both the difficulty and the possibility of controlling the validity of knowledge (knowledge of knowledge). Knowledge of knowledge, according to Morin, immediately finds itself up against an inexorable paradox.

To understand this, we must use the negative evidence found in Tarsky's logic and in Goedel's theorem. Tarsky sustains that no semantic system can entirely explain itself. Goedel holds that a complex formalized system will not contain within itself the proof of its validity. However, both Tarsky's logic and Goedel's theorem tell us that it may be possible to correct a system's deficient self-knowledge by setting up a *metasystem* that includes it, thereby considering it an object-system, the knowledge of which the metasystem can then either verify or falsify.

This consideration led us to ask ourselves whether one could not, by positing the therapeutic system as a metasystem encompassing both the family and the team, consider the team an object-system, the knowledge of which the metasystem can then hold up for scrutiny. At first blush, the whole idea sounds far-fetched and obscure: We will try to clarify it by synthetically recounting our doubts and what we did to try to dispel them.

Our tentative approximation of a general schema of how interactive processes in a family can lead to a member's symptomatic behavior opened up a whole congeries of new questions. For a while, after the schema had been drawn up, the team members felt as though they had finally reached their objective and there seemed to be some cause for celebration. Hadn't we been saying for years now that what we most needed was a set of "roadmaps" to help the therapist gain access to understanding the nature of psychotic games? Now that we had done all this work, why was doubt creeping back in? Were we still really as sure as we had been that understanding a game was tantamount (or almost) to knowing how to break it up?

In order to tackle this crucial issue, we realized we would have to roll up our sleeves and, in a certain sense, start from scratch. First of all, we understood that with each new family coming for treatment we would need to test our general model. How was this to be done? By the process of fitting our model over that family's specificity. Verbal and nonverbal reactions that the family—or rather its individual members—would show when we told them we "knew about" their game would act as a control of this "knowing" of ours. In other words, enmeshed as we inevitably were in our own constructs, we were certainly in no position to self-validate our knowledge (of knowledge) if we were to use only our instruments for obtaining it. However, by organizing a therapeutic metasystem comprising the family, such a metasystem, by virtue of comprising us (the team) as well, could consider us as an object-system and would hence be able to control our knowledge with a certain degree of objectivity. Verification would come to

a greater extent from the single members' behavioral reactions, both immediate and delayed, than from their verbal response. Whether this feedback,
even were it to be verified, would give rise to any change was quite another
matter, and remained to be seen.

More: There seems to us to be another powerful tool that could help us
remedy the deficiencies of our self-knowledge—the reactions of any of our
colleagues who may find it of interest to test our model in their own
clinical work. This is an idea that has been with us for some time now. It
prompted us to get the present work-in-progress report down in writing
now, despite the fact that the scene is as yet a dark, largely unexplored one
in which there are only a few flickering lights to guide us.

It is our fond hope that teams in various corners of the earth may wish
to adopt our model when working with families of psychotic patients, thus
subjecting it to an invaluable control. Our intellectual capacity is incapable
of grasping the maelstrom of feedback effects and reciprocal influences
such a proposition might unleash: If the schema that describes a family
process (and especially that of anorexia, particularly falsifiable[3] because it is
particularly well-defined) is found by others to be "true" and to elicit
change, what could we conclude from this? What would this tell us?

THE CASE FOR A SCIENTIFIC THEORY
OF THE SUBJECT

As explained in the first part of this book, systematic use of the invariant
set of prescriptions, by leading us to realize that individual members of a
family react differently to the prescription, prompted our gradual rediscovery of the individual. Faced with a vast range of differing behaviors, some
of them strange and unexpected, we were obliged to find explanations for
them all. How were we to do this? By setting each individual player concep-
tually into the ongoing family game and trying to figure out what his
special expectations, frustrations, intentions, objectives and strategies
might be—in other words, what stake he had in that particular game at that
particular time. We are, however, also quite positive that going beyond the

---

[3]We are referring here to Popper's argument that the scientific character of any
assertion is inseparable from its falsifiability. A concept, an assertion, or a theory is
scientific to the degree to which it is falsifiable. The schema we have devised for
the anorectic process as it develops in the family, although there is a range of
specific variants to which it is generally applicable, purports, by refining and
dating, to diverge from models for the social sciences so general and sweeping as
to be virtually unfalsifiable. Moreover, identification of the numerous factors
(inherent to sociocultural ecology) that combine to bring on the anorectic symptom in a family establishes the multidimensional character of the anthropo-social
reality of which we must take heed. Such a reality, in fact, always has a biological, a
psychological and a social dimension.

systemic conceptual model requires a multidimensional study of the *subject.*

In this connection, in volume II of the *Méthode* (1980, p. 371), Morin proposes the idea of macroconcepts, as opposed to the disjunctive, atomizing concepts peculiar to traditional science. As to the individual, Morin argues that a concept such as that of "individual" cannot be recovered unless the individual's fundamental complexity is fully acknowledged. The concept of the individual, he says, needs to be defined in a complex manner as a multidimensional macroconcept that embodies the macroconcept of "subject," which in turn embodies the macroconcept of computation, which is inseparably linked to the concept of self-referral and to that of ecological niche (Morin, 1980, p. 372).

From this host of macroconcepts, all of them converging on the macroconcept of "individual," we need to briefly extrapolate "computation," which we consider very stimulating and significant for speculating about our own work. Morin devotes a long chapter to computation in the third part of the *Méthode* (1986), in which he deals with knowledge. How are we to interpret this concept of computation? The word intuitively suggests an operation centered on self-interest, entirely self-serving. Even the lowliest form of life, for instance a bacterium, possesses self-referential abilities which are constantly directed towards solving the problems of living and surviving. "Computation," when we speak of living things, "means *self-computation*. It leads from the self, acts in function of the self and upon itself" (Morin, 1986, p. 43).

Computation of this sort is basic to life. This concept of computation places the subject at the center of its own world, where the subject "computes" this world and "computes" itself, by effecting a separation between that which is "itself" and that which is not, based on what is advantageous for it. This is how self-egocentricity is engendered and gets instated: It is the primary and fundamental characteristic of subjectivity. Hence, computation appears to be the primary, elementary form of knowledge—a knowledge that is quite definitely self-knowing, i.e., a being's knowledge of itself. The bacterium "knows" itself when it feeds (by knowing what to feed on), when it regenerates, defends, or reproduces itself (by, in each case, knowing how to go about it). This translates into its effecting *choices* and computing *risks*. However, the bacterium is not aware of its knowledge—it neither knows *that* it knows nor *what* it knows. In other words, even the lowest form of life, on a level of simple reckoning, possesses appropriate strategies for its own survival and that of the species, but does not *know that it knows* these strategies.

The ability to compute would seem to be a basic cognitive tool of life itself. Morin has it that the notion of *computation as knowledge* developed out of the Cartesian "cogito"—"I think, therefore I am"—which, however, presupposes conscious *auto-communication* from the individual to himself.

This is a reflexive process, which has auto-information going from the "I think" state back to the "I am" state, and is the prerogative of human beings only. Conversely, computation may be considered elementary self-knowledge in that it does not recognize itself as knowledge *and cannot be dissociated from concrete actions* such as organizing, self-production, reproduction, all of them in the service of its survival and that of the species.

The team discussed at length the distinction Morin points up between elementary self-knowledge (computation) and knowledge "that one knows" (cogito). The distinction has important consequences for the way we interpret our observations in our work with families. The human family is undoubtedly an organization geared to life and survival in every sense, both of the individual and of the species. Its internal interactive organization consists of an exchange of behavioral sequences that mutually influence one another. If we apply the game metaphor to such an internal game, we can view each of these internal pieces of behavior as individual moves obeying choice and decision (which implies a strategy). To which level of knowledge should we then assign each of these behavior pieces? Which should be assigned to the level of simple reckoning (computation), which to the level of "cogito"?

The very word strategy, with its martial overtones, alludes to an egocentric, utilitarian, competitive directive, even when considered at the level of conscious thought. Hence, we may assume that there are strategies on the "computation" level and strategies that belong on the "cogito" level. And we may likewise assume that the former are the more numerous and important, and have far more significant implications for our work. It is quite obvious, in fact, that the members of a family will enact seemingly very skillful, winning strategies of which, however, in a Cartesian sense, they are totally unaware and would be at a loss to describe. When such strategies are detected and revealed to them during the session, they will react nonplussed at first and then, after the shock wears off, acknowledge the revelation to be true.

This is highly important, for a number of reasons. First, it establishes beyond doubt that when a family therapist describes a family game he will not be referring to something done by people moved by lucid, clear-headed, and sometimes unscrupulous intentions. In the second place, and as corollary to the first reason, it tells us that we must cast aside all moral indignation and adopt instead a respectful, understanding, and compassionate attitude. A third and very important reason is that it reveals to us how human beings are often the victims of self-deception (warped awareness). This is possibly the most frequently recurring phenomenon in family games.

A case in point is that of the father of a chronic anorectic girl. During the first session, this man was roundly accused by his young son-in-law, the husband of his other (elder) daughter, Donata, of phoning her every single evening punctually at 8:30, just when the newlyweds were sitting down to their dinner. He would call just to have a chat. It must be said that Donata and her father worked together, so that the phone calls would come only about two hours after they'd last seen each other.

This item of information gave the therapist a chance to comment on how the father, who had suffered greatly from his wife's strong ties to her own father, could not help reenacting this same game with his son-in-law, thereby signaling to the young man: "I'm only calling so you'll know I'm the *real* man in Donata's life." The therapist went on to say that Donata probably had very good reasons of her own for tolerating her father's interference.

What came of all this during the second session? Despite all that had been said, the father had kept on phoning Donata every evening—not at 8:30 as before, however, but at 10 o'clock, so as not to spoil his son-in-law's dinner. It also turned out that Donata's mother would always remind her husband, as the appointed time drew near, that it was getting late and he should hurry and call his daughter.

This change in the father's behavior clearly revealed how the father/son-in-law rivalry was nothing but a pseudo-problem masking the real one, i.e., the father needed to get back at his wife for the strong attachment she had shown in the past for her father and did this by exhibiting his equally strong attachment for his elder daughter. How did his wife react? Translated into explicit language, this is what she was signaling: "You see, I am encouraging you to phone Donata because I'm not in the least put out by your attachment to her; in fact, I consider it is something that you need, you poor dear, and I think you ought to be granted this little treat." So, the real issue, the "feral" nature of this couple's stalemate, had remained buried under a false (and therefore presentable) façade—that of the stereotyped jealous feelings of a father towards his young son-in-law.

Reality is immense. It extends far beyond our intellectual capacity to grasp it. If we are to explore the complex universe of human relations without losing heart, we must first of all learn to be very humble. We must proceed step by step: first by inventing little strategies to help us to both gain knowledge and solve our immediate, single, local problems, as they occur in the present time-dimension; then by integrating the information thus gained into our patterns for further action; then by studying the effects these actions elicit; and so on and on. This is probably the only road open to us in our patient progress towards greater knowledge.

None of the oversimplifying theoretical models, such as those pertaining to psychoanalysis and systemic thought, are able to meet the challenge of the extreme complexity of serious mental disorders, especially schizophrenia. They provide no adequate answers. If, as is the case, the human being is a highly complex entity set in a complex universe, interactive processes of organization (such as the process leading to schizophrenic symptoms) compound, when they develop in a family, to reach a level of almost unfathomable complexity. The effort required to progress towards greater knowledge of these organization patterns will then need an appropriate method for acquiring this knowledge we *must* have, a method more adequate than either the linear or the systemic one, a method that renounces mutilating simplification and lets us work steadily, persistently, to find a dynamic point of convergence for what is plural, multidimensional, and heterogeneous.

References

Anderson, C., Hogarty, G., & Reiss, D. (1980). Family treatment of adult schizo-phrenic patients: A psychoeducational approach. *Schizophrenia Bulletin, 6,* 490–505.

American Psychiatric Association (1980). *Diagnostic and statistical manual of mental disorders* (3rd ed.). Washington, DC: American Psychiatric Association.

American Psychiatric Association (1987). *Diagnostic and statistical manual of mental disorders* (3rd ed., Revised). Washington, DC: American Psychiatric Association.

Arieti, S. (1955). *Interpretation of schizophrenia.* New York: Robert Brunner.

Ashby, W. R. (1954). *Design for a brain.* London: Chapman and Hall.

Bateson, G. (1972). *Steps to an ecology of mind.* San Francisco: Chandler.

Berne, E. (1964). *Games people play.* New York: Grove Press.

Bertalanffy, L. von (1968). *General system theory.* New York: George Braziller.

Bocchi, G., & Ceruti, M. (a cura di). (1985). *La sfida della complessità.* Milano: Feltrinelli.

Bogdan, J. (1986). Do families really need problems? *Family Therapy Networker,* July–August, 30–35, 67–69.

Boszormenyi-Nagy, I., & Framo, J. (Eds.). (1965). *Intensive family therapy.* New York: Harper & Row.

Bowen, M. (1966). The use of family theory in clinical practice. *Comprehensive Psychiatry, 7,* 345–374.

Calvino, I. (1979). *Se una notte d'inverno un viaggiatore.* Torino: Einaudi.

Cancrini, L. (Ed.). (1977). *Verso una teoria della schizofrenia.* Torino: Boringhieri.

Ceruti, M. (1986). *Il vincolo e le possibilità.* Milano: Feltrinelli.

Cirillo, S. (1986). *Famiglie in crisi e affido familiare.* Roma: La Nuova Italia Scientifica.

Covini, A., Fiocchi, E., Pasquino, R., & Selvini, M. (1984). *Alla conquista del territorio.* Roma: La Nuova Italia Scientifica.

Crozier, M., & Friedberg, E. (1977). *L'acteur et le système.* Paris: Seuil.

Dell, P. (1981). Some irreverent thoughts on paradox. *Family Process, 20*(1), 37–42.

De Shazer, S. (1982). *Brief family therapy.* New York: Guilford.

Di Blasio, P., Fischer, J. M., & Prata, G. (1986). The telephone chart. A cornerstone of the first interview with the family. *Journal of Strategic and Systemic Therapies, 5*(1–2), 31–44.

Fisch, R., Watzlawick, P., Weakland, J., & Bodin, A. (1972). On unbecoming a family therapist. In A. Ferber, M. Mendelsohn, & A. Napier (Eds.), *The book of family therapy* (pp. 597–617). New York: Science House.

Framo, J. (1965). Rationale and techniques of intensive family therapy. In I. Boszormenyi-Nagy and J. Framo (Eds.), *Intensive family therapy*. New York: Harper & Row.

Fromm-Reichmann, F. (1950). *Principles of intensive psychotherapy*. Chicago: University of Chicago Press.

Guntrip, H. (1961). *Personality structure and human interaction*. New York: International Universities Press.

Haley, J. (1959). The family of the schizophrenic: A model system. *Journal of Nervous and Mental Diseases, 129*, 357–374.

Haley, J. (1963). *Strategies of psychotherapy*. New York: Grune & Stratton.

Haley, J. (1976). *Problem solving therapy*. San Francisco: Jossey-Bass.

Haley, J. (Ed.). (1971). *Changing families*. New York: Grune & Stratton.

Hoffman, L. (1981). *Foundation of family therapy*. New York: Basic Books.

Horney, K. (1937). *The neurotic personality of our time*. New York: Norton.

Jackson, D. D. (Ed.). (1960). *Etiology of schizophrenia*. New York: Basic Books.

Jackson, D. D. (1965). The study of family. *Family Process, 4*(1), 1–20.

Jackson, D. D., Haley, J. (1963). Transference revisited. *Journal of Nervous and Mental Diseases, 137*, 363–371.

Kaye, K. (1977). Toward the origin of dialogue. In H. R. Schaffer (Ed.), *Studies in mother-infant interaction*. New York: Academic Press.

Keeney, B. (1983). *Aesthetics of change*. New York: Guilford Press.

Le Moigne, J. L. (1985). Progettazione della complessità e complessità della progettazione. In G. Bocchi and M. Ceruti (Eds.), *La sfida della complessità*. Milano: Feltrinelli.

Lidz, T., Fleck, S., & Cornelison, A. (1965). *Schizophrenia and the family*. New York: International Universities Press.

Luhmann, N. (1975). *Macht*. Stuttgart: Enke.

Maturana, H. R., & Varela, F. S. (1980). *Autopoiesis and cognition: The realization of living*. The Netherlands: D. Reidl.

Mc Farlane, W. R. (Ed.). (1983). *Family therapy in schizophrenia*. New York: Guilford Press.

Minuchin, S. (1974). *Families and family therapy*. Cambridge: Harvard University Press.

Minuchin, S. (1984). Interview in family therapy. *The Family Therapy Networker, 11, 12*, 26–31, 66–68.

Minuchin, S., Rosman, B. L., & Baker, L. (1978). *Psychosomatic Families*. Cambridge: Harvard University Press.

Montalvo, B., & Haley, J. (1973). In defense of child therapy. *Family Process, 12*(3), 227–244.

Morawetz, A., & Walker, G. (1984). *Brief therapy with single parent families*. New York: Brunner/Mazel.

Morin, E. (1973). *Le paradigme perdu: La nature humaine*. Paris: Seuil.

Morin, E. (1977). *La méthode I. La nature de la nature*. Paris: Seuil.

Morin, E. (1980). *La méthode II. La vie de la vie*. Paris: Seuil.

Morin, E. (1982). *Science avec conscience*. Paris: Fayard.

Morin, E. (1985). Le vie della complessità. In G. Bocchi & M. Ceruti (Eds.), *La sfida della complessità*. Milano: Feltrinelli.

Morin, E. (1986). *La méthode III. La connaissance de la connaissance*. Paris: Seuil.

Neumann, von J. V., & Morgenstern, O. (1947). *Theory of games and economic behavior*. Princeton, NJ: Princeton University Press.

Pao, P. N. (1979). *Schizophrenic disorders*. New York: International Universities Press.

Pizzini, F. (Ed.). (1980). *Famiglia e comunicazione*. Milano: Feltrinelli.

Popper, K. (1934). *The logic of scientific discovery* (Logik der Forschung), First edition Wien, first English edition 1959.

Prigogine, I., & Stengers, I. (1979). *La nouvelle alliance.* Paris: Gallimaro.

Rabkin, R. (1977). *Strategic psychotherapy.* New York: Basic Books.

Ricci, C. (1984). Complessità e giochi sociali. In A. Quadrio (a cura di). *Questioni di psicologia politica* (pp. 301–326). Milano: Giuffrè.

Rigliano, P., & Siciliani, O. (1988). *Famiglia schizofrenia violenza.* Roma: La Nuova Italia Scientifica.

Rohrbaugh, M., Tennen, H., Press, S., White, L., Raskin, P., & Pickering, M. R. (1977). *Paradoxical strategies in psychotherapy.* Paper presented at 1977 meeting of American Psychological Association, San Francisco.

Savagnone, E. (1978). Il caso di Claudia, *Rivista Sperimentale Freniatria,* 1408–1430.

Savagnone, E. (1982). Onora il Padre-Dio, *Il Ruolo Terapeutico,* 30, 14–18.

Schaffer, H. R. (1977). *Studies in mother-infant interaction.* New York: Academic Press.

Scheflen, A. (1981). *Levels of schizophrenia.* New York: Brunner/Mazel.

Searles, H. (1959). The effort to drive the other person crazy: An element in the etiology and psychotherapy of schizophrenia. *British Journal of Medical Psychology,* 32, 1–18.

Selvini, M. (Ed.). (1988). The work of Mara Selvini Palazzoli. New York: Aronson.

Selvini, M., Covini, A., Fiocchi, E., & Pasquino, R. (1987). I veterani della psichiatria. *Ecologia della Mente,* 4, 61–76.

Selvini Palazzoli, M. (1972). La famiglia con paziente anoressica: Un sistema modello. *Archivio di Psicologia Neurologia Psichiatria,* 4(23), 311–344.

Selvini Palazzoli, M. (1978). *Self starvation.* New York: Jason Aronson.

Selvini Palazzoli, M. (1983). Jeu instigateur et syntôme psychotique. Proceedings International Congress, Terapia Familiar e Comunicatria, Lisbona.

Selvini Palazzoli, M. (1984). Preface of the German edition of *The hidden games of organizations (Hinter den Kulissen der Organisation).* Stuttgart: Klett-Cotta. Partially translated in M. Selvini (Ed.) (1988).

Selvini Palazzoli, M. (1985a). Anorexia nervosa: A syndrome of the affluent society. *Transcultural Psychiatry Research Review,* 22(3), 199–205.

Selvini Palazzoli, M. (1985b). The problem of the sibling as the referring person. *Journal of Marital and Family Therapy,* 11(1), 21–34.

Selvini Palazzoli, M. (1986). Toward a general model of psychotic family games. *Journal of Marital and Family Therapy,* 12(4), 339–349.

Selvini Palazzoli, M., Boscolo, L., Cecchin, G. F., & Prata, G. (1978). *Paradox and counterparadox.* New York: Jason Aronson.

Selvini Palazzoli, M., Boscolo, L., Cecchin, G. F., & Prata, G. (1980a). The problem of the referring person. *Journal of Marital Family Therapy,* 6(1), 3–9.

Selvini Palazzoli, M., Boscolo, L., Cecchin, G. F., & Prata, G. (1980b). Hypothesizing, circularity, neutrality: Three guidelines for the conduct of the session. *Family Process,* 19(1), 7–19.

Selvini Palazzoli, M., & Prata, G. (1980). Die macht der ohnmacht. In J. Duss, v. Werdt, & R. Welter Enderlin (a cura di). *Der familienmensch.* Stuttgart: Klett-Cotta.

Selvini Palazzoli, M., Anolli, L., Di Blasio, P., Giossi, L., Pisano, I., Ricci, C., Sacchi, M., & Ugazio, V. (1987). *The hidden games of organizations.* New York: Pantheon.

Selvini Palazzoli, M., & Prata, G. (1983). A new method for therapy and research in the treatment of schizophrenic families. In H. Stierlin, L. C. Wynne, & M.

Wirsching (Eds.). *Psychosocial intervention in schizophrenia. An international view*. Berlin: Springer.

Selvini Palazzoli, M., Cirillo, S., Selvini, M., & Sorrentino, A. M. (1985). L'individuo nel gioco. *Terapia Familiare*, *19*, 65–73.

Selvini Palazzoli, M., & Viaro, M. (1988). The anorectic process in the family. A six-stage model as a guide for the individual therapy, *Family Process*, *27*(2), 129–148.

Sluzki, C. E., & Ransom, D. C. (1976). *Double bind: The foundation of the communicational approach to the family*. New York: Grune & Stratton.

Sorrentino, A. M. (1987). *Handicap e riabilitazione*. Roma: La Nuova Italia Scientifica.

Speed, B. (1984). How really real is real. *Family Process*, *23*(4), 511–520.

Stanton, D. (1981). Strategic approaches to family therapy. In A. S. Gurman & D. P. Kuykern (Eds.). *Handbook of family therapy*. New York: Brunner/Mazel.

Stierlin, H., Simon, F. B., & Schmidt, G. (Eds.). *Familiar realities*. New York: Brunner/Mazel.

Sullivan, H. S. (1966). *Conceptions of modern psychiatry*. New York: Norton.

Sullivan, H. S. (1968). *The interpersonal theory of psychiatry*. New York: Norton.

Viaro, M., & Leonardi, P. (1982). Le insubordinazioni. *Terapia Familiare*, *12*, 41–62.

Viaro, M., & Leonardi, P. (1983). Getting and giving information. Analysis of a family interview strategy. *Family Process*, *22*(1), 27–42.

Viaro, M., & Leonardi, P. (1986). The evolution of the interview technique: A comparison between former and present strategy. *Journal of Strategic and Systemic Therapies*, *5*(1–2), 14–30.

Watzlawick, P. (1978). *The language of change*. New York: Basic Books.

Watzlawick, P., Beavin, J. H., & Jackson, D. D. (1967). *Pragmatics of human communication*. New York: Norton.

Watzlawick, P., Weakland, J., & Fisch, R. (1974). *Change: Principles of problem formation and problem resolution*. New York: Norton.

Weakland, J., Fisch, R., Watzlawick, P., & Bodin, A. (1974). Brief therapy: Focused problem solution. *Family Process*, *13*(2), 141–168.

Weeks, G., & L'Abate, L. (1982). *Paradoxical psychotherapy*. New York: Brunner/Mazel.

Wynne, L. C., & Thaler Singer, A. (1963). Thoughts, disorders, and the family relations of schizophrenics. *Archives of General Psychiatry*, *9*, 191–206 and *12*, 187–220, 201–212.

Zappella, M. (1984). *Non vedo, non sento, non parlo*. Milano: Mondadori.

Index

active provocation, 167
adoptive families, 62
affluent society and anorexia nervosa, 177–78
agent, victim as, 123–26
alliance:
  of the loser and the patient, 189–90
  see also therapeutic alliance
altruistic behavior, ambiguous, 157
Anderson, C., 238n
anger, as a trigger for change, 224–25
Anolli, L., 154
anorectic behavior:
  process in, 177–82
  type A and type B, 181, 220
  volte-face in development of, 181–82
  Western cultural model for, 177
anorexia-bulimia, 91–97, 146–47
anorexia nervosa, 13, 16–17, 73–77, 85–88, 170–71, 174–76, 213, 215–17, 224–25, 227–28
  enslavement of parents, 59
  imbroglio in, 72–77, 86–87
  and parents' divorce, 89
  reaction of family to disappearance, 55
  in a single-parent family, 62
anti-wife, role of daughter, 197
Aristotelian logic:
  limitations of, 3
  utility of, 266
Ashby, W. R., 154
autistic disorder, 123–26, 187–89, 233–35, 255–56
  and instigation, 123–26
  interviewing the mother alone, 222
  recovery from, 159
auto-communication, 271–72
autonomy:
  for the couple, 248
  development in adolescence, 170
  through disappearance, 58–59
  and privacy, 26–27

and psychotic behavior, 8
of siblings of the patient, 176
auto-organization, 264

Baker, L., 179
Bateson, Gregory, 33, 83, 151, 154, 167n, 260, 268
Beavin, J. H., 3, 4, 154, 156, 159, 242
Bertalanffy, L. von, 154, 159
betrayal, and symptom development, 67–68
bipolar disorder, 213–15
blackmail, psychosis as, 185
Bocchi, G., 265
Bodin, A., 5
Bogdan, J., 156
boomerang effect of instigation, 118–19
Boscolo, L., 5, 12n
Bowen, Murray, 212
bulimia, 174–76
  see also anorexia-bulimia

Calvino, Italo, 11
causative levels of symptoms, 193
Cecchin, G. F., 5, 12n
Ceruti, M., 265
change:
  anger, as a trigger for, 224–25
  discontinuous, 242–43
  through prescription, 248
  and therapy, 242–50
child as center of the family, 178
chronic patients:
  individual therapy for, 228
  and prolonged disappearance, 61
chronology of onset of symptoms, 207
circularity:
  in family interactions, 160–61
  of inquiry, session two, 20
  interactive, 159–60
  therapeutic instilling of, 6
Cirillo, S., 243n
coalition, mother/son, 131